Sermons You Can
from the Types and
Metaphors of the Bible

By Jabez Burns, Edited by Barry L. Davis, D.Min., Ph.D.

Copyright©2017 Barry L. Davis

Visit us at: www.pastorshelper.com for more great ministry resources!

About the Author: Jabez Burns committed his life to studying the Bible and preaching the Gospel. He was a well-known author and publisher of many relevant Christian works.

About the Editor: Barry L. Davis is the owner of The Pastor's Helper ministry offering many ministerial helps to ministers all over the globe. He is also the author of numerous Christian books.

Table of Contents

1. ADAM A TYPE OF CHRIST

"Who is the figure of him that was to come."—Rom. 5:14.

THE person, offices, and work of Christ, were not only predicted by the prophets, who all bear witness to him, but a variety of striking types shadowed him forth. Hence Christ is called the truth; that is, the exemplification of what before had been exhibited in figure. The term type, as one observes, signifies the mark or impression made by one thing upon another; but the term is usually employed to denote a prefigurative action or occurrence, in which one event, person, or circumstance, is intended to represent another, similar to it in certain respects, but future and distant.

It must be observed, that none of the personal types could perfectly represent the Savior, as they were all fallible, sinful men; so that it is necessary, while we pursue the parallel points existing in their history, not to forget the things in which there was an obvious disparity.

The text refers us to Adam, the father of mankind, and says, that "He is the figure of him that was to come."

Let us then, in noticing the typical character of Adam, consider,

I. The Points of Resemblance between Adam and Christ.

1. Both were formed and directly proceeded from God.

All, except our first parents, have been born in the usual mode of generation; and one generation has descended from another. Not so, however, with Adam; his body was molded and fashioned by God. Jehovah breathed into his nostrils the breath of life, &c. See how this typified the wonderful formation of the nature of Christ. He was conceived of a virgin, by the overshadowing of the Holy Spirit, and was thus immediately formed by the power of God.

2. They resembled each other in the perfection of their nature.

Both were formed in the glorious likeness of God. "He created man," &c. Thus, too, Jesus was holy, undefiled, &c., the express likeness of the Father. "Whoso hath seen me hath seen the Father."

3. They resembled each other in their fatherhood of a numerous race.

Adam was the father of mankind. All have descended from his loins; and all have borne the general features of then first progenitor.

Jesus Christ is called the first-born of many brethren And, by Isaiah, he if styled, "Everlasting Father," or "the Father of the age to come." All spiritual persons are Christ's seed. Hence the promise, "He shall see his seed," &c., Isai. 53:10,11 And all his descendants resemble him. All bear his image. As they bore the image of the earthly, by nature; so, by grace, they bear the image of he heavenly.

4. They resemble each other in the lordship and dominion with which they were invested.

God made Adam but a little lower than the angels, &c., Ps. 8:5. He gave him a kind of proprietorship over all earthly things. Now Jesus is fully invested with authority and power over all things. "The Father loveth the Son," &c., Heb. 1:2, 4. Eph. 1:20-23, "And set him at his own right hand," &c.

5. They resembled each other in the conjugal union appointed by God.

God cast Adam into a deep sleep, and took from his side woman, who was thus found a help-meet and companion for him. Now the union of the husband and wife is one of the most striking types of Christ's union with the church. He is the bridegroom, and the church is the bride, the Lamb's wife. See Eph. 5:25-32. Now the sleep of Adam seems to exhibit in a striking typical manner how Christ obtained the bride—the church. It behooved him to sleep the sleep of death. His side had to be opened; his heart pierced. "Christ also loved the church, and gave himself for it," Eph. 5:25.

Such, then, are some of the more striking points of resemblance between Adam and Christ.

II. The Points of Contrast.

1. The first Adam was earthly, the second Adam is heavenly.

He came from heaven, was in heaven, and ascended to heaven.

2. The first Adam effaced the divine image from his mind, and polluted human nature; the second Adam was the express image of God, and came to restore our nature to purity and glory.

3. The spirit of apostatizing Adam was proud, unbelieving, discontented, and rebellious; the spirit of the second Adam was humble, submissive, obedient, and faithful.

4. The first Adam brought sin and death upon his species; the second Adam brought salvation and life.

5. By the first Adam paradise was lost by the second Adam paradise was regained.

In the paradise lost, we were deprived of the pleasures of earth; but in the one regained, we obtain the felicities of heaven 6. By the first Adam all men were brought beneath the curse; by the second Adam's death, redemption from that curse has been procured for every man, Rom. 5:15, 16.

Application

1. Learn our natural connection with the first Adam. We are all his posterity. Have all his fallen nature. Heirs to all pains and miseries his fall produced.

2. We have all imitated Adam's sin. He proudly aspired after that which was beyond his reach. He desired what was prohibited. He disobeyed Sod. Which of us has not done the same? "We have all gone astray," &c.

3. See then the importance of an interest in the second Adam. Here is our help. "O Israel, thou hast destroyed," &c. We must be of the nature of the second Adam We must be coheirs with him. We shall then have a sure and certain hope of a resurrection with the just, and the enjoyment of eternal life.

2. NOAH A TYPE OF CHRIST

"Noah—a preacher of righteousness."—2 Pet. 2:5.

FEW lives have had so many incidents of a striking nature crowded into them as that of Noah. He lived at a very interesting crisis, and had to do with events of the most solemn and important character. His personal history is repeatedly brought forward to command the imitation of the servants of God, and as a model of sterling, although not infallible rectitude. In considering his eventful history as typifying that of the Savior, most of the prominent traits and occurrences of his life will necessarily be brought before us. Noah seems to have been a type of the Redeemer,

I. In his Name.

Noah signifies comfort or rest; and of him it was prophetically said, "This same shall comfort us concerning our work and toil of our hands," &c. Gen. 5:29 Now Jesus is emphatically the "consolation of Israel," and the rest of a heavy-laden and guilty world. He imparts spiritual rest to the weary soul. The believer rests on him as the only foundation of hope; and he has provided, and it is his prerogative to admit to that heavenly rest, which remains for the people of God.

II. In his Holy Life.

"Noah was a just man and perfect in his generation, and Noah walked with God." Gen. 6:9. What a testimony does God give in this verse of the excellency of Noah; "just, perfect, and walking with God." Yet how much more fully were these features observable in Jesus. He was the "*Just One.*" His nature was immaculate,—without spot, or sinful infirmity. He lived in closest fellowship with God. Ever walked before him in all well-pleasing. His whole life reflected the purity of the Father, and, in all things and every moment, God approved, and loved, and delighted in him.

III. In his Public Ministry.

Noah was a "preacher of righteousness." No doubt it was by the truth which Noah delivered, that the Spirit strove with the wicked and infatuated antediluvian world. We have every reason to believe that in discharging this office, he was faithful, self-denying, earnest, and persevering. How fully did this office point out the ministrations of the Son of God. Jesus was appointed to preach the gospel of righteousness to the poor. To this he devotedly attended, and faithfully did he persevere in publishing the righteous doctrines and precepts of his heavenly kingdom. His preaching was eminently spiritual, yet clear, plain, and often clothed in the language of figure and parable, so that the common people heard him gladly. It is remarkable, too, that, as preachers, both prophesied of the just vengeance of God. Noah with respect to the old world, Jesus with respect to Jerusalem and Judea.

IV. As the Deliverer of his Family.

God directed him to prepare an ark for the saving of himself and house; and he obeyed God, built the ark, and thus saved himself and family from the destructive flood. Jesus expressly came to save his people from their sins, and thus to deliver them from the wrath to come. The ark, in this sense, seems strikingly to represent the church of Christ.

> 1. Thus, as in the ark the family of Noah were together, and separated from an ungodly world, so believers are redeemed out of the world, and are united together under their one head, Jesus Christ.

> 2. As the ark was of divine construction, so the church is the workmanship of Christ, fashioned in all things after his own infinite wisdom and skill.

> 3. As the ark was the instrument of safety, so we are brought into the church out of the condemnation under which the whole world lies.

> 4. As those in the ark escaped the vengeance of God, and became the inhabitants of the new world; so all believers, united together in the church of Christ, are heirs of God and of the kingdom of eternal life.

V. As the Priest of the World.

Noah evidently acted as such, and his offerings were clearly typical of that which Christ has presented for the guilt of the world. See Gen. 8:20, 21. The sacrifice which Noah presented consisted of clean beasts, and also of every clean fowl, a sacrifice which was peculiarly acceptable to God, and through which he expressed his gracious regards to the future generations of mankind. Jesus offered the perfect sacrifice of himself, for all the nations and families of the earth, a sacrifice which made atonement for the transgressions of man, and through which God has expressed his favor and mercy to all who sincerely repent and believe the gospel of his Son.

Such are the leading points of typical resemblance between Noah and Jesus. Many instances of *disparity* will be obvious to the contemplative mind.

> 1. Noah was only perfect in his generation, contrasted with those around him; he had the infirmities pertaining to sinful nature, and after his deliverance fell into temptation, and became inebriated with the fermented juice of the grape. Jesus was sinless, absolutely holy, and guile was not found in his mouth.

> 2. The ark which Noah built was for the temporal deliverance of a few persons Christ's salvation is spiritual and eternal and will embrace, of all nations and tongues, a multitude which no man can number.

Application

1. Sinners who reject the message of life by Christ Jesus, must be involved in endless and irremediable ruin.

2. The guilt of such is exceedingly aggravated, above those who perished in the time of Noah.

3. Let all men listen to the gracious overtures of mercy as made known in the gospel.

4. All who believe and enter into the ark shall be saved.

5. There is ample room in the ark, and a free invitation to every sinner.

6. Be wise, and enter in, and be saved.

3. MELCHIZEDEK A TYPE OF CHRIST

"After the order of Melchizedek." —Heb. 7:11.

IT is impossible to conceive of a more clear and manifest type of Jesus than Melchizedek. As such he was spoken of by the psalmist in one of his most direct and beautiful prophecies of the Messiah, Ps. 110:4. The apostle quotes the language of that prediction, and applies it directly to the Savior; and the chief part of this chapter serves to illustrate the corresponding traits of resemblance between Melchizedek and Christ. The chief features of similitude obviously center in the character of their priestly office, but there are other particulars not unworthy of our consideration:—Melchizedek typified the Savior,

I. In the Mysteriousness of his Personal History.

This mystery particularly refers to his descent being unrevealed. We have no account of his father or mother; we know nothing of his stock or ancestry: he appears in his own striking character, standing forth alone in the pages of revealed truth. Now that which is unrevealed of Melchizedek, (for doubtless he had both father and mother,) literally applies to Jesus.

1. As divine.

He had no father or mother, no beginning of years, and will have no end of life. Thus, he is self-existent, immutable, and eternal; the wise and blessed God, who hath unchangeableness and immortality dwelling in himself.

2. As human.

He had no father; he was conceived of the Virgin by the Holy Spirit As it was written, "A virgin shall conceive," &c.

II. In the Offices which he sustained.

He was "King of Salem and Priest of the most high God." See Heb. 7:2. In these how strikingly he represented Jesus the Messiah, who is eminently styled,

1. Prince of peace and righteous governor.

The holy, the just one. Whose reign is a righteous administration; whose scepter is eminently mild, pacific, and merciful.

It is impossible to conceive of one who so fully bears out these distinguished features in his person and government as Jesus. The righteous ruler; the prince of peace. See Ps. 45:1; Isaiah 32:1, Jer. 23:5; Zech. 9:9; Rev. 7:14.

2. He is, too, the priest of the most high God God's especially anointed and holy one. The priest of his universal church. Whose sacrifice is the richest and most precious ever offered on the altar of the Lord. A priest, whose office, work, and glory, were but dimly prefigured by those who served at the Jewish altar. A priest, in whom Jehovah's approbation centered, and whose incense ever came up so as to secure his highest delights.

3. Both the regal and priestly offices were united in him.

These offices were generally separate. Uzziah incurred God's displeasure for presuming to enter on the work of the priesthood. See 2 Chron. 26:18. But of Jesus it was distinctly predicted that he should be "a priest upon his throne," Zech. 6:13. And as the sacrifice of his body was suspended upon the cross, a true inscription represented his regal glory,— "Jesus of Nazareth, King of the Jews." As king and priest he now dwells in the most holy place. There he has his heavenly throne. There he wears his royal diadem. There he sways his righteous scepter. But there, too, he has on his sacerdotal vestments, and touched with the feeling of his people's infirmities, he ever lives to make intercession for them. Like Melchizedek,

4. He had no predecessor or successor in the offices he held.

No monarch left for Jesus a throne or kingdom. And as to his priesthood, he was not of Aaron's line, nor of the tribe of Levi. In both capacities he stood forth in his own divine right, to govern and to atone. To reign over men, and to redeem them to God by his own infinitely precious blood. He will never transfer either the crown or the miter. None will ever succeed him, is prince of righteousness, or priest of the most high God. His sacrifice once offered, possessing boundless virtue, avails forever in behalf of all who believe. And his throne abideth forever and ever. Melchizedek was a type of Jesus,

III. In the Blessing he bestowed.

Now mark here,

1. The person blessed.

Abraham, the father of the faithful. The rich blessings of Jesus are confined to believers, those who are the spiritual seed of that godly patriarch.

2. The ceremonial medium of the blessing.

"He brought forth bread and wine." How strikingly significant of that sacred medium through which Jesus blesses his people. The very symbols of his body and blood. Those symbols he chose to perpetuate the remembrance of his death in the ordinance of the supper. All our blessings come to us through the body which bare our guilt, and through the blood which was offered for our sins.

15

3. The blessing itself.

It was the "blessing of the most high God," Gen. 14:19. Now that of which Jesus is the medium, and which he bestows, is the favor and love of God. The smile of God. The peace of God With which every good in time and in eternity is connected. Which include present happiness and eternal life. Melchizedek was a type of Christ,

IV. In the Homage and Tribute he received.

Abraham greatly honored Melchizedek, and gave him tithes of all. How much more ought every believer to honor Jesus, and cheerfully consecrate to him their hearts, lives, influence, and their all. To him we belong; we are not our own but his. He has bought us, redeemed us to himself, so that if we live, we are solemnly obligated to live to him; or if we die, to die to him: so that living or dying, we are ever the Lord's.

Application

1. Learn the true dignity of the Savior, both in his kingly and priestly offices.

2. Both these he sustains for our welfare. He died to bless us; and now he reigns and lives to bless us.

3. The affectionate and supreme homage which we should render

4. ISAAC A TYPE OF CHRIST

"And Abraham called the name of his son that was born unto him, whom Sarah bare unto him. Isaac."—Gen. 21:3.

THE piety and faith of Abraham in surrendering his beloved son, at the demand of Jehovah, has ever been held up, as an extraordinary act of love and devotedness to God. In scripture the event stands forth as one of peculiar interest; and we are not only to admire the patriarch, but to imitate his self-denial and resignation; and to follow him, as one who now through faith and patience inherits the promises. But I fear in contemplating the subject we forget that the piety and faith and resignation of Isaac could not be greatly inferior to that of his father, for Isaac might have rebelled and refused to have submitted to a death so apparently unnatural and cruel, for at this time he was twenty-five if not thirty years of age. But at present let us glance briefly at the leading points of resemblance between Isaac and Jesus.

We see it,

I. In the Appropriateness of his Name.

Isaac signifies "laughter" or "rejoicing." Jesus, as the Messiah, was to be the consolation of Israel. As the Redeemer, the joy of the whole earth. No name so full of gladness to a disconsolate world as that of Christ's:

> "'Tis music in the sinner's ears,
> 'Tis life and health and peace."

II. In the peculiar Circumstances of his Birth.

1. His birth was specially predicted. God had communicated this both to Abraham and Sarah, Gen. 17:10, and 18:13. To the birth and coming of Jesus most of the prophets bare witness. Every event connected therewith had long been written on the roll of prophecy by the finger of God. 2. His birth was extraordinary When his mother was past age, Heb. 11:11. The birth of Jesus was still more extraordinary. Born of a virgin. According to the prediction of Isaiah,7:14 Luke 1:34. 3. His birth was connected with great joy, Gen. 21. Still greater rejoicing was associated with the birth of Christ. A host of angels descended to celebrate it in songs of rapturous joy. "And suddenly here was with the angel a multitude of the heavenly host," &c. Luke 2:13, 14.

III. In being intentionally offered as a Sacrifice.

Observe,

1. The description of the sacrifice which was given,

"Thy son, thine only son Isaac, whom thou lovest." How naturally our thoughts are led by this language to Jesus, the only-begotten son of God, the son of his delight, his dearly beloved son.

2. He was to be presented as a sacrifice.

"Offer him there for a burnt-offering," Gen. 22:1, 2, &c. Here again we are directly led to Jesus. He came to be a sacrifice. The apostle says of him, "For by one offering," &c., Heb. 10:14, evidently referring to the death of Jesus.

3. He was to be devoted and sacrificed by his father.

To Abraham God said, "Take now thy son," &c. Jesus was God's gift to the world. He so loved the world, that "he gave" &c., "He spared not his own son," &c., Rom. 8:32. The prophet Zechariah presents this before us in a form peculiarly striking, when Jehovah speaks, "Awake, O sword, against my shepherd," &c., Zech. 13:7. See also Acts 3:18.

4. He was to be offered on mount Moriah.

To this spot with his father he travelled for three days, &c. Near the same spot,—on Calvary, Jesus was sacrificed for the sin of the world.

5. Isaac bare the wood, which was designed to burn the offering.

Christ also bare the cross on which he was to be crucified.

6. Isaac freely submitted to be bound and tied upon the altar.

Jesus voluntarily went forth to death, and freely surrendered his spirit into the hands of his Father. But here the typical resemblance terminates. For Isaac a substitute is provided. The uplifted hand is stayed: God orders a ram to be bound and slain by Abraham in the stead of his son, Gen. 22:13. For Jesus there was no substitute. It behooved him to suffer. He was sent and appointed of his Father to his end He was born and lived that he might give himself a sacrifice for the sin of the world in the return of Isaac to his father's house, we have shadowed forth the resurrection of Christ from the dead, and his ascension to heaven, where he now appears at the right hand of the majesty on high.

Application

1. Let the subject lead us to contemplate the true desert of sin—which is death. And to this death as sinners all men are exposed.

2. Consider the necessity of an atoning sacrifice, "Without shedding of blood," &c.

3. Consider the infinite merit and preciousness of that sacrifice which God has provided,—his own son. The precious blood of Christ.

4. The necessity of a believing personal interest in the death and resurrection of Jesus Christ.

5. The awful consequence of neglecting the propitiation the love of God has provided—eternal death.

5. RESEMBLANCE BETWEEN JOSEPH AND CHRIST

"And the patriarchs, moved with envy, sold Joseph into Egypt, but God was with him."—Act 7:9.

ALL kinds of readers are charmed with the history of Joseph. So full of incident we do not wonder at young persons feeling deeply interested in the striking details of holy writ. So evidently distinguished by the finger of divine providence, the pious and contemplative must adore the wisdom and goodness of God, which overruled every event for the furtherance of his own designs, the glory of his name, and the ultimate advancement and happiness of Joseph. The piety of Joseph was striking and exemplary, and runs, like a golden thread, through the entire narrative of his life. But the very peculiar coincidence in many of the events of his history, and similar events in the life of Jesus, has led many to consider him as an eminent type of the Savior. Without either affirming or denying this, it cannot fail to edify our minds, while tracing the very numerous features of resemblance which exist between them. Observe this,

I. In the Significance of Joseph's Name.

It signifies especially, *increase,* or fruitfulness. As such it seemed to point out the ultimate prosperity with which God would bless him. Of Jesus it was predicted, by the prophet Isaiah, that "of the increase of his government and peace there should be no end," ch. ix. 7. John, the harbinger of Messiah, said of him, "He must increase," &c. His name is to endure longer than the sun; all men are to be blessed in him, and call him blessed. His progeny is to outnumber the stars of heaven, and the sands on the seashore. The resemblance is observable,

II. In his Father's preeminent Affection.

Joseph was the first-born of the beloved Rachel. And it is said, "Israel loved Joseph more than all his children," Gen. 37:3. We do not vindicate the evidence which Jacob gave of this, allowing the feeling to be right. But we turn to Jesus and his heavenly Father. He is God's only-begotten Son. The first-born. The Son of the Highest. And on him all the heart's affections of the Father were fixed. He was his chosen. God's soul ever delighted in him, and he proclaimed from the excellent glory, "This is my beloved Son, in whom I am well pleased," Matt. 3:17 "The Father hath loved the Son, and hath given all things into his hand," John 3:35.

III. In the Trials and Sufferings which he endured, and the Advancement which followed.

1. Joseph was the subject of his brethren's envy and dislike.

So Jesus came to his own, but they hated him, and received him not. From envy did they persecute and malign him.

2. While Joseph was on a mission of kindness to them, they conspired against him.

The Jews, the kinsmen of Jesus, after the flesh, also conspired against him, and took counsel to put him to death.

3. Joseph was sold by his brethren for twenty pieces of silver.

So Jesus was delivered for thirty pieces into the hands of his enemies.

4. Joseph was falsely accused and cast into prison.

So was Jesus arraigned, and many false accusations were brought against him. As a prisoner, too, he was scourged and delivered up to his accusers.

5. The predictions of Joseph in his abasement respecting the chief butler and baker, seem to coincide with the declaration of mercy which Jesus made to the dying thief, of an entrance into paradise, while we fear the other perished in hardness and unbelief.

6. The deliverance of Joseph somewhat resembles the resurrection of Christ from the dead, and the rolling away of the stone from the mouth of the sepulcher where he had been laid.

7. The advancement of Joseph to honor, and riches, and dominion, beautifully sets forth the glorious exaltation of Christ to the right hand of his Father, who hath committed all judgment and authority into his hauls.

8. Joseph provided the bread of life for those who would otherwise have perished So Jesus has provided the bread of everlasting life for a dying world.

9. Joseph mercifully forgave his brethren, and dealt bountifully with them.

So Jesus prayed for his murderers, and gave the first offer of salvation to the guilty sinners of Jerusalem.

10. Joseph provided a dwelling for hi kindred in the rich and fruitful Goshen.

So Jesus has prepared for all his followers everlasting mansions in the kingdom of his glory.

11. Joseph exercised power and authority over all the people.

So Jesus has unlimited power and universal authority, for the Father hath given all things into his hands.

12. God overruled all events, even the malice and wickedness of his brethren, for his final good and exaltation.

So all the affairs of earth and time are under divine control, for the final and universal establishment of Christ's kingdom and glory, until the kingdoms of this world shall become the kingdom of Christ, and he shall reign forever and ever. Such are the chief points of resemblance between Joseph and Jesus.

Application

1. Let the interesting narratives connected with the history of Joseph only serve to incite us to peruse more intently the all-important history of Jesus the Son of God

2. While we honor and admire the stern integrity and sincere piety of Joseph, we are called upon to imitate and walk in the footsteps of Jesus.

3. Joseph conferred temporal benefits upon the people and upon his kindred; Jesus hath obtained eternal redemption for all who obey him. He gives the bread of life, the mercies of salvation, and everlasting glory to all who love him.

4. Joseph endured many sufferings, out now feeble were they when contrasted with the agony and death of the Son of God; and let it not be forgotten, while Joseph suffered on his own account, Jesus suffered expressly and voluntarily for us, and for our salvation, that he might bring us to the enjoyment of the favor, image, and glory of God.

6. MOSES A TYPE OF CHRIST

"A prophet—like unto me."—Deut. 18:15.

No other person so fully and clearly typified Christ as Moses. His life was crowded with events which evidently shadowed forth the long-predicted and expected Messiah. In addition to these prominent events, God expressly commanded him to inform the people, that he would raise up for them a prophet *like* unto himself, one who should have Jehovah's words in his mouth,—who should speak all his words unto the people, and whose commands all the people should be solemnly required to hearken and obey. Let us notice then the great leading incidents in the history of Moses, which seemed to typify the character and work of the Redeemer. Notice,

I. The peculiar Circumstances connected with their Birth.

A cruel edict was in force when Moses was born, for the extermination of the male children of the Israelites, Ex. 1:16. A similar edict was issued by Herod, at the birth of Jesus, when the children of Bethlehem and the coasts thereof were slain, Matt. 2:16. Moses was mercifully delivered by the providence of God; in like manner Jesus was saved by the direct interposition of heaven, Matt. 2:13. Thus, as the life of Moses was preserved from the cruel designs of Pharaoh, was the life of the Savior delivered from the murderous hand of Herod. Notice,

II. Their voluntary Abasement and Humiliation.

Moses, a resident in the palace of Pharaoh, surrounded with the honors, and riches, and pleasures of Egypt, when he was come to years freely surrendered them all, and chose rather to be the companion of the suffering people of God. Jesus, the prince of heaven, possessed of all the honors and riches of glory, for our well-being and salvation, cheerfully condescended to assume our nature and condition, to tabernacle in our world, to become a servant ministering to all, that we, through his humiliation and poverty, might be made rich, and obtain exalted honors and eternal life. Observe,

III. Both were especially appointed to be the Deliverers of the Afflicted and the Oppressed.

Moses was sent to deliver the groaning Israelites from the bondage of Pharaoh and the slavery of Egypt. Jesus came to deliver the world from the bondage of sin and the slavery of the devil. Moses was sent by God, expressly commissioned and fully qualified by miraculous power for the accomplishment of this great work. Jesus was also sent immediately from the Father to deliver the world from the power of Satan, and to save immortal souls from the destroying vassalage of sin. For this he was anointed with the Holy Spirit, and possessed all strength, so that all things were subjected to the word of his power. No one ever performed the mighty works which were done by Jesus. See Peter's reference to Christ's miraculous deeds, Acts 2:22.

IV. Both of them delivered the Laws and Mind of God to the People.

On Sinai Moses received from God the moral law, and made it known to the Israelites. Jesus delivered the spiritual exposition of the law in his sermon on the mount. See Matt. 5, 6, and 7. This one great office Christ sustained to make known unto men all the will of his Father, to bring life and immortality to light by his gospel, and to give a perfect code of laws to mankind.

V. Both of them were appointed Leaders of the People.

Moses stood at the head of the old dispensation, and having given God's law to Israel, he conducted them through the desert towards the land of promise Jesus was given as a witness and leader to the people. He came as the head of the new dispensation to conduct the numerous host of believing followers to immortal glory.

VI. Both of them acted as Mediators between God and the People.

Moses stood forth between the people and God, when his avenging wrath would otherwise have destroyed them. For their safety he faithfully, perseveringly, and successfully interceded. In this he but faintly exhibited the mediatorial office and work of Jesus. Jesus engaged himself as the surety of ungodly, condemned sinners; he freely sought to bear their sins, and be wounded for their transgressions; and by the virtue of his atoning blood he honorably turned aside the just wrath of God, and delivered a guilty world from condemnation and eternal death. If Moses pleaded for his ungrateful and guilty countrymen, Jesus with his dying breath pleaded on behalf of his murderers, and said, "Father, forgive them, they know not what they do."

VII. Both of their Engagements were connected with the Ministrations of Angels.

The law was ordained by angels in the hand of Moses, as mediator. See Acts 7:53; Ex. 23:20, &c. The whole life of Jesus was associated with the ministry of angels. They announced his conception, proclaimed his birth, succored him in the desert, witnessed his transfiguration, strengthened him in the garden, watched over his sepulcher, rolled away the stone at his resurrection, and were as his attendants, when he ascended to glory.

VIII. Both were distinguished for high moral Endowments.

Moses was the obedient, faithful servant of God. He was eminently holy, the meekest of all men. He held intimate fellowship with God. Fasted forty days and forty nights. His countenance was irradiated with the beams of the divine glory. And God greatly distinguished and honored him before the people. Jesus was obedient and faithful as a son. He was spotless, guile was not in his mouth. He did no sin He was gentle and meek; he strove not, neither did he cry, or lift up his voice in the street. The law of love was in his heart. Kindness and benignity in his conversation. He exhibited great self-denial, and fasted, too, forty days and nights in the wilderness. He held the most intimate and unbroken fellowship with God. At his transfiguration his countenance shone as the sun, and his garments appeared to be of glittering brightness, and God, on several occasions, declared him to be the Son of his delight, in whom he was well-pleased.

IX. Both were eminent Prophets of the Most High God.

As a prophet God spoke to Moses more directly than to other prophets, "face to face." He prophesied largely, and his predictions, although extending probably to the end of the world, were full, comprehensive, and clear. See many parts of the book of Deuteronomy. Jesus possessed the spirit of prophecy without measure. At all times he had access to his heavenly Father, knew all his mind, and on any occasion, could reveal his will to the people. Like Moses, his prophecies included the displeasure of God, towards the impenitent seed of Abraham, and his predictions had respect to succeeding events from the lime of his first advent to his second coming, in majesty, power, and glory, to judge the world.

X. Both obtained unspeakably valuable Blessings for the People.

Not only did Moses lead Israel from the galling yoke of Pharaoh, but when in the desert he obtained for them "manna from heaven," water from the flinty rock, and turned aside from them fearful plagues. See Ex. 32:30; Numb. 16:46. Jesus Christ in the days of his flesh went about doing good, healing their infirmities, delivering those who were bound and tormented of the devil. He also fed multitudes in the desert, and gave himself as the true bread of life to a dying world.

XI. Both lived and labored for the Wellbeing of others.

Moses displayed the most astonishing benevolence for his countrymen. He ever sought their happiness, and exhibited the greatest kindness and patience towards them: rather than they should perish, he besought the Lord that his name might be blotted out of God's book. In this how vastly the antitype exceeds the type. Jesus exhibited inexpressible goodness to his ancient people. He embodied his immeasurable love in all his conduct towards them. And he actually became a curse for sinners, that they, through his death might obtain everlasting life.

XII. Both were treated with Ingratitude by those whose Welfare they lived to promote.

How often did the Israelites rebel against him, and would have thrown off his authority; they frequently murmured against him, and with the greatest ingratitude did they often attribute their own miseries to him, instead of confessing and forsaking their iniquities. Thus, too was Jesus treated by the Jews; he came unto his own, but his own received him not. They even preferred a murderer to him, and by wicked hands did they put him to a cruel and shameful death.

Application

1. Justly distinguished as Moses was, he was yet frail, a man of like infirmities with others; as such he offended God, by speaking rashly with his lips. Jesus was immaculate. All holiness dwelt in him.

2. Moses was but a servant; Jesus was the Son of God.

3. Moses was the head of that dispensation which was legal and ceremonial, and which passed away. Jesus is the head of that ceremony which is spiritual, gracious, and abiding. To the supreme excellency and glory of Jesus did Moses and the prophets bear witness.

25

4. Let us rejoice that we are not come to Sinai, but Zion; not under the law, but under grace; not the followers of Moses, but the disciples of Christ.

5. If disobedience to Moses and his law was visited with God's displeasure, how shall those escape who neglect Christ's salvation, and obey not his gospel.

7. JOSHUA A TYPE OF CHRIST

"The Lord spoke unto Joshua, the son of Nun." &c.—Josh. 1:1-5. See Heb. 4:8.

THE life and history of the most celebrated individual could not fully and perfectly typify the life and work of the Son of God. In several things Moses could not represent the coming Messiah. His sin against the Lord, and his exclusion from the goodly land, especially illustrate this idea. The great designs of God respecting his people were not perfected by Moses. Joshua had to take up and complete those designs, after Moses had died in the mountain of the Lord. Joshua appears, in many respects, to have been an illustrious type of the Savior. Notice the typical character of Joshua,

I. In his Name.

Joshua signifies precisely in Hebrew what Jesus does in the Greek tongue, viz., SAVIOR. See Heb. 4:8. Both names were appropriate to the work in which they engaged, and the achievements which they obtained. In this only, as Saviors, did they differ, that while Joshua had to do with the temporal salvation of the hundreds of thousands of the Israelites, Jesus came to save unnumbered hosts of believers from spiritual and eternal death.

II. As the Successor of Moses.

Moses gave the law to the people, but did not put them in possession of the promised rest. For this he must have Joshua as his successor. So it. was with respect to the legal dispensation, would not give rest to the weary and heavy laden sinner; but our spiritual Joshua came expressly to do that which the law could not do, and to give that to transgressors which the law could not give. As such, the law, with its requirements and its threatenings to the guilty, came by Moses; but grace that is, favor to condemned sinners, came by Jesus Christ. Moses showed the people what they owed to Jehovah, Joshua exhibited what the goodness of God had provided even for the unworthy.

III. As the Commander and Leader of the People.

As such he was required to make known unto the people all the words of God's law, and to exemplify perfect obedience thereunto in his own person and life. He was also to lead them in their marches, and conduct them onwards to the land of promise. How strikingly did Joshua thus typify Jesus! He was appointed to be God's witness and a leader to the people, Isa. 55:4. All the law of God did he exhibit in his holy and spotless life. He was righteousness, living and speaking to the world, the ten commandments, in all their spiritual meaning, alive. He announced himself as the way, the truth, and the life, and engaged to conduct all who followed him to a glorious immortality and eternal life. "For it became him, by whom are all things," &c., Heb. 2:10,

IV. In the astonishing Events of his Life

1. There was the miracle at Jordan.

The waters of Jordan were divided before him, and the people passed through as on dry ground. In the same river the glories of Jesus were witnessed by the people. It was there that he began his ministry, by being baptized of John, while the heavens were opened, and the voice from the excellent glory pronounced him to be the Son of God's delight, in whom he was well pleased. In this ordinance, too, is it not where men, having forsaken the world, profess their faith in Christ and their love to his name, and by which they become the partakers of that spiritual rest which all who believe experimentally possess? See Rom. 6:4; Col. 2:12.

2. He threw down the walls of Jericho, ch. 6:5.

And that by an instrumentality apparently powerless and insignificant. How indicative of that subjugation of the world to the authority of Christ, by the preaching of his cross. Yet, as in the one case, the walls fell down at the sound of the rams' horns, so in the other, by the publication of the gospel, the strongholds of sin have been beaten down, and by this simple and, to the wise men of the world, foolish agency, small all the kingdoms of the world ultimately bow down before the scepter of Jesus, call him blessed, and be blessed in him, 1 Cor. 1:18-28.

3. He subdued all their enemies.

Faithful to all which God had spoken to him, the divine help made him at all times victorious, and placed his feet on the necks of his enemies. In this we again turn to contemplate the Captain of our salvation, who came to encounter all the deadly foes of mankind, and who, by his life and sufferings, by his miracles and death, by his conflicts and resurrection, triumphed over all the powers of darkness, bruised the head of the old serpent, and effectually destroyed the works of the devil, Col. 2:13, 14; Rev. 1:18.

4. He gave the people possession of the good land. See ch. 14:1.

Thus Jesus, having overcome all our enemies, and accomplished all the Father had given him to do, ascended on high, and took possession of the heavenly Canaan, on behalf and in the name of his people. He said, "In my Father's house are many mansions," &c., John 14:1, "I ascend to my Father and to your Father," John 20:17. &c.,; Rev. 3:21 Such are the leading traits of resemblance between Joshua and Jesus, in the one case, Joshua was the leader of one nation, in the other, Jesus is the captain and conductor of countless hosts of every nation, and people, and tongue. The achievements of Joshua were temporal, and the land he obtained was but an earthly, temporary possession. The achievements of Jesus were spiritual, and the inheritance he bestows is heavenly, and does not pass away. Happy the hosts who had Joshua for their leader, and Canaan for their inheritance, but unspeakably more happy the followers of Jesus, and the expectants of that kingdom which shall not pass away.

8. SAMSON A TYPE OF CHRIST

"And the angel of the Lord appeared unto the woman, and said unto her, Behold now, thou art barren and hearest not; but thou shalt conceive and bear a son," &c.—Judges 13:3-5.

FEW persons of scriptural renown appear to less advantage than Samson. There are no evidences of superior piety or distinguished goodness exhibited in his life, and we might almost have hesitated whether to place him among the ranks of the godly, had we not found this already done by the apostle, who gives us a brief view of Old Testament worthies, in his epistle to the Hebrews, (ch. 11:32,) and concludes by saying, "All these died in the faith." While the private life of Samson is however so lamentably deficient as to traits of elevated piety, yet the public events of his wonderful career seem expressly typical of the person and work of the Messiah Observe this in the following particulars:

I. In the Events associated with his Birth.

His conception was announced by an angel, and his future character and history predicted, Judges 13:5. How exactly do we see a similar messenger, announcing a similar event to the virgin mother of Jesus. "And the angel said unto her, Fear not, Mary; for thou hast found favor with God. And behold thou shalt conceive in thy womb, and bring forth a Son, and shall call his name Jesus. He shall be great and shall be called the Son of the Highest, and the Lord God shall give unto him the throne of his father David," &c., Luke i 30-33. He seemed to be a type of Christ,

II. As a Nazarite.

It was ordained of him that he should be a Nazarite from the womb. The Nazarites were considered separated from common purposes, and devoted to God. In this how did he typify Jesus, who although not a *legal* Nazarite, yet was called a Nazarene, Matt. 2:23. And who exhibited in all his actions his devotedness to his Father's work, and who was holy, harmless, undefiled, and separate from sinners. Yes, how truly was the very spirit of the Nazarite exemplified in Christ. He associated not with those engaged in the pursuit of wealth, fame, or earthly glory. His was not companionship with the great and the learned, with the nobles and princes of this world. He came to do the work of God, and he wearied not, until he could say, Father, "I have finished the work which thou gavest me to do."

III. In his Achievements

1. In the destruction of the lion.

The history of this event is given, Judg. 14:6, and the sequel of the bees and honey in the carcass is peculiarly singular; as SCOTT justly observes, "the carcass of a lion was a most unlike place for a swarm of bees, being, as might have been supposed, both inconvenient and offensive to that delicate insect, which draws honey from she most odoriferous flowers and plants." In this we see the temptations and victory of Christ singularly exhibited. Christ, on his entrance on the great work of his mission, retired into the wilderness, and there conflicted and overcame Satan, the roaring lion. And this conquest of Christ's is full of sweetness to the tempted believer, for he not only sees the limited power of the wicked one, but also learns how effectually to put him to flight by the sword of the Spirit, which is the word of God. See Matt. 4:1-11.

2. He marvelously discomfited his enemies.

Unto these enemies he was delivered by his own people, Judg. 15:11, &c. Yet by his own mighty arm, nerved with power from on high, did he overcome them. See Judg. 15:14-20. And so also at his death did he slay still more of his enemies than during his life, Judg. 16:26. The whole life of Jesus was one struggle with those who were the enemies of his person, doctrine, and reign. By his words and miracles did he confound both the Pharisees and scribes and teachers of the people. But at his death he gained a final conquest over earth and hell, and triumphantly shouted, "It is finished," and gave up the spirit In the sufferings and indignities offered to Samson before his death, we have shadowed forth the shame, and contumely, and cruelty with which Jesus was treated in the court of Herod, and after the sentence of death was pronounced upon him. Com pare especially Judg. 16:25, and Matt 27:29.

3. In beaming away the gates of Gaza.

See Judges 15:2, 3. It is impossible to read the scripture account of this event and not see a striking coincidence in it, and the resurrection of Christ from the dead.

Just as the enemies of Gaza must have marveled at Samson's escape, bearing on his shoulders the ponderous gates of the city, so marveled both the soldiers and the Jews at the resurrection of Christ from the tomb, with the earthquake and glory with which it was attended. We shall not attempt to show the great disparity between Samson and Jesus, as one was the least perfect of Old Testament saints, and the other the source and pattern of unsullied purity and goodness. It may indeed be said that many New Testament saints, under a more favorable dispensation, exhibit equal frailties to those displayed in the life of Samson. Our reply is, Jesus is the model of Christian excellency, we are called with a high and holy calling, and it behooves us to show forth a conversation becoming the gospel of Christ. While Samson acts as a beacon, let Jesus be the magnet, directing us to walk in his holy and heavenly steps.

9. DAVID A TYPE OF CHRIST

"They shall serve the Lord their God, and David their king, whom I will raise up unto them." —
Jer. 30:9.

No one ever more fully typified Jesus than David, who, notwithstanding his lamentable defects
of character, was an eminently holy man, and an illustrious servant of the God of Israel. His
history is exceedingly eventful, and highly adapted to instruct and edify the contemplative
believer. Few were more visibly under the guidance of a benign and wise providence than David.
God indeed was his refuge, his help, and his shield. He stands forth justly celebrated as a wise
and good monarch; his ardent devout piety, the prophetic sphere in which he moved, and his
sanctified poetic powers, rendered him an eminent blessing in his day and generation. His psalms
have comforted and strengthened the people of God in every age, and his songs of praise will be
joyfully sung in the assemblies of the righteous to the end of the world. But at present we have to
do with David as a type of the Savior. This typical resemblance is observable,

I. In his Name.

David signifies beloved. Such was David, beloved of God, a man after God's own heart. We see
in the text that the very name is given to Jesus, for the prophecies of Jeremiah could have respect
to none but to the Messiah. See also Ezek. 34:24; Hos. 3:5. If David's name appropriately
belonged to him in its signification of beloved, how much does it apply to Jesus. He is essentially
and in the most comprehensive sense the BELOVED. Beloved of God, Jehovah's everlasting
delight. (See Prov. 8:30.) Beloved and adored of angels. The joy of heaven and the one supreme
object of celestial worship and praise. Beloved of the church, in every age and country, and
among every nation and people, where the gospel has been preached, and his sweet odoriferous
name made known. This is our beloved, and this is our friend.

II. In his Parentage and Birth-place.

Jesse, a man of no worldly celebrity or greatness, was the father of David; Bethlehem, a village
or small town of Judea, his birthplace. How clearly did these shadow forth the humble condition
of Jesus. He was the son of Mary, a poor virgin espoused to Joseph a carpenter. And precisely
the same place, Bethlehem, gave birth to David, and to David's Lord, the world's Messiah. Hence
it was written by the prophet, "And thou Bethlehem, in the land of Juda," &c., Matt. 2:5, 6.

III. In his Occupation.

David was originally a shepherd. It was emphatically said of him to Samuel, "He keepeth the
sheep," 1 Sam. 16:11. In his pastoral employment how strikingly he typified Jesus, the "Great
Shepherd of the sheep." To a shepherd Christ often likened himself. He said, "I am the good
shepherd." As such he evinced unequalled affection and tenderness for his flock.

He gave his life for his sheep. He leads them into green pastures. He preserves them from the roaring destroying lion. He restores them when they wander. He heals all their diseases. And finally he receives them into his heavenly fold, and causes them to lie down, by the rivers of his pleasure, forever and ever.

IV. In his Person and Moral Endowments.

The personal beauty of David is the subject of inspired testimony. His pious and holy character are expressly described and exhibited in the history of his life. Of Jesus, he said, when speaking by the power of inspiration, "Thou art *fairer* than the children of men, grace is poured into thy lips," &c., Ps. 41:2. All moral excellencies were concentrated in Jesus. In him light and truth centered, holiness and love dwelt. Righteousness and peace were perfected. He was the express image of the purity and goodness of God.

V. In his Exaltation to the Throne of Israel.

In the exaltation of David we behold the direct interference of God. The evident work of his all-wise and blessed providence. See 1 Sam. 16:3, &c. For this exalted station God qualified him in the day of his anointing, by giving him his Holy Spirit, 1 Sam. 16:13. In this how forcibly are we led to contemplate the royal character of Messiah the Prince. That David whom the Lord anointed to be king in Zion, whose scepter is a scepter of righteousness, and whose dominions are destined to encircle the whole earth, and whose reign is to be a reign of everlasting mercy and truth. For his kingly office God anointed his son Jesus, with the oil of gladness above his fellows, Heb. 1:8.

VI. In his Prophetical Office.

David was richly imbued with the spirit of prophecy. His predictions are numerous. He predicted extensively of the person, work, suffering, glory, and kingdom of the Messiah. Jesus is also a prophet. A prophet possessing the powers of inspiration in himself. For the Spirit dwelt in him in all its immeasurable fulness. He is also the source and the chief subject of prophecy. To him bear all the prophets wit ness.

VII. In his Sufferings and Enemies.

David had to bear the malignant, envious dislike of Saul. The opposition of the surrounding nations. The blasphemous rage of Goliath. The deceitful conspiracy of his own subjects. And the unfaithfulness and crimes of his own family. What room for enlargement here, on the sufferings and enemies of Christ! Jesus had to conflict with the powers of darkness. The envy of Herod and the chief priests. The hypocrisy of the scribes and Pharisees. The defection of his own disciples, and the wicked perfidy of Judas, who betrayed him. Many of David's psalms were clearly expressive of his own sufferings and enemies, and yet prophetically alluding to the sufferings and enemies of Christ.

VIII. In his signal Victories.

The victories of David were signal and numerous. See these celebrated, 2 Sam. 18:10. God often went with him, and in the name of the Lord he mightily triumphed over his enemies. The lion and the bear, Goliath and the Philistines, were all vanquished by the son of Jesse. Jesus too triumphed over all his foes. He overcame the wicked one in the wilderness. He overcame the powers of darkness and sin, in the mighty miracles which he wrought. He overcame death and hell, by his resurrection from the dead. He is the mighty and blessed conqueror, who is represented by John, in the visions of Patmos, as seated on a white horse, and going forth from conquering to conquer.

But David was a frail man; his victories were obtained by the shedding of blood, and his course was connected with the misery of his fellow-men. Our David is the perfect and immaculate Christ; his victories are bloodless, and his course is one of universal happiness and joy.

How happy are his loyal subjects! How precious the privileges of his kingdom! And how universally glorious shall be his dominion and reign!

10. SOLOMON A TYPE OF CHRIST

"A greater than Solomon is here." —Luke 2:31.

THE history of Solomon is connected with much that is dark, mysterious, and distressing. He commenced his public career under the most bright and encouraging circumstances. The son of the pious David, he had been favored with his religious instructions and example He had been interested, too, in many fervent prayers which had ascended to God in his behalf. He began his course in a way so devoutly and wisely, that God greatly approved of him and gave him largely beyond what he had sought of him in prayer, and for a time the prospects before him were more fraught with hope and promise than any who had swayed the scepter in Israel. But he did not maintain that piety and purity with which he commenced his reign; he wandered awfully from God, and exhibited in his own conduct the weakness and frailty even of the wisest and best of men, when they do not closely and faithfully depend upon God for assistance and strength. It is to be hoped that the book of Ecclesiastes was written after he had experienced the emptiness of the world, and the bitterness of sin, and as such that it indicates his repentance and restoration to the favor and service of God. It is very clear in his public movements, that he was an eminent type of Jesus Christ. He was so,

I. As the Descendant of David.

Jesus is described as both the root and offspring of David. And there is one scripture which was originally expressly applied to Solomon as David's son, 2 Sam. 7:14, which is afterwards as distinctly applied to Jesus. "I will be to him a father, and he shall be to me a son," Heb. 1:6. We need not try to prove the genealogical descent of Jesus from David, Matt. 1:6-16.

II. In his extraordinary Knowledge and Wisdom.

Solomon prayed for wisdom, and God richly endowed him with it. He seemed to understand all the principles of nature. He was celebrated as a sacred poet, and his proverbs exhibit the supernatural attainments which heavenly inspiration conferred upon him. Jesus is the wisdom of God. In him dwelt all the treasures of wisdom and knowledge. Peter said truly to him, "Lord, thou knowest all things." He is emphatically wise of heart, and his understanding is infinite.

III. As Monarch of Israel

No king in Israel ever possessed equal glory and riches with Solomon. His reign seemed typical of Christ's regal character.

1. In its righteousness and equity.

2. In its riches and glory, representing he true spiritual riches and dignity of the kingdom of Christ.

3. In its peaceableness. Jesus is "The Prince of peace." His kingdom is a peaceable kingdom. He brought peace and good will to a rebellious world. He confers peace, which the world can neither give nor take away.

IV. In his Connection with the Temple

He had it in his heart to honor God by erecting a splendid edifice for his worship and glory. He entered zealously on the work. He persevered till the erection was completed. He dedicated it, with the greatest solemnity and devotion to God. In these things Christ and his church are evidently typified in the spirit and conduct of Solomon.

Jesus came expressly to rear a spiritual edifice in the world for the honor and glory of the living God. The materials of which it is composed, he redeemed to God by his own blood. These by his Spirit and word he prepares and builds up, into a house and dwelling or habitation for God. These he sacredly dedicated to God by intercessory prayer, John 17. All the services and ordinances of this temple, Jesus, as supreme Prince, and great High-priest, he solemnly fixed and established. And he is still rearing this glorious building, and shall do so until the head-stone is elevated amid shouts of "Grace, grace unto it!"

The heart of Christ is fully set on this, and all the dispensations of time, and events of providence, are tending to this one august and inconceivably grand consummation.

But a *greater* than Solomon is here. Greater even in those things for which Solomon was most justly celebrated. Greater in wisdom,—greater in true glory,—greater in the extent of his dominions,—greater in the happiness of his subjects,—greater in the righteous and benevolent characteristics of his administration. Solomon's glory declined, and his honors faded away. His kingdom has been revolutionized, and the site of the temple he erected has been ploughed up. Christ's glories are increasingly resplendent. His honors are ever increasing. His kingdom cannot be moved. His reign shall be forever, and his scepter shall be swayed from the rivers to the ends of the earth.

Application

1. How happy, dignified, and secure the subjects of Christ's kingdom.

2. How unspeakably wonderful his per son and perfections.

3. Let his people celebrate his praise.

4. Let his foes fall down before him and kiss the scepter of mercy which he extends to all.

5. His obdurate enemies shall be covered with shame and perish forever.

11. JONAH A TYPE OF CHRIST

"No sign shall be given but that of the Prophet Jonah." —Matt. 12:39

JONAH was one of the least amiable or interesting of the prophets. Neither as to piety, talents, or usefulness, will he bear any comparison with his fellow seers, who were employed to reveal the mind of God to the people. How greatly is this disparity seen, when we compare him with the assiduous and devoted Samuel, with the devotional psalmist, with the evangelical Isaiah, with the sublime Ezekiel, or the moving Jeremiah. Yet, as in a great house there are necessarily vessels of wood and clay, as well as of silver and gold, so we see the same variety among the saints of God's family, and the officers of his spiritual kingdom. Jesus has greatly honored Jonah, in referring to his history and sufferings as being figurative of his own mission, death, and resurrection from the grave. In glancing at the typical character of Jonah, we may notice,

I. The striking Signification of his Name.

Jonah signifies dove,—a striking emblem of the meek and gentle Jesus. He was meek and lowly of heart. He did not lift up his voice and strive, but with open arms of affection did he receive the weary and afflicted, and gave them rest. When he was anointed for the great mission, "the Holy Spirit descended like a dove lighting upon him," Matt. 3:16. Jonah was a type of Christ,

II. As a Proclaimer of God's will to Men.

Jonah's message was one which charged the people with guilt, called them to repentance, and assured them of the readiness of God to exercise mercy if they repented, but declared the vengeance of God if they repented not. These four leading particulars are evidently discernible in the preaching of Jesus Christ. He charged men with sin. He enjoined repentance. He offered forgiveness. He predicted God's wrath to the incorrigibly guilty.

III. In his Sufferings and Deliverance.

Jonah in attempting to flee from God's presence, was overtaken by a fearful tempest. The superstitions of the crew suggested the casting of lots. The lot fell upon Jonah. He offered himself to be the propitiatory victim, and said, "Take me up, and cast me into the sea," Jonah 1:12. After vainly striving against the storm, at length they took Jonah and cast him into the sea. For his preservation God provided a great fish, which was the ark of his safety for three days and three nights, ch.1:15-17. In the belly of the fish, by reason of his affliction, he cried unto God, and the Lord heard and mercifully delivered him, ch. 2:1-10. How strange and wonderful this series of events in reference to Jonah! How significant when viewed as typifying the sufferings and resurrection of Jesus!

1. In the storm we have a striking representation of God's righteous displeasure and wrath against a sinful world. 2. In Jonah's willingness to be thrown into the sea, we have the voluntary

engagement of Christ as the substitute for guilt. 3. In the cessation of the storm we have the perfect satisfaction of God, with the sufferings of his Son, and his desire for the reconciliation of the world to himself. 4. In the distressing sorrows and mournful complaints of Jonah, when surrounded by the waters of the great deep, we have a faint picture of the overwhelming anguish and grief of Christ, when presenting his soul an offering for sin. Especially when prostrate in Gethsemane, and when expiring on the cross. See Matt. 26:36-39, and Matt. 27:46. 5. In the preservation of Jonah we have clearly prefigured the care which Jehovah took of the body of Jesus; his resurrection from the dead the third day. In this Jonah was an express type of Christ's burial and resurrection from the dead, and as such this was to be the last great sign which God would give to the Jews of the Messiahship of Jesus. A sign so great and peculiar that nothing but the deepest unbelief and infatuation could possibly reject. 6. In the success of Jonah's preaching after his deliverance, we have brought to our remembrance the successful proclamation of the gospel of Christ, and the rapid spread of divine truth in the days of the apostles.

Jonah after all very imperfectly typified Christ. His unwillingness to obey God, how unlike the cheerful obedience of Jesus, and his readiness at all times to do the will of his Father. His envious spirit at the repenting of the Ninevites, how unlike Christ rejoicing in spirit where he beheld the progress of his gospel, and the kingdom of Satan falling as lightning from heaven. His discontented and fretful temper, how opposite to the holy, calm, resigned spirit of Jesus. Indeed a greater, one infinitely surpassing Jonah, is here. Greater in the mission he undertook—the salvation of a world. Greater in the sufferings he endured. Greater in the deliverance he effected. A few mariners escaped death in the one case, a world was delivered from the curse in the other. Greater in his personal dignity and glory. Greater in his office, character, and work. Jesus was Jonah's master, Jonah's Lord. This very Jonah must have exercised faith in the coming Savior, to have escaped the just wrath of God, and the true desert of his own sin.

Application

1. Christ as the propitiation for sin we would make known to all men.

2. The peril of sin and unbelief we would urge upon all careless lethargic sinners.

3. Faith in Christ as the only Savior we would proclaim to all who are inquiring, "What must we do to be saved?"

12. CHRIST TYPIFIED BY JACOB'S LADDER

"And behold a ladder set up on the earth, and the top of it reached to heaven and behold the angels of God ascending and descending on it." —Gen. 28:12.

AT sundry times, in divers manners, God spoke unto the fathers. He revealed his mind to Noah as to the deluge. To Abraham as to his will respecting him, and his promise that in his seed would all the families of the earth be blessed. To Jacob God revealed himself on several occasions The scene at Bethel was peculiarly solemn and interesting. Jacob was now alone; far from the dwelling of his affectionate parents. Fleeing from the face of his incensed brother. On his journey to Padanaram, overtaken by the shades of evening, he laid himself down to sleep. The earth was his bed, the canopy of heaven his only covering. A stone his pillow. There, overcome by the fatigue of travelling, having doubtless commended his soul to God, he fell asleep. In a vision of the night God appeared, and said, "I am the Lord," &c., ver. 13. God evidently designed to cheer and strengthen the mind of Jacob, and the whole was intended to give him an assurance of his interest in the kind arrangements of a benign and watchful Providence. But the vision of the ladder seems to present a beautiful emblem of the Savior; to this, then, lot us direct our present attention. See Christ's authority for this, John 1:51. It might typify,

I. The Person of the Savior.

The top of the ladder "reached to heaven." Jesus, the second Adam, was of heaven, heavenly. He dwelt there in the bosom of the Father. His glory filled heaven. He was the Prince royal of heaven. The Most High and blessed Potentate. But the ladder "was fixed upon the earth." And in this we have shadowed forth the humanity of Christ. God with God, he became man with men. He became an inhabitant of the earth. He was born into it. He took upon him the nature of man— was of the seed of Abraham, Gal. 4:4. He dwelt upon the earth, tabernacled amongst us, and displayed his "glory, the glory of the only-begotten of the Father," &c., John 1:14. He sojourned for more than thirty years upon the earth, and blessed mankind with the riches both of his providence and grace; filling heaven with the rays of his glory, yet, at the same time, he was filling the earth with his goodness and mercy. See this strikingly stated by Christ, John 3:13. It might typify,

II. The Mediatorial Work of Christ.

The ladder reached from heaven to earth, therefore *united* both. This was the grand object of the Savior, to connect heaven with earth. Earth had revolted, thrown off its allegiance, was in a state of rebellion. Jesus sought to restore it to rightful authority, and thus to bring it beneath the smile and favor of God. That separation which sin had effected he came to make up. That ruin which sin had produced he came to repair. That misery which sin had entailed, he came to remove. He came to bring down heaven to earth, and to raise earth to the holiness and bliss of heaven. Or it might typify,

39

III. Christ as the only Way to the Father.

God appointed Jesus to be the medium of communication between himself and man. And Christ is the only way of access for the sinner to God. Jesus said, "I am the way." "*No* man cometh unto the Father but by me." In Christ God is well pleased, and all who are in Christ are accepted of him. Here he requires that all we do be done in Christ's name. Faith must be in Christ's name. Prayer and thanksgiving must be in Christ's name All obedience must be presented to him in, and through, Christ Jesus. If we go to God for pardoning mercy—renewing grace—or adopting love, Christ is the only way. He is the true propitiatory, where we have access to God, and enjoy fellowship with him. It might typify,

IV. The Accessibility of Christ to this perishing Sinner.

The ladder was placed upon the earth, close to the spot where Jacob lay and slept Now herein we see how near Christ is to us. Not a Savior in heaven only, but on earth. A Savior for us and with us. Need not say, "Who shall ascend," &c. A Savior who has stooped to our very condition, and brought his mercy within the reach of every perishing sinner. It seemed to typify,

V. The Connection of Angels with the Work and Kingdom of Christ.

"For behold the angels of God ascending and descending on it." Angels, although not personally concerned in the nature Christ assumed, or in the sacrifice he presented, yet manifested the deepest interest in all that related to Christ, when upon the earth. We meet them in company with Christ in Bethlehem. In the desert. On the mount of transfiguration In the garden. At the sepulcher, and or. the summit of Olivet. With Christ's personal work on earth, their visits of mercy did not terminate. They ministered to Peter. Conveyed messages to Philip, to Cornelius, and others; and, it is evident they feel overflowing joy on the conversion of sinners, and minister cheerfully to the heirs of salvation. Or it might typify,

VI. The Heavenly State to which Christ will exalt his People.

The ladder "reached to heaven;" led to the presence of God. A striking view of the salvation of Christ. Present in its enjoyment. Progressive in its character, raising us higher and higher above the world, and terminating in heaven. Christ will exalt all his followers to enjoy the presence of his Father, forever and ever.

IMPROVEMENT

Let the subject lead us,

1. To rejoice in the reconciliation which Christ has effected for us. Every obstacle is removed out of the way of the sinner's recovery to God.

2. To avail ourselves of the invitations which the gospel presents to us to come to Christ and have abundant life.

3. To remember there is but *one* way to heaven, and that way is Christ.

4. Believers must advance in divine things. "Grow in grace." "Go from strength to strength," &c. "Giving all diligence," &c.

5. Let the glorious consummation cheer the Christian in this, the house of his pilgrimage.

13. THE BURNING BUSH A TYPE OF THE CHURCH

"Behold, the bush burned with fire, and the bush was not consumed." —Exod. 3:2.

THE striking phenomenon which arrested the attention of Moses, was intended doubtless to suggest a variety of important particulars to the mind of that servant of God. God chose it for the purpose of revealing his mind and designs respecting his afflicted and oppressed people. One of the most sublime emblems of deity is fire; and here, out of the midst of the flame, Jehovah spoke, and proclaimed himself the God of Abraham, the God of Isaac, and the God of Jacob. He also made known his gracious purpose of delivering his people from their Egyptian task-masters, and bringing them unto the good land flowing with milk and honey. It is impossible to conceive of a scene more solemn and magnificent than that the text presents before us. In the dreary deserts, where Sinai and Horeb lifted their awful summits and sublime grandeur, behold, a bush enveloped in flames. Moses, the servant of God, witnessing with devout astonishment the bush still unconsumed, is about to draw near to inspect the wondrous sight, when God makes known the sanctity of the spot, and commands him to draw near with reverence, for the place on which he stood was holy ground. The voice of God—the burning unconsumed bush—the prophet Moses—the projected emancipation of the hundreds of thousands of enslaved Israelites. What topics for instructive meditation! But we confine ourselves to the bush, and in that we see a striking type of the church of God. Observe.

I. The Metaphor itself.

"A bush." Apparently mean, worthless, and perishing. Just what the church appears to be, and the estimation in which it is held by the world. Nothing in it of worldly grandeur. No earthly pomp. No human embellishments. No temporal glory. Like its head and Lord, as "a root out of a dry ground, without form and comeliness." Was it not so in the time of Moses, oppressed and grieved in Egypt? In the time of the Savior? Behold his disciples Not many great or learned, chiefly the poor, &c. Has it not ever been so to a very great extent? Is it not so now? The true church of Jesus, but composed of the humbler ranks of life; still a mere bush; overlooked, despised, contemned; deemed insignificant and worthless.

II. Its present Condition.

A bush in the "desert." Such is the condition of Christ's church, situated in a desert. In the desert of the world. Brought out of Egypt, yet not established in Canaan. To the spiritual soul, the soul is in a dreary, barren wilderness. Bleak, sterile, and deficient in those supplies the renewed soul requires. Exposed to tempests and storms. Liable to the fierce attacks of beasts of prey. The very opposite of what she shall be, when caught up to the verdant scenes of the heavenly paradise. Observe,

III. Its suffering State.

"The bush burned with fire." It has often happened that the people of God have had literally to go through flames to heaven. In the first Christian persecution the fires of martyrdom were scarcely ever extinguished. But fire is the symbol of extreme suffering. The state of the church in the world is that of suffering. Thus Peter speaks of the trial of faith being more precious than of gold that perishes, though it be tried with *fire*," 1 Pet. 1:7. again, he says, "Beloved, think it not strange concerning the fiery trial which is to try you," ch. 4:12. In all ages and countries the spirit of the world has been opposed to the spirit of the people of God. The seed of the serpent have ever hated, and, to the very utmost of their ability, persecuted the people of God. Thus Cain murdered Abel. Ishmael mocked Isaac. Pharaoh oppressed the Israelites. And all generations of God's people have experienced that only through much tribulation could they enter the kingdom. These fiery sufferings are, however, purifying in their nature. They are allowed and overruled for the church's real good, and they not only conform the members to their suffering head, but. work out for them a far more exceeding and eternal weight of glory.

IV. The Divine Preservation.

"And the bush was not consumed." Fire was adapted to destroy it. A mere bush is soon burned. But not so here. The flame consumes it not. It is preserved amid hottest flames. Now consider this,

1. As an historical fact.

The church has ever been hated and persecuted, yet never destroyed. Ever in flames, yet never consumed. Indeed, her sufferings preserved her purity, and in proportion to her purity has she ever flourished. The winds of persecution scattered the disciples everywhere, and wherever they sojourned, the truth was established and prevailed. From the ashes of the martyrs a numerous progeny sprang forth, which no power could destroy; which no fires could burn. Amid all the changes, and wars, and revolutions of the world, the feeble bush has remained "unconsumed." Consider this,

2. As to its true cause.

"God has *dwelt* in the *midst* of the bush." God has been on her side; yea, he has been in the midst of her, therefore she has lot been consumed. Thus did he preserve he three Hebrew worthies in the fiery furnace. What he did for them he has ever done for his people. He has been with them, and round about them, and therefore their enemies could not prevail against them. He has witnessed all the malignity with which she has been treated. He has seen every weapon which has been formed against her. He has hearkened to all the stratagems of her foes. And when they have counselled to raze her foundations, or to consume her with flames, he who dwelt within her, held them in derision. He who sat on high, laughed, when the kings of the earth set themselves, and the rulers took counsel together, Ps. 2:1-4.

Application

1. The subject admonishes those of God's people who complain of sufferings. This is the necessary state of the church here. Suffering must precede glory. The cross must be borne before the crown is given. "If we suffer with him," &c. All have been meetened and gone to heaven this way.

2. The subject is full of consolation. In every trial God is in the midst of her. He is our help and our shield. He will never leave nor forsake, neither shall his cause ever perish from the earth.

3. Let persecutors remember that they fight against God. They cannot prevail their madness will involve them in awful and interminable ruin. The enemies of the church of Jesus have perished, but the cause they hated and persecuted still lives. Still in flames, yet unconsumed!

4. Let Christians act worthy of the divine presence. God is with us; then how seriously, and reverently, and holily, should we walk before him. His eye is upon us every moment: then with what hallowed care should we strive to do those things pleasing in his sight. Be patient and resigned, yet unyielding and resolved; stand fast in the faith; quit yourselves like men; be strong in the Lord, and in the power of his might. If God be for us. and with us, who can be against us?

14. CHRIST TYPIFIED BY THE PASCHAL LAMB

"Christ our passover is sacrificed for us." —1 Cor. 5:7

THE apostle has already shown us, in this passage, the true typical character of the paschal lamb. That sacrifice, and the ceremonial connected with it. seems rich-ly fraught with incidents peculiarly applicable to the person and work of Christ. Doubtless, both the officiating priest and the devout worshipper ever looked beyond the literal passover, to the true Lamb of God, who should take away the sin of the world. The appointment of the paschal lamb was immediately connected with the deliverance of the Israelites from Egyptian bondage, and, throughout, had direct reference to the redemption of the world by the sacrifice of Christ Jesus. Observe,

I. The Victim appointed.

This was a "lamb." Now it was required that this lamb should be—a *male*—a year old—without blemish. In other words, it was to be one of the most perfect of its species. The best the flock and fold could yield. Herein was typified the innocence, meekness, and excellency of the Son of God.

> 1. He was the perfection of our nature. Without frailty, without spot.

> 2. He was offered in the vigor of life. When of full age. In the midst of his manhood, he offered himself to God.

> 3. In him the innocence and meekness of the lamb were fully exhibited. "He was led as a lamb, &c., Isa. 53:7; 1 Pet. 1:19; Rev. 5:6, &c. Consider,

II. The Mode in which it was to be presented to God.

> 1. It was to be separated from the flock. Thus *Jesus* was fore-ordained and set apart by the Father to the great work of redemption. As such the prophets all bare witness of him, and predicted his mission of mercy to our world. "In the fulness of the time," &c.

> 2. After the separation, the lamb was to be kept alive *four* days. Thus *Jesus* appeared about four thousand years after the promise was first revealed to our first parents. And it was in the *fourth* year after his public consecration to his work in Jordan that Jesus laid down his life a sacrifice for sin.

> 3. The lamb was to be presented to God on the fourteenth of the first month, (March,) at the full of the moon. Thus was Jesus literally offered on the precise day, when the paschal lamb was slain. When the high priest was about appearing before the Lord, with the blood of the Passover, did Jesus expire, when the veil of the temple was rent in twain, &c. How wonderfully exact the type, and the great antitype.

4. The lamb was to be *slain.* By the *priest; publicly,* and in the *evening* of the day. Thus Jesus was put to death. He, as the priest, offered himself, laid down his own life. Gave himself, publicly, before the thousands of the inhabitants of Jerusalem, and that both in the evening of the world, and in the evening of the day, about three o'clock in the afternoon.

5. The lamb was to be *roasted* with *fire.* In the manner in which this was done, was strikingly exhibited the very form of Christ's death upon the cross. And the fire seemed properly to set forth the extreme severity of Christ's sufferings, especially those mental and spiritual agonies which he endured when he "made his *soul* an offering for sin." Observe,

6. Not a *bone* of the lamb was to be *broken.* How very singularly did the providence of God preserve Jesus from having his legs broken, as was common with those crucified, and which took place with both of those who were suspended by his side. See John 19:32, 33. Such are the chief points of resemblance in the *preparation* of the paschal lamb and Christ. Notice,

III. *The Way in which the Paschal Feast was to be regarded.*

1. The flesh of the paschal lamb must be eaten.

Thus showing the necessity of personally participating of Christ's virtue and merits, John 6:54. And there are several things in the original institution deserving of attention.

1. All the lamb must be eaten. So Jesus, in all his offices and work, must be received. We must have a whole Christ undivided, fully and entirely ours.

2. It was to be eaten only by the seed of Abraham; the circumcised. So Jesus is only and can only be received by faith. Unless we believe in him, we cannot enjoy the benefits of his death.

3. It was to be eaten standing, to denote their readiness to leave Egypt, and commence their pilgrimage towards the land of promise. So Christ is only really received by those who are ready to forsake the world, and to take up his cross and follow him.

4. It was to be eaten with bitter herbs. Faith in Jesus Christ is ever associated with godly sorrow for sin. Repentance an believing are inseparable. "They shall look on him whom they have pierced," &c., Zech. 12:10.

5. It was to be eaten with unleavened bread. And Christ must be received with sincerity of heart. In the exercise of love and truth, with purity of motive and purpose. Without malice or hypocrisy.

6. The reception of the lamb was as a social feast, and not private or solitary. In this was typified the social character of Christ's church, and especially the unity of those who surround the table of the Lord, and have fellowship in Christ's death.

2. The blood of the paschal lamb was to be sprinkled on the door posts of their houses, Exod. 12:22.

Thus the blood of Christ must be sprinkled on our consciences, that we may be cleansed from all sin, Heb. 10:22; 1 John 1:7.

3. In the reception of the paschal lamb, they were to commemorate the delivering hand of the Lord. See Exod. 12:26, 27.

Thus believers, in receiving the symbols of the body and blood of Jesus, are to do it in celebration of the great salvation which Jesus has wrought out for all who obey him. In doing this, they testify their faith and hope in Christ's death as an atoning sacrifice for guilt, and show forth their love to it, and their trust in it, until he shall come again.

Application

1. The observance of the Passover was that which distinguished those who were preserved from the destroying angel. Faith in Jesus, and obedience to him alone, will enable us to receive the saving benefits of his death. He who believeth in Christ will certainly love and obey him, and such only shall be saved. The unbeliever will assuredly perish.

2. To Christ, as the true paschal lamb, all sinners are freely invited. He taketh away the sin of the world. He is the Savior of all men, but especially of them that believe.

3. In the Lord's supper, the great doctrines of our ruin and help are prominently set before us. Let that ordinance be highly valued, and seriously and regularly regarded.

4. To celebrate the glories of the Lamb will form a portion of our employment is heaven, forever and ever

15. CHRIST TYPIFIED BY THE SMITTEN ROCK

"And the Lord said unto Moses, Go on before the people, and take with thee the elders of Israel; and thy rod, wherewith thou smotest the river, take in thine hand, and go. Behold, I will stand before thee there upon the rock in Horeb; and thou shalt smite the rock," &c.—Exod. 17:5, 6.

"That rock was Christ."—1 Cor. 10:4.

THE apostle could not mean more than that the rock of Horeb was a type of Jesus. That it had a distinct reference to him, and was intended not merely to supply the Israelites with water in the wilderness, but to point to Christ, the rock of salvation, from whom should flow the waters of life for all people. As such let us examine the original narrative, and see the various typical points presented for our consideration. We notice,

I. The Rock typified the Person of Christ.

The rock exhibits Christ,

    1. In his exaltation and glory.

As the rock lifts its head above all around, and stands forth with sublime prominence—so Jesus, in his divine nature, is higher than the kings of the earth, yea, higher and more glorious than angels, above all, God blessed for evermore.

    2. The rock typified the strength and power of Jesus.

Rock is the emblem of strength. Unlike the yielding earth or gliding sand. It will bear pressure. It stands before the tempest and the storm. The lightning of heaven and the roaring torrent affect it not How emblematical of Jesus. He possesses all power. All the elements of nature are subject to him and under his direct control. By his fiat he created all things, and "he upholds all things by the word of his power."

    3. The rock typified his unchanging stability.

No other object in nature seems at all expressive of immutability. The sea, the air, the heavenly bodies, in their respective movements, all indicate change. The rock is the emblem of fixedness, and here the term everlasting is by accommodation applied to the hills. Jesus is the blessed and immutable one who changes not, the name yesterday, today, and forever. "His years fail not;" "I am what I am," is his unalterable prerogative.

    4. The rock typified the humble and mean appearance of Jesus.

The rock amid all its loftiness, &c., bears sterility on its surface. The opposite of the fertile and fruitful earth. How unlikely to supply the wants of the thousands of Israel. Thus did Christ appear when clothed with pur nature. There was nothing to the carnal eye attractive He was to the Jews as a rock of offence, and stone of stumbling. And the doctrine of salvation through his cross, was to the Jews a stumbling-block, &c. Observe,

II. The Smiting of the Rock was typical of the Sufferings of Jesus.

1. The rock was smitten by God's command. Christ suffered by the will and appointment of God. God gave him, and sent him forth, expressly to suffer as a propitiatory sacrifice. He was the Lamb of God, raised up to take away the sin of the world, see Zech. 13:7.

2. The rock was smitten by the rod of Moses.

Moses, as the lawgiver smiting the rock, is strikingly a representation of Jesus meeting the claims of the law, bearing its penalties in his own person. Being made a curse for sinners, although he knew no sin. He obeyed all the enactments of the law, and so far was clear; but as the sinner's substitute, he had to sustain all the wrath which transgression had incurred, Gal. 3:13.

3. The rock was smitten in the presence of the elders of Israel.

Christ suffered publicly. He was arraigned, tried, condemned, scourged, and crucified before the elders of Israel. His sufferings were to be open and manifest, (not done in a corner, secretly,) as they were to be the leading facts the apostles and disciples were to make known to the world.

III. The gushing Stream was typical of the benefits flowing from Christ's Death to Mankind.

1. The stream was that which was needed by the people.

Salvation was that of all things most precious to the guilty condemned sons of men. As nothing could be a substitute for the water the Israelites desired, so there is nothing to be compared, and nothing can be substituted for the saving mercy and grace of God.

2. The stream flowed not till the rock was smitten.

All the blessings of providence and grace come to us through the merits of the mediator. "It behooved him to suffer," &c. "Without shedding of blood," &c.

3. The stream issued forth abundantly.

The supply was ample, more than equal to their wants. So the benefits of Christ's death meet all the exigencies of sinners. There is no lack. It is an overflowing and exhaustless fulness.

> Enough for all, enough for each,—
>   Enough for evermore."

4. The stream was free and gratuitous to all the children of Israel.

As there was no limitation, so there was no restriction. All required it; and it was for all. So the benefits of Christ's death are for all men. No exclusion on God's part. "He willeth not the death of a sinner," &c. None on Christ's part, for he "died for all." None on the Spirit's part, for "the Spirit, as well as the bride, says, Come, and all that will, may come and take of the water of life freely." Rev. 22:17.

Application

1. The water which flowed from the rock was obtained by the will of God. The water of life by the unknown agonies of the Son of God.

2. That water only supplied the thirst of the body. The water of life, the vast and boundless desires of the soul.

3. That was for Israel, this for the world. Let every sinner come, then, and receive the living waters of salvation freely, without money and without price.

4. To reject or neglect this water, is to expose our deathless souls to irretrievable ruin.

16. CHRIST TYPIFIED BY THE MANNA

"Your fathers did eat manna in the wilderness and are dead. This is the bread which cometh down from heaven that a man may eat thereof and not die." —John 6:49, 50.

JESUS has graciously explained to us the spiritual signification of the manna with which God supplied his people in the desert To them it was one of the chief blessings he bounty of God provided. It was the staff of their life. But it also was designed to lead their minds to that gift which God had promised to their fathers—the Messiah, who was emphatically to be "the bread of life" to a perishing world. We do not envy the Jews who were privileged with the type, and who were fed with angels' food; but we rejoice with Jew and Gentile, that we now possess "the bread which cometh down from heaven," &c. Let us contemplate, the subject, with a view of discerning the resemblance between the "manna," and Christ "the bread of life." Notice,

I. The Origin of the Manna.

It was food from heaven. It came from he munificent storehouse of God. The Israelites were in a condition of need. God graciously compassionated them, and bountifully sent them food from heaven. Christ as the bread of life is the free gift of God. He came down from heaven to supply the wants of our starving race. He gave himself for the life of the world. Observe,

II. The Peculiarities of the Manna.

The manna was a small grain, as little as a seed of coriander. It was particularly sweet, like wafers of fine honey. In form it was round, and in color white. In each of these particulars it seemed to prefigure the Savior. In his appearance to the sons of men, he was as a root out of a dry ground, nothing of earthly dignity or glory was associated with him. In his nature, offices, and merit, he is unspeakably sweet and precious to the believer. The roundness of the manna shadowed forth the completeness or perfection of Christ. Immaculate, eternal, and unchanging. In the color of the manna, we are led to contemplate the holiness of his person and the righteousness of his administrations. Notice,

III. The Manner in which it was bestowed.

The manna was bestowed freely, abundantly, every morning. Jesus Christ as the heavenly bread was given freely, the result of God's wise and overflowing grace. In Christ there is an abundance of mercy and grace. An exhaustless fulness; even all the fulness of God. Jesus too is the daily bread of the soul. He is the morning portion of his people, He was given, too, by promise in the morning of the world As the manna fell in double quantities or the sixth day so as to supply their need on the sabbath, so Christ was more fully revealed, and more plentifully made known and more graciously offered on the morning of the sixth day, when he appeared in our flesh as the Messiah and Savior of the world. Notice,

IV. The Way in which it was received and used.

1. It fell round about the camp. So Jesus is made known by the preaching of the gospel and the ordinances of Christianity. 2. It was designed specifically for the Israelites. So Jesus for believers. Offered freely to all men, yet *faith* is requisite in each and all who savingly enjoy his gracious benefits. 3. The Israelites had to go forth and gather it. So Jesus, the gift of God, must be received into the heart, by a believing appropriation of him to our souls. 4. They gathered it early and daily. And Christ is to be the chief object of our solicitudes and desires. He must be preferred to all things. In all things have the preeminence. And daily must we live upon him. He is our souls' unfailing support, and essentially needful to us every moment. 5. The manna was to be prepared by being ground and baked with fire. Thus it was necessary that Christ should suffer and bear our iniquities, that the wrath, justly denounced against sin, should consume him as the great sacrifice, in order that we might have reconciliation and life through his name. And this is the essence of the gospel, that "Christ died for our sins according to the scriptures," &c., 1 Cor. 15:1-3. 6. All the manna was to be eaten. Jesus must be received wholly and fully. In his twofold nature—God and man. In his threefold offices—as prophet, priest, and king. In his obedient life, sacrificial death, resurrection power, and heavenly glory. 7. The manna, if laid up, and not used, putrefied, &c. So Christ preached and offered and not personally received, will be the savor of death, and expose such to more aggravated punishment; seeing they have rejected the anointed Jesus, and done despite to the richest exhibition of the grace of God. But the manna could not fully typify the excellencies of Christ. The manna was designed for the body. Jesus is the bread of the soul, and the Savior both of body and soul. The manna was only a temporary provision, it ceased when they got to Canaan. Jesus is the present and everlasting good of his people. On earth and in heaven, in time and eternity, he will be all their joy and salvation. Those who ate the manna died. Jesus is the eternal life of his people. The bread which if a roan eat thereof he shall never die. The manna was limited to the thousands of Israel; Jesus is given and freely offered to the whole world, 1 John 4:14; John 3:14-17.

Application

1. Now is Christ Jesus as the bread of life freely offered to you.

2. You cannot reject him and live.

3. Your opportunities and mercies are rapidly passing away. Procrastination has been ruinous to countless myriads of souls.

4. Then gratefully, humbly, and believingly receive Jesus as the only Savior, suited to your state, and now graciously offered you in the gospel of life.

5. The health, and vigor, and joy of Christians, greatly depend on feeding freely and constantly on this bread sent down from heaven. See John 6:53, 54.

17. CHRIST TYPIFIED BY THE TWO GOATS

"And he shall take the two goats, and present them before the Lord at the door of the tabernacle of the congregation. And Aaron shall cast lots upon the two goats; one lot for the Lord, and the other for the scapegoat." —Levit. 16:7, 8.

NONE of the ancient sacrifices more fully exhibited the work and expiatory sacrifice of Jesus, than the institution of the goats, both of which were necessary to give a true typical representation of the Messiah. In reading the divine account of this offering, the mind is led, as it were instinctively, to those striking passages of holy writ, where Jesus is described as "bearing our sins," as "bearing the sins of many," and, as "taking away the sins of the world." How very great a portion of the epistle to he Hebrews is occupied in giving full and vivid illustrations of the ancient sacrifices, as referring to, and ending in, the vicarious sufferings and death of the Son of God. In contemplating the two goats, let us observe what is said.

I. As to the Goat that was put to Death.

The goat which was to be sacrificed was decided by lot. And thus it was considered as the choice and appointment of God. And it was also considered, especially for the Lord; that is, devoted to a sacred purpose by the will of God. How this applies to the choice and appointment of Jesus, by the express will of his Father, to be the redeemer of the world, and to redeem it by the shedding of his blood. He was sent forth by the Father. He was the elect of chosen of the Father. "Him did God, by his determinate counsel and foreknowledge, deliver up, Acts 2:23. Hence, just before Jesus went to the garden, he said, "The Son of man goeth as it is written of him," &c. Matt. 26:24. To die, as a sacrifice for human guilt, was the great end of his life, and mission into our world. Thus was he represented by the goat that was sacrificed. Notice, how the figure was still further carried out,

II. In the Goat which was kept alive.

1. Over the head of this goat the sins of the people were confessed, and on it symbolically laid. Thus, Jesus came to be our surety and substitute. He placed himself between our guilt and ruin, and the law, with the penalty it denounced against us. Thus, he really and virtually suffered in our stead, the "Just for the unjust," &c.

2. Iniquities, transgressions, and sins, were confessed and laid on the scapegoat Showing us here the extent of Christ's sacrifice for all kinds of guilt, whether arising from neglect of God's commands, or the willful violation of his righteous prohibitions. In the sacrifice of Christ, then was an atonement for every kind of sin and for all grades and classes of sinners We cannot conceive of a more heinous crime than that of murdering, with envious hate and malice, the Son of God. Yet the offer of mercy was first of all to be proclaimed to the populace of Jerusalem showing the extensiveness of his atonement for all iniquity, transgression, and sin 3. The scapegoat was dismissed into the wilderness, with the imputed iniquity of the people upon it.

Thus, has Jesus truly borne our guilt away. He has obtained for a world of transgressors, the offer of pardon. For the polluted race of Adam, the means of purity. For condemned and dying sinners, the favor of God and the gift of eternal life. Notice.

III. How the Benefits of the Scapegoat were conferred upon the People.

Aaron was to lay both his hands upon the head of the scapegoat, and there confess all the sins of the people. How clearly does this show us the appointed medium by which, we enjoy the salvation of Christ. 1. There must be implicit faith or confidence in his person and sacrifice. This was symbolically taught in the priest laying his hand upon the head of the live goat, ver. 21. Here we are to bring our sins, our misery, our helplessness, and place our entire confidence, our whole hope and trust, in the sacrifice of Christ. We are to place our whole burden of guilt and ruin where God's mercy has placed our help and salvation. And how worthy is Christ that all our dependence should be implicitly reposed upon him. 2. Faith in Jesus will ever be accompanied by sincere repentance. It will be connected with ingenuous confession, deep contrition, entire self-abasement, and self-loathing before God, with earnest forsaking of the paths of impenitence and sin.

Application

1. We see here the connection between sin and death. Sin deserves death, exposes to death; where it is unforgiven, it will involve in eternal death. "The soul that sinneth," &c.

2. In Christ's death is the only real sacrifice for sin: "He died for our sins." What a glorious truth! How precious! How momentous!

3. Faith is the only medium of securing to the soul the benefits of that death. "He that believeth," &c.

18. THE BRAZEN SERPENT A TYPE OF CHRIST

"And as Moses lifted up the serpent in the wilderness, even so must the Son of man be lifted up."
—John 3:14.

HERE we have the authority of Jesus for considering the brazen serpent as directly typical of himself. Without this divine testimony we might have been struck with the points of coincidence, and have legitimately illustrated the one by the other. Seeing Christ has done this for us, we approach the subject with peculiar confidence, and rejoice that the merciful precision of the serpent of brass was designed to point to that great act of mercy, by which God designed to save all believers through Christ Jesus.

I. The appointment of the Serpent of Brass originated in the Mercy of God towards his rebellious Creatures.

Ungratefully murmuring against the benign providence of God, he righteously visited their rebellion with the tokens of his displeasure. He sent among them fiery serpents, whose bite was fatal. Thus, the wrath of Jehovah spread disease and death through the Israelitish camp. For this evil it is obvious there was no human remedy or help. Had not God mercifully interposed they would all have been consumed. But because his compassions failed not, he remembered them in their perishing state, and devised means for their deliverance.

Now we have here an exact and faithful representation of our fallen and ruined state by sin. Satan, the old, subtle, fiery, and deadly serpent, deceived our first parents. He tempted them to sin against God, and most awfully prevailed. Thus they became corrupt, guilty, and were condemned to die. Their condition was beyond human help. They had no skill to deliver themselves, or power to avoid the calamitous results of their transgression. The mercy of God, however, prevailed over all the worthlessness of the sinner, and from the boundlessness of his grace he provided a ransom and a deliverer. God so loved the dying Israelites as to appoint a remedy for their misery, and "He so loved the world," &c. John 3:16. Notice,

II. The striking Resemblance in the Instrument of Death and the Means of Recovery.

A serpent inflicted the fatal wound, and a serpent of brass was the medium of cure By man sin entered into the world, "with all our wo." By Adam apostacy and guilt and ruin were introduced. By the second Adam, the Lord from heaven, who became really man, made of a woman, &c., was the curse sustained the penalty paid, and salvation procured. Through man we became aliens, diseased, and exposed to death. By man also we were brought nigh, receive healing, and everlasting life See this fully illustrated by the apostle Paul, Rom. 5:12, to end.

III Both Remedies were to be similarly exhibited.

The serpent of brass was to be affixed to a pole and lifted up. Thus Jesus says, "As Moses *lifted* up the serpent, even so must the son of man be lifted up," &c. Now in the antitype we see this,

1. In the crucifixion of Christ.

He was lifted up on the cross. Lifted up there as the victim for sin. Lifted up there to die publicly as an atoning sacrifice for a guilty world. And this was necessary and essential. "It behooved Christ to suffer," &c.

2. In the lifting of Christ up by the preaching of the gospel.

Ministers are standard-bearers. It is theirs to go forth unfurling the banners of salvation. On this is the emblem of the Lamb slain. It is their great work to make known the cross of Christ to all the perishing children of men:—

"'Tis all their business here below,
To cry, Behold the Lamb."

IV. Both Remedies were effectual.

The serpent of brass was an antidote to the bite of the fiery serpent. It saved the diseased and dying victims from death. It was invariably effectual. So Jesus, as God's remedy, is in every case efficacious to the salvation of the soul. He possesses all ability and all merit. None availed themselves of the remedy Moses lifted up and died, and none come to God by Christ and perish

"He is able, he is willing,
Doubt no more."

V. The Application to both Remedies was the same.

The virtue of the serpent of brass was derived by looking. Whoso "looked," lived. Now faith is the soul looking to Christ. It is the eye of misery and helplessness, directed to the all-meritorious and all-sufficient Savior. In this looking or believing on Christ, the eye of desire and trust is withdrawn from every other object, and directed only to Christ. It is an act in which there can be no merit. An act which alone is effective, through the virtue there is in Christ. An act which displays the gratuitousness of salvation, the very opposite of merit, &c. An act which is followed invariably by the enjoyment of *life*. Whoso looked lived, and whoso believes is saved. Saved into spiritual life, and into the hope of eternal life in heaven Yet do we see a great *disparity* between these remedies. The one was but for a temporal malady, and imparted natural life; the other is for all the maladies of the soul, and relates to spiritual and everlasting life. The one was but a temporary remedy, suited to a limited period; the other is an abiding, and the only remedy throughout all time. The one was for the Israelitish camp; the other for the whole world

Application

Learn,

1. Sin is a disease, painful, universal, and fatal. Have you felt it? Do you desire healing and deliverance?

2. Christ is the remedy. The one and only remedy. No other name. No other sacrifice, &c. A remedy gratuitous, free and infallible.

3. Faith is the only means of obtaining restoration. O look unto him and be saved. Look now, before the exhibition of Christ to you ceases. Look all of you, and thus your souls shall live.

19. CHRIST TYPIFIED BY THE ARK OF THE COVENANT

"The ark of the covenant." —Heb. 9:4.

IT is manifest that most of the furniture as well as the services of the tabernacle were of a typical character. Of these the ark of the covenant deserves to occupy a prominent place. We shall see in a variety of striking instances, how it distinctly pointed to Jesus, the substance of all the shadows connected with the ceremonial of the Mosaic economy. For a description of the ark read Ex. 25:10-17. Notice,

I. The Ark typified the Dignity and Purity of Christ's Person

The ark was made of *incorruptible wood,* was overlaid with *pure gold;* and had *crowns of gold* wrought round about it, Here is distinctly pointed out to us, 1. The holiness and incorruptibility of Christ's human nature. That holy thing conceived of the virgin. That which God had decreed should not be left in the sepulcher, and see corruption, Acts 2:27. 2. The divinity of Jesus is represented by the fine gold. For not only did he possess human nature in its sinless condition, but he also had in connection with that, the divine nature of the Father. For in him dwelt "all the fulness of the Godhead bodily." 3. The encircling golden crowns typified the regal glory of Jesus. As King of kings and Lori of lords. And as these crowns encircled the ark, so they exhibited the eternity of Christ's authority and kingly power. We may just add here, that the shape of the ark might point out the perfection and completeness of Christ's person and work.

II. The Contents of the Ark typified the Fulness and Work of Christ.

1. In it were the two tables of the law.

In Jesus these laws were embodied. He had them in his heart. He exemplified them in their fullest extent. "He magnified the law and made it honorable."

2. In it was the golden pot of manna. So in Jesus is the bread of life. He is the heavenly manna. "His flesh is meat indeed." He is the soul's satisfying portion. In him is treasured up provision for a starving world.

3. In it was Aaron's rod that budded.

Typifying Christ's exalted and abiding priesthood. A priest forever. His priestly office will only terminate when the Mediatorial kingdom shall be delivered up to the Father, 1 Cor. 15:24.

III. The Achievements of the Ark typified the Victories of Christ.

1. The ark opened a passage through Jordan to the promised land So by Christ a way has been opened through the grave to the heavenly Canaan. He has gone forth before his people to prepare for then: mansions of bliss and glory, John 14:1-3.

2. By the ark's compassing the walls of Jericho they were thrown down.

So Jesus by his divine power spoiled the powers of darkness, and he shall finally overthrow all the bulwarks of Satan's empire, and shall obtain a universal conquest over all his enemies. Wherever Christ is present in his preached gospel, there Satan's kingdom falls as lightning from heaven.

3 The presence of the ark broke the idol Dagon to pieces.

So shall the Savior cast down all the idols of the heathen, and he alone shall receive the worship and homage of all the nations of the earth. Then shall be sung with universal gladness and delight, "The kingdoms," &c., Rev. 11:15.

IV. The Movements of the Ark typified the Progress and Consummation of Christ's Kingdom.

The ark was possessed by the Israelites, then it was in the hands of the Philistines, and finally it was laid up in Solomon's temple. Thus Christ was first preached to the Jews; the gospel kingdom was first set up among them, afterwards it was extended to the Gentiles; and when consummated, it shall consist of all nations, and kindreds, and tongues, and people, in the heavenly temple, there to be permanently glorious forever and ever.

The ark has long since perished with all that appertained to the first and second temples. Jesus is the imperishable ark, who abides forever. The ark was destructive to the Philistines, and the men of Beth-shemesh perished for looking into it. Christ our gracious ark is acceptable to all, and the vilest are invited to approach freely, that they may not perish but have everlasting life

Application

Learn,

1. The privilege you possess in having Christ the true ark with you. In it you have treasured up a fulness of all spiritual blessings.

2. With believing reverence draw rear to it, and receive mercy, enjoy fellowship with God, and obtain grace to help you in every time of need.

3. Despisers of Christ must inevitably perish.

20. THE MERCY-SEAT A TYPE OF CHRIST

"And over it the cherubim of glory shadowing the mercy-seat." —Heb. 9:5.

"Set forth to be a propitiation (or mercy-seat)." —Rom. 3:25

IT is clear from the apostle selecting this term, and applying it to Christ, that he considered it a? typically shadowing him forth. We have already seen, in several particulars, how the ark itself was a type of Jesus; let us then call our attention to that which covered the ark, and which was most significantly styled the "mercy seat." Notice,

I. The Mercy-seat covered the Ark, in which were the Tables of the Law.

Thus, Jesus obeyed and honored all the laws of God. He was subject to the law in all its moral claims and ceremonial institutions, and he was perfectly conformed to all its requirements. And it was necessary that he should do this, that the purity, justice, wisdom, and goodness of God might be vindicated. And also that by his perfect obedience, he might render to God an acceptable holy sacrifice for the sin of the world, Heb. 7:26, 27. Thus redemption is based on the personal rectitude and obedience of Christ Jesus.

II. The Mercy-seat was made of Pure Gold.

This signifies both the purity and preciousness of Christ. Christ in his twofold nature was possessed of unsullied holiness. He was without spot. The holiness of Jehovah dwelt in him. But it also pointed out the preciousness of Christ. He is the peerless pearl, beyond all price. He enriches all who possess him, with the unsearchable riches both of grace and glory.

III. Upon it were the Cherubim.

Here was expressed the interest which holy angels take in the things of Christ, and which pertain to human redemption. Doubtless the apostle refers to this, where he says, "Which things the angels desire to look into," 1 Pet. 1:17. They take delight in all the ways and works of Jehovah, but it is probable that they feel interested in a peculiar degree in the mysteries of redeeming love. Here they obtain a fresh manifestation of Deity.

"For God in the person of his Son,
Has all his mightiest works outdone."

And the poet represents them as being tilled with reverent awe and wonder, and says—

"The first archangel never saw,
So much of God before."

IV. Here God was enthroned, and communed with Moses.

"There will I meet with thee, and I will commune with thee from above the mercy-seat." See Ex. 25:17-23. How applicable the language of the apostle, "God was in Christ reconciling the world unto himself," 2 Cor. 5:19. Jesus was God manifested in the flesh. God with us. God holding intercourse with men. So that whoever had seen Christ, had also seen the Father John 14:9.

V. Here God revealed his Mind and Will

Here God said, I will give thee of all things in "commandment unto the children of Israel," Ex. 25:22. Thus as God spoke in divers manners in times past to the fathers by the prophets, "he hath in these last days spoken unto us by his Son," Heb. 1:2. Jesus came to show us the will of his heavenly Father. He revealed the mind of God to man. Portions of truth had been published by prophets and holy men of old, but Jesus was the embodied truth of God He came to be the light of the world. God says to all inquirers after life and blessedness, "Hear ye him." As the Messiah he came to show us all things, and to bring life and immortality to light, &c

VI. At the Mercy-seat Prayer and Offerings were presented.

So it is in and through Christ we have access to God. Whatsoever we ask it must be in his name. God is unapproachable to the guilty except through the per son of his Son. He is the one mediator &c. Our persons and all our services, must be presented to God, by and through Christ. Here too the mercy of God is alone dispensed. All our blessings descend to us through him. Here we find mercy and obtain grace to help in every time of need. We come to the Father by this way, and here God meets and blesses his believing people.

VII. The Mercy-seat was to be approached through the sprinkling of Blood.

"Then shall he kill the goat of the sin-offering that is for the people, and bring his blood within the vail, and do with that blood, as he did with the blood of the bullock, and sprinkle it upon the mercy-seat and before the mercy-seat," Lev. 16:15. The apostle alludes to this, Heb. 9:7, &c. Now here we are taught the supreme efficacy of Christ's blood. And that to this we must have especial regard in all our intercourse with Deity. That without shedding of blood there is no remission. That in Christ's blood we have redemption. And that our faith and hope must ever respect the blood of sprinkling, &c. The death of Christ is the great meritorious fact, on which we are to rest for pardon purity, peace, and everlasting life

Application

1. As sinners we need a mercy seat. Guilty we are justly condemned and exposed to death. We have no merit or help in ourselves.

2. Christ is the only and the all-sufficient mercy-seat. There is no other. He is ever near. Full of efficacy. Almighty to save. Overflowing with tenderness and grace. His heart and arms open to a lost world.

3. Personal approach indispensable. We must draw near to him. In humble penitency. In unwavering faith. In earnest prayer.

21. THE HIGH-PRIEST A TYPE OF CHRIST

"A great High-priest." —Heb. 4:14.

THE high-priests under the law were persons of high official dignity, and whose duties were of the most solemn and important character. At the head of those engaged in the sacred services of the tabernacle, or temple, they were greatly venerated by the people, and occupied a sort of midway station between the worshippers and the great Being unto whom their services were presented. It is clear that they were evident types of the expected Messiah; and that not only in the sacrifices offered, but also in the illustrious official person who entered into the holiest place with the blood of the victim, the pious worshipper was led to exercise faith and hope in the promised Savior of the world.

The points of resemblance are numerous and striking: let us contemplate them with a direct view to our spiritual knowledge and comfort. This is seen,

I. In their Personal Distinctions.

1. They were to be men of one specified tribe, to be free from bodily infirmities and defects; they were to avoid touching any dead body; and they were not to mourn for the dead as others. See Lev. 21:9-23. In this was very strikingly pointed out the perfection and holiness of Christ Jesus, our high priest, "was holy, harmless, undefiled, and separate from sinners," Heb. 7:26. He had not one defect of character. He was free from every sinful infirmity, and reflected the perfectly holy and righteous image of God.

2. As the high priest too was fully devoted to sacred purposes, and did not engage in temporal affairs, so Christ was entirely engaged in the execution of his great sacerdotal calling. He lived to glorify his Father, and make known his mercy and grace to the miserable guilty sons of men.

II. In their Calling and Appointment to this Office.

To this great and holy calling, they were appointed by God, no man took this honor upon himself. So Jesus our high priest was especially called and appointed of the Father. As such God is represented as "sending him forth," "delivering him up," "giving him for the life of the world." And Jesus ever acknowledged himself as his Father's "called" and "chosen servant." "I come," he said, "to do thy will, O God."

III. In their Consecration to Office.

In this,

1. They were to be washed with water, Ex. 29:4.

2. They were to be anointed with oil, Ex. 29:7.

3. A sacrifice was to be presented to God, 5:10.

In all these things we have a clear reference to Christ.

1. Christ was consecrated to his great work by baptism.

2. Here too the anointing oil of the Holy Spirit descended upon him.

3. And from this period to the moment he expired on the cross, he was a living sacrifice, presented to God for the salvation of the world. See Matt. 3:13-17.

IV. In The Sacerdotal Vestments, &c., which they wore.

1. They were to be clothed round about the loins with *fine white linen.* Expressive of the purity and righteousness of Christ's person and worth.

2. They had the EPHOD, a costly and beautiful flowing garment, representing the rich graces, and heavenly beauties, of our great high priest. In this was set, in precious stones, affixed to the shoulders, the names of the twelve tribes of Israel. Expressive of Christ bearing upon his shoulders all the interests of his spiritual kingdom, and sustaining all the concerns of his believing people.

3. They had the BREASTPLATE. This was to be made of twelve costly and precious stones. These were to be set in four rows, so as to form an exact square And this was affixed to the breast of the high priest. In this was typified the love of Christ to his people. That he had them on his heart. That they were distinctly recognized and known of him. And that they were his peculiar treasure and delight The form of the breastplate might signify the perfection and security of the church of Christ. In all Christ's offices and undertakings, he ever bears his people on his breast, indicating his tender and changeless love and solicitude for them.

4. They had the URIM and THUMMIM. Of these it is difficult to speak. See Ex. 28:30. But they signified *"Light and Perfection"* and it is supposed by and through these the priests obtained the will of God in all cases of judgment, and thus were preserved from error in all their decisions. Jesus Christ is the true light and perfection of all things. In him dwelt all the wisdom and knowledge of God. He spoke most fully, and clearly, and infallibly the will of God. Through him we know all the will of God concerning us, and the love and mercy of God towards us.

5. They had the MITER and the CROWN. This was a kind of head-dress, made of blue silk and fine linen, in shape like a half-coronet. Beautified with a golden plate, on which was engraved, "Holiness to the Lord," Ex. 28:36. Here we have represented the royal glory and absolute purity of Jesus. His dignity is unrivalled, his nature immaculate. His work is emphatically a holy work. He came to exhibit the holiness of God, and to redeem to

64

himself and present before the Father a holy people to celebrate his praise forever. These were the chief distinctions in the garments of the high-priests. They typified Christ,

V. In their Sacred Work.

Now of these duties we refer only to the following:

1. They were to make an annual atonement for the people.

See Lev. 16:3-16. See this fully illustrated in the office and work of Christ, Heb. 9:7-14.

2. They were to make intercession for the people.

With the blood of the annual sacrifice, they went into the holiest of all, and there presented their prayers to God for the people. Thus Jesus has entered into the holiest place of all, and with his own blood appears before God, ever living to make intercession for us.

3. They blessed the people in the name of the Lord.

So Jesus Christ, as our exalted high priest, has obtained for all believers remission of sins, and all the gifts and graces of his Holy Spirit. He ascended and entered the holy place, that he might receive gifts for men, yea, even for the rebellious. But the high priest,

4. Had to give judgment and decide all matters of controversy.

This power and authority Christ possesses. All judgment is committed to him. He is the one infallible Head and Lord of his church, and he will finally judge the world in righteousness, and give to every man according as his works shall be.

But the high-priests under the law were but frail men Jesus is the immaculate Son of God. They were required to offer sacrifices first for themselves. But Christ had no sin. He was ever well pleasing to God. They had to repeat their sacrifices often: Jesus, by one sacrifice, has fully atoned for sin, and obtained salvation for every believer. They had their successors, for they did not continue by reason of death. Jesus is the one great *High-priest,* who ever lives.

Application

1. See in Christ the priest of heavenly dignity, and the sacrifice of infinite merit.

2. Come to him with penitence and in the exercise of faith, that you may personally be interested in this great salvation.

3. There is no other sacrifice for sin, of hope for the sinner.

22. THE PRIESTS TYPICAL OF BELIEVERS

"A royal priesthood." —1 Pet. 2:9.

THE ancient priesthood passed away, when the Christian dispensation was established. Jesus is now the only priest, who has presented one great sacrifice for sin, and who "ever lives to make intercession for us." But in a spiritual sense, all believers are now priests, and as such they are designated by the apostle in our text, "A royal priesthood." The kingly and priestly offices were separate and distinct under the Mosaic economy. In Jesus they were united; he was a royal priest, or a "priest upon his throne." Believers in Christ's right and by virtue of union to him, are made kings and priests unto God and the Father, &c. At present let us view the priesthood of the Christian, as typified by the priests under the law. They were so,

I. In their Separation to the Priestly falling.

The priests were separated from the other tribes and devoted to the worship of God. Believers are called out of the world, and separated to the service of God. Hence they give themselves to the Lord. Present themselves as a living sacrifice, &c. Consecrate their service to the Lord. They cease to be of the world, and come out of it, bearing Christ's cross and following him. Besides, as the priests under the law were required to be sound in body and free from deformity, so none are of the spiritual priesthood but those who are sincere in heart, and fully devoted in life to the service of the Lord.

II. In the Manner in which they entered upon their Office.

They did this,

> 1. By being washed in pure water, Ex. 29:4.

> A striking emblem of baptism, by which we commence our Christian profession, and put on the Savior before men. To this doubtless the apostle refers, "Let us draw near," &c., Heb. 10:22.

> 2. By being clothed with the sacerdotal vestments.

> Without dwelling minutely on these, we may observe that believers are clothed with that holiness which is likened to fine linen. That they wear the girdle of truth,—the robe of salvation,—the breastplate of righteousness,—and the shoes of the preparation of the gospel of peace. On their heads too they have, as their miter and helmet, the hope of salvation.

> 3. By being anointed with consecrating oil.

In this was typified the communication of the Holy Spirit. Compare Ex. 29:7, with 2 Cor. 1:21, and 1 John 2:20.

4 By the whole being ratified through the blood of sacrifices, (Ex. 29:10,) with which also they were hallowed for their sacred service.

In this we are distinctly led to behold the acceptance of the believer, through the merit of Jesus Christ, the great sacrifice for sin; and the application of his blood to the sanctifying of the conscience before God.

III. In the Duties which devolved upon them.

They were,

1. To offer sacrifices, Heb. 5:1.

The nature and manner of doing this was revealed to them by the Lord. Thus also do believers present their sacrifices to God. They present themselves as a living sacrifice. "The sacrifices of God are a broken spirit," &c. They present the sacrifice of prayer and thanksgiving, with that of benevolence, and liberality, and mercy, with which God is well pleased, Ps. 51:16, 107:22; Heb. 13:15, 16.

2. They were to offer intercession for their fellow-worshippers.

And this duty belongs to the Christian priesthood. See 1 Tim. 2:1. They are to pray one for another, James 5:13, 18.

3. They were to instruct and bless the people.

To feed the people with knowledge. To explain and enforce the will of the Lord, Mal. 2:7. And in the name of the Lord to bless the people. The Christian priest is, in like manner, to diffuse abroad the light of the gospel, holding forth the word of life, and by his life and influence to be a blessing to those around him. God says of such, "I have blessed thee and will make thee a blessing," "Ye are the salt of the earth," &c.

4. They were to carry on the services of the tabernacle, and to keep the fire continually burning on the altar.

In this too we behold the trust which God has committed to his church. It is for his spiritual priests to maintain the ordinaries of the gospel in all their purity, and to convey them down to posterity. They are to maintain the celebration of Christian worship, the preaching of the word of life, and to offer up their united prayers for the extension of the church, and the salvation of the world. Consider,

IV. The Privileges which they enjoyed.

1. Their support was ordained of God and fully provided for them.

Certain portions of the sacrifices were to be for Aaron and his sons, Lev. 2:10 The great Sacrifice for sin, provides all his spiritual priests with "meat indeed." Christ in all his fulness is to be received for the support and strengthening of the soul. Jesus said, "Verily, verily, I say unto yon, except ye eat the flesh of the Son of man, and drink his blood, ye have no life in you," John 6:53.

2. Their office was one of peculiar dignity and honor.

Separated from secular pursuits. They were dedicated to a holy calling, and raised to occupy as it were a sacred place between God and the people. This honor have all God's saints. They are a people sanctified to the Lord. His chosen servants. The Lord's delight and heirs to his eternal kingdom and glory.

3. They had more direct intercourse with Deity.

Through the blood of the sacrifices, by their offering of incense, and their intercessions, they came immediately before the Lord. Of believers the apostle says, "Through him (Christ) we both have access, by one Spirit unto the Father," Eph. 2:18. So also, "Having boldness to enter into the holiest of all," &c., Heb. 10:19.

Application

1. Let believers rejoice in their high and heavenly calling. "Unto him who hath loved us," &c.

2. With fervor and delight attend to the duties of their sacred avocation. Especially never allow the fire of devotion to expire on the altar of their hearts.

3. To have respect in all things to the great sacrifice for sin. Here alone is merit, and righteousness, and acceptance with God.

4. To anticipate the more perfect services of the heavenly temple.

23. THE TABERNACLE A TYPE OF THE CHRISTIAN CHURCH

"I will abide in thy tabernacle forever: I will trust in the cover of thy wings." —Ps. 61:4.

OUR text contains the expression of David's devoted attachment to the tabernacle of the Lord. Among the very numerous excellencies which distinguished the psalmist, this was one peculiarly prominent. He loved the house of the Lord, and desired above all other things to dwell in it all the days of his life, that he might behold the beauty of the Lord, and inquire in his temple. Here he affirms the resolution of his soul, "I will abide in thy tabernacle," &c. Is it not our duty and privilege and interest to cherish a spirit like that of David! Our souls ought to be glad when we are invited to go up to the house of the Lord. Here God manifests himself. Here we have the rich provisions of his grace. Here we behold the divine glory, and have fellowship with God and the excellent of the earth. But let us consider the subject typically, and view the ancient tabernacle as a symbol of the church of God on earth. The tabernacle was a spacious movable tent, created for the celebration of Jehovah's worship. It was built in the time of Moses, was of divine origin and construction, and the cost of the materials was provided by the voluntary liberality of the people. In many things it very much typified the person of Christ. In some things the heavenly state.

I. The Tabernacle was a type of the church of Christ on earth.

1. It was so in its divine origin and construction.

God called for its erection. It was not of human devising. And in all things it was made according to the pattern which God showed to Moses in the mount. Such too is the church of God. A spiritual house or tabernacle formed for Jehovah's praise, and in all things fixed and established by the infallible wisdom of God. Not an angel would interfere. The plan is perfect as its author. The materials the order, and their use, are all settled by the unerring skill of God.

2. It was so in its design.

It was to be the depository of holy things The place of holy exercises. The scene of holy manifestations. Here was the ark, the mercy-seat, the oracles, the golden pot of manna. Here sacrifices were offered. Incense burned. Praises and supplications presented. Here the glory of God was seen. The blessings of his love imparted. How truly applicable to the church of Christ. Here is deposited all the riches of his grace, &c.

3. It was so in its costliness and worth. The most valuable materials were employed,— gold, silver, and precious stones. Herein we see shadowed forth, &c., preciousness of believers, the true and only materials of which the church of Christ is constructed. See 1 Cor. 3:12. All the members of Christ's church are precious but in different degrees of value; 2 Tim. 2:20. All the materials are blood-bought—highly prized of God and endued with immortality.

70

4. It was so in the voluntary spirit of those who erected it.

Ex. 35:4, 5, 20, 21, 36:56. What an astonishing instance of zeal, and liberality, and devotedness to the service of God. In this we have a typical resemblance of the voluntary character of all those spiritual services which God will accept. In Christianity our profession, our baptism, our regard to all the ordinances and duties must be voluntary, &c. "We are to present our bodies and give ourselves to the Lord," &c., serve him with a cheerful and willing heart.

5. It was so in its moveableness from place to place.

Notwithstanding the great excellence of the tabernacle, yet it was easily taken down, and went in all sojournings. Now God has ever had his church in the world, yet not always in the same locality. Once a flourishing church in Jerusalem, Corinth, &c. It moved from the eastern to the western world. It has never been fixed and stationary, but ever changing and in motion.

6. It typified the church as it was superseded by the temple at Jerusalem.

So the church of Christ on earth shall be consummated, and all its members be removed to the celestial temple in heaven. Of that temple John had a sublime vision. Read Rev. 20. Such are the chief points of typical resemblance. Notice,

II. The Psalmist's pious Resolution.

"I will abide in the tabernacle." Now what does this imply and include?

1. That, he was already a resident in it.

No abiding without first being in it. He had chosen it as the place of his spiritual abode, and "Blessed are they who dwell in thy house," &c. The Christian has been born into the church and kingdom of Christ. He lives in it; it is his spiritual home.

2. It implied fare-eminent attachment to it.

He was not weary of it. Not indifferent to it. Full of love to it. It was nearer his heart than his own palace. He preferred it to his chief good. How dear is the church of Christ to the believer. How he loves the assembly of the saints. He rays for her peace, and labors for her prosperity. It is his banqueting house.

&c., and he had rather be a doorkeeper &c.

A desire to enjoy its meetening influences for the heavenly state Communion with God on earth will prepare for communion above. Plants of righteousness, we must bear fruit till we are meet for being transplanted to the paradise above. O yes, there is a delightful nearness and connection between the church on earth and the church above! Like the holy and the most holy place.

It is desirable to die in visible union with Christ and his people. Well may we say, "I will," &c. Wherefore should we forsake it? Where shall we go, &c. Observe, he also resolves to trust in the shadow of the divine wings. God's house is his joy, and God's outspread wings his defense. Happy the people in such a case, &c.

Application

1. How satisfied the Christian should be with his portion as a citizen of Zion. A member of God's family.

2. Improve your privileges. Be diligent, devout.

3. Promote its welfare. Do all you can by your example, influence, &c.

24. JERUSALEM A TYPE OF THE CHURCH OF CHRIST

"But Jerusalem which is above is free, which it the mother of us all." —Gal. 4:26.

THE apostle is evidently contrasting the two dispensations. That of the law and the gospel. That of Moses and Christ. That of the ancient Zion and Jerusalem, with that spiritual New Testament dispensation, the Jerusalem from above, the mother of all believers, whether Jews or Gentiles. Between these dispensations there is indeed a striking contrast. One an economy of terror, of law, and legal ceremonies; the other a dispensation of love, grace, and spiritual freedom and rest. But we now design to consider the ancient Jerusalem in its typical representation of the church of Christ.

I. It was the City of the Divine Choice.

The Lord close Zion; he said, "Here will I dwell," &c., Ps. 132:13-18. Now the church is the choice of the Lord; it contains the united congregation of his saints, those who have been called by his gospel, who have believed in his Son, and who have been the living partakers of his heavenly grace. Over these God rejoiced. With these he has his delights. Unto these he manifests himself as he doth not unto the world. Jesus says of each of these, "If a man love me he will keep my word, and my Father will love him, and we will come unto him," &c., John 14:23. See 1 Pet. 1:23, 24.

II. It was the City of Divine Rule and Authority.

Here God made known his laws and judgments. Here he deposited his living oracles. His holy statutes. Here he revealed his will, and recorded his blessed word. And by these the inhabitants of Jerusalem were to be governed. Obedience to these secured the favorable tokens of God's love and favor. So in the new Jerusalem of his church. Here he has revealed his holy will, not by the oracle, or over the material mercy-seat, but by his own Son, and by making his living church the pillar and ground of truth. By depositing within it the doctrines, and commandments, and ordinances of the gospel. And the divine presence and favor is only secured, by unswerving fidelity to the charge with which God has entrusted her.

III. Jerusalem was the City of Divine Services

Here met the tribes of Israel, who came to worship before the Lord. Here were presented the sacrifices and the offerings of the people. Here God was worshipped and adored Here the voice of prayer and praise was heard in God's holy temple. Here the religious festivals were celebrated, and God honored in his sacred institutions. Such is the church of Christ, the Jerusalem, &c. Here those who have believed, and are of the saved, are united together, in the holy bonds of fellowship and love. Here they meet to observe all things their divine head has commanded them, and to continue "steadfastly in the apostles' doctrine and fellowship, in breaking of bread and in prayers," &c., Acts 2:41.

IV. Jerusalem was the City of Divine Blessings.

"The Lord loved the gates of Zion," &c. His especial love and care was directed to it. His providential benignity surrounded it. The Lord was the keeper and protector of the holy city. Within it he poured down the blessings of his grace and caused his favor to dwell, even life for evermore. See his gracious engagements and promises, Ps. 132:15, &c. So God preeminently blesses his spiritual Zion. Unto his people he gives exceedingly great and precious promises. They are blessed with the unsearchable blessings of his grace. With all the fulness of his love. With all the blessings of providence and grace. God supplies all their need. Defends from all their enemies, and keeps and saves unto eternal life.

V. Jerusalem was a City of distinguished Immunities and Privileges.

It was an honor to have been born in her. Her sons were freemen of the most favored city under heaven. Her inhabitants had numerous opportunities of enjoying religious services, they had the presence of the priests, and teachers of the law of God. "Happy were the people in such a case," &c. Still greater and more precious the immunities and privileges of the people of God. They enjoy spiritual liberty, have exalted titles, and possess immunities of the most glorious and heavenly character. Access to God's gracious throne. The sweet fellowship of his Holy Spirit. Delightful seasons of refreshing from the divine presence, and experimental overflows of that peace which passes all understanding

Application

1. Are we the citizens of the Jerusalem from above? Have we been born into her? Born from above? Born of water and the Spirit? Do we possess the spirit of her heavenly inhabitants?

2. How great the responsibility of such. It is theirs to exhibit the glory of divine grace, in calling and saving them, by a conversation which becometh the gospel of Christ. "To show forth his praises," &c. To pray for her peace and to labor for her prosperity. To display the spirit of love and harmony towards all the citizens, and to yield loyal subjection and hearty obedience to Christ the rightful Lord and King.

3. Unlike the earthly Jerusalem, she shall never become a prey to her enemies Her walls shall never be cast down, nor her streets become waste. "The gates of hell shall never prevail against her."

25. SOLOMON'S TEMPLE A TYPE OF THE HEAVENLY STATE

"And the house, when it was in building, was built of stone made ready before it was brought thither," &c.—1 Kings 6:7

WE recently contemplated the tabernacle as a striking type of Christ's visible church, and one of the typical resemblances was, that it was finally superseded by the temple of Solomon. Thus the church of Jesus on earth is preparatory to the church above. This is the union of good yet imperfect beings; that of the perfect and the holy. This is distinguished by mutability; that by its fixed, abiding, and eternal unchangeableness. The glory of that holy state we must die to realize and enjoy; and in its magnificence, and purity, and bliss, it will infinitely surpass all we ever saw or heard, or it ever entered into the heart of man to conceive. In treating of the heavenly state all expressions and images must necessarily fail. But let us look at some of the points of resemblance between Solomon's temple and what is revealed of the heavenly world. We notice,

I. That it typified Heaven in the Costliness of its materials.

See in reference to this, ch. 5:17, and 6:21-30. One part of the temple, the holy of holies, was overlaid with gold to the value of six hundred talents of gold, or the immense sum of four millions, three hundred thousand pounds of our sterling money. Of the entire expense we can form no probable idea. The spiritual, celestial temple above is not formed of earthly material stones, however precious. It is not overlaid with fine gold. It is constructed of spiritual beings. The souls of the redeemed. To estimate the value of these is beyond an angel's power. A soul outweighs in worth the material world. Jehovah's mandate brought suns, and systems, and worlds into being. He spoke, and it was done. He commanded, and it stood fast. But the outlay connected with the erection of the heavenly temple involved the gift of Christ, the impoverishing of heaven, the humiliation and sacrifice of God's only Son. "Not redeemed with corruptible things," &c.—but with the "precious blood of Christ." It typified the heavenly state,

II. In its Magnificence and Extent.

It was built according to the wisdom and kill of God. In every respect its appearance was that of grandeur and magnificence In form and size it was an exact square one thousand, four hundred, and sixty feet long on each side. Being considerably above a mile in circumference. Everything, however, like verbal description must be inadequate, to give you even a faint idea of its glory and extent. How much the grandeur and vastness of the heavenly kingdom. If a building erected by an earthly monarch should be so vast and magnificent, how splendid and glorious will that temple be, of which God is the immediate architect, and which is to show forth his glory throughout the ages of eternity. "In my Father's house are many mansions," &c.

III. In the Variety of the Materials of which it was composed.

75

Here were various kinds of wood and precious stones, and silver and gold. Many of these materials were brought from afar. How exactly the antitype agrees with this The heavenly temple shall be formed of countless numbers of believers. A multitude which no man can number. Persons of every age, and clime, and country, and tongue. Jews and gentiles, bond and free: all of whom shall unitedly constitute the celestial temple of the Lord. The typical analogy is seen,

IV. In the Preparation of these Materials before they were brought together.

To this our text especially refers. "I was built of stone made ready before it was brought thither." Now of these materials observe,

 1. They were originally unfit for such a use.

 In their native state, a part of the rocky quarry. Such was the original condition of every glorified spirit. They were once afar off. "Dark, polluted, hard, in a state of nature, and unfit for the glory of God." See Isaiah 51:1.

 2. They were made fit by a process of preparation.

 Separated from the mass, hewn out squared, and polished; each fit for its proper place in the erection. Thus, the materials of the celestial temple are "made ready." They are brought out of then natural sinful state. Renewed by the spirit of divine grace. Qualified for certain duties and stations of usefulness. And progressively polished by the sanctifying influences of the Holy Spirit. Until they possess a "meetness," or adaptation, for the inheritance of the saints in light.

This process of preparation was before the stones were brought to the building.

When brought they were ready to be fixed, and to form their part of the wall of the temple. So that there was not heard the sound of axe or hammer, while the house was in building. So it is with the erection of the heavenly temple. All the process of preparation is confined to this world, and to time. Here the hammer of the word is employed and heard. "Is not my word a hammer," &c. Here conviction is produced. Here the cry of anxious desire is heard. Here the bemoaning of contrite spirits, and reformation of life is witnessed. In short, sin is forgiven. New nature imparted. And the soul made fully holy and fit for heaven here. No heralds of mercy above. No sanctuaries. No baptisteries. No providential sanctifying dispensations. The souls are made fit before they are brought there. This is illustrated by the wise virgins. By the man with the wedding garment. By the ripe grain fit for the garner, &c. Observe the typical resemblance,

V. In the glorious Design of its Erection.

 1. The happiness of human beings.

 Here they were to have privileges and blessings worthy of God to bestow. Here they were to be exalted to the enjoyment of the highest and loftiest exercises. Here enjoy visible communion with the divine majesty of heaven and earth. God thus magnified and blessed his people. And the celestial temple is one of exalted enjoyment. The whole stupendous fabric formed of redeemed spirits is vocal with melody and joy. Here is the fountain of bliss and pleasures for evermore. Here he saints enjoy close and uninterrupted fellowship with God forever.

2. The manifestation of Jehovah's glory. God filled the temple with the cloud of his presence, the symbol of his glory. Heaven will be the scene of the brightest display of the glory of God. Here it would overwhelm us. "No man can see my face (says Jehovah) and live." On the mount the disciples were overwhelmed with the transfigured appearance of the Savior. At his resurrection, the guards fell down as dead men. But in the celestial temple God's glory shall be fully revealed. His face shall illumine it He shall be its sun. And the saints shall behold it, and live, in unutterable ecstasy forever. And here we see the disparity:—Solomon's temple was after all earthly and mutable, and finally passed away the celestial temple is heavenly, immutable and everlasting.

Here, were the sacrifices of beasts and the services of dying priests; above, there are the services of the saints, who are all priests, and who, through the sacrifice of Christ, will be acceptable to God forever and ever.

Application

Learn,

1. The benevolent and glorious design of God, in erecting a spiritual temple of redeemed souls, to show forth his praises through all the ages of eternity.

2. Do we personally enter into this great design? Are we anticipating a place and portion in his heavenly kingdom? Have we a good hope, to which we have been begotten, by faith in the resurrection of Christ from the dead?

3. Are we undergoing the preparatory process? Are we being made ready by the gracious means which God has appointed? How anxious, and diligent, and fervent we should be concerning this. Forget it not, that all which is prerequisite must be done and obtained here. Then let it be our wisdom and business to "Give diligence," &c., 2 Peter 1:10, 11.

26. THE JEWISH NATION TYPICAL OF THE CHRISTIAN CHURCH

"A chosen generation. A holy nation. A peculiar people." —1 Peter 2:9.

THE apostle here has obvious reference to the Jewish people as a type of the Christian church. And if the various sacrifices and services were typical of Christ and the Gospel, we need not be surprised to find a striking analogy between the Jewish nation and the spiritual kingdom of the Savior. The apostle uses three terms in the text, which we shall endeavor to illustrate in their typical signification.

I. The Church of Christ is a chosen Generation.

God selected Abraham and called him to be his servant, and promised that he would make of him "a great nation," and said, "I will bless thee and make thy name great, and thou shalt be a blessing," &c., Gen. 12:1-3. We enter not into the principles of this choice; we know not why and wherefore God made the Jews his chosen generation; but, he did so, although it is evident in this choice Jehovah had respect to an election to privileges, and which did not secure, irrespective of faith and obedience, either his favor or everlasting life. See Heb. 3:7, 19; 4:1. Thus believers are called and chosen to the fellowship of the gospel. In their collective capacity they are the delight of God. The objects of his love, the recipients of his blessings, a generation to show forth the praises and glory of God. They are chosen "through sanctification of the Spirit, unto obedience and sprinkling of the blood of Jesus," 1 Peter 1:2.

II. They are a Holy Nation.

A nation distinct and separated to God, us were the Jews, the seed of Abraham. Now we shall find a striking analogy in the following particulars, between the Jewish nation and the church of Jesus.

1. As a nation originally they had no supreme ruler or king but Jehovah.

Theirs was a theocracy, and their laws were all divine. The spiritual nation of believers has no head and king but Jesus. He is the head over all things to his church. The only king in Zion.

2. As a nation they were distinctly separated from all other people.

So the church is a distinct spiritual nation or kingdom, not of this world. Redeemed out of it, and separated manifestly from it. "Ye are not of the world," &c.

3. As a nation they had their especial religious laws and ordinances.

So the church of Jesus has the revealed laws of the Son of God. He has given her his holy word, and established within her holy ordinances and institutions.

4. As a nation they enjoyed many immunities and blessings.

God was their kind benefactor, guardian, and friend. So the church of Christ possesses distinguished privileges and favors. The Most High dwells within her. He is constantly imparting the riches of his grace. And he is as a wall of fire to his Zion, and their glory in the midst. He watches and Keeps his holy hill in perfect safety.

III. They are a peculiar People.

That is, distinct and differing from others. Now many things which were peculiar to the Jews we have adverted to. But we may add, of God's spiritual people,

1. They are the subjects of peculiar love.

"What manner of love hath the Father, &c. "Herein is love," &c.

2. They are peculiar in their experience.

Passed from death to life. Plucked as brands from the fire. Brought out of vassalage, &c. New creatures in Christ Jesus. Much about them paradoxical. Alive, yet dead. Rich, yet poor. Sorrowful, yet rejoicing. Princes, yet beggars. Weak, yet strong. As nothing, yet heirs of God, and possessing all things. Dying daily, yet having a sure hope of life and immortality.

3. As a people they were distinguished by their peculiar costume, habits, and language.

So the disciples of Christ are a spiritual nation, influenced by spiritual principles, distinct in their appearance by the graces and fruits of the Spirit, and have a holy conversation and speech, unlike that which prevails in the world. And this leads us to the next particular.

4. They have peculiar enjoyments.

Food to eat, of which others are ignorant. Sweet visitations from God. God manifests himself unto them, &c. They have peculiar peace, which passeth all understanding. Peculiar joy, with which strangers cannot intermeddle; joy unspeakable and full of glory. Bright providences, and glowing hopes of future blessedness.

Application

Learn,

1. Believers only, whose faith worketh by love, and produces obedience to God, belong to this chosen generation, &c. Let us not depend upon the logical peculiarities or doctrinal notions, and from these infer our character and condition. The safe test is living, purifying faith. "Dost thou believe in the Son of God?"

2. Let such walk worthy of their high and heavenly calling. As the chosen, holy and peculiar people of God, let their conversation and spirit honor God, and practically recommend religion to those around them. "So let your light shine before men," &c.

27. CHRIST TYPIFIED BY THE CITIES OF REFUGE

"Who have fled for refuge." —Heb. 6:18.

IT is clear that the apostle, when uttering these words, had especial reference to the cities of refuge, and the security the manslayer had by fleeing to them. A full description of these cities is given in the book of Numbers 35:9-28; and Joshua 20. Their appointment was designed for the security of those who accidentally or unwittingly slew a man, and who were exposed to death by the next of kin to the deceased, as the avenger of blood. Now observe,

I. Every Sinner is justly exposed to Death.

The penalty of transgression is death. The soul that sinneth shall die. All whose guilt and transgressions are uncancelled, unforgiven, are condemned already, and the wrath of God abideth on them. Natural death is the result of sin. In death and trespasses all ungodly men are now involved, so as to be dead while they lire. But the justice of God will punish, with eternal death, all who remain in final impenitence and unbelief. And this is the condition of all mankind. All countries, all classes, all degrees of sinners are in the way of death. Pursued by the righteous AVENGER of blood, who will cast the wicked into hell, with all the nations that forget God.

II. God hath appointed Jesus as the Refuge for condemned Sinners.

He came that men might not perish, but have everlasting life. He came not to destroy men's lives, but to save them. Now in this, he was strikingly typified by the cities of refuge.

1. In their number we are reminded of the sufficiency of Christ.

There were six of these cities. Doubtless amply sufficient for the cases which might require them. Jesus is the *sufficient* Savior of all men. In him is room for the whole world. Merit, mercy, and willingness, for every child of man.

2. In their diversified localities we see the accessibility of Christ.

These cities were placed in various parts of the land, so as to be near to every quarter, and accessible to the inhabitants throughout. Here we see at once pointed oat to us, the nearness of Christ to every portion of the family of Adam. Throughout our wide world, in every region and city and spot tenanted by a sinner, is Christ near at hand, and not afar off. All the world may have ready access to Christ, and live.

3. In the spacious well-directed roads to the cities of refuge, we are reminded of the free, full, and plain declarations of the gospel of Christ.

The cities were to be on distinct elevations, so as to be seen afar off. The roads to them were to be wide and unobstructed. Finger-posts were to be placed at every turning, on which were to be inscribed Refuge! Thus every aid was afforded to the manslayer in his flight for mercy. How truly does this show us the very spirit of the gospel. Here the way of mercy is fully revealed. The mode of salvation clearly detailed. The most gracious directions given. And every facility afforded to the soul who is inquiring what he must do to be saved.

4. In the signification of the names of the cities, we also perceive the glorious excellency of Christ.

One of these cities was called "KEDESH," which signifies "HOLY." Jesus is the Holy One of God. His person is holy. His work is holy. He redeems and saves men to holiness. Another was called "SHECHEM," which signifies "SHOULDER," representing Christ as bearing the sins and burdens of the sinner. "He hath borne our griefs and carried our sorrows." The whole church of God is sustained by him and rests upon him. Another was called "HEBRON," signifying "FELLOWSHIP." Thus Christ is the medium and ground of fellowship between God and men, and between the whole body of believers. In Christ we become the sons of God, and members one of another. Another was called "BEZER," which signifies a "STRONGHOLD." Christ is often thus described. He is our refuge, our fortress, and a stronghold in the day of trouble. In him we are more secure than if surrounded by a munition of rocks. Another of the cities was called "RAMOTH," which signifies "EXALTATION." Jesus is the exalted Son of God. The Prince of life The Lord of glory. After the work of his humiliation and sorrow. God raised him from the dead and exalted him to the right hand of the majesty on high. He is exalted by the uplifting of the cross, in the hearts and supreme love of all his people, and shall be exalted in the songs of the redeemed forever and ever. The name of the last city of refuge was "GOLAN," which signifies "EXULTATION," or "JOY." Christ is the joy and rejoicing of his people. His gospel is the message of joy. His kingdom is not only righteousness and peace, but joy in the Holy Spirit. He is the joy of his church on earth, and the ecstasy of the heavenly world.

5. In the deliverance of the manslayer we see typified the salvation which is in Christ Jesus.

Within the city he was safe. Death was averted. Provision was made for him. But it was necessary that he should abide, at least until the death of the high priest. Now, by believing repentance, the sinner flees to Christ, and becomes interested in his all-extensive merit and saving benefits. But he must be *in* Christ. And he must *abide* in him, John 15:1-7. Thus he shall be delivered from present condemnation, and from eternal death. In Christ is ample provision for his comfort, safety, and well-being.

Application

From this subject,

1. We see the awful misery and peril of the careless sinner.

2. The absolute necessity of repentance towards God and faith in the Lord Jesus Christ. And how necessary that this should be prompt and immediate. Without delay, seeing that the avenger of blood is pursuing every sinner. "Agree with thine adversary quickly," &c.

3. How urgently should ministers make known the terrors of the Lord and persuade men.

4. How happy are those who are delivered from the power of Satan, and have been brought to enjoy the forgiving love of God. Within the city of refuge, all their interests are secure both for time and eternity.

28. THE GOSPEL ERA TYPIFIED BY THE YEAR OF JUBILEE

"To preach the acceptable year of the Lord" —Luke 4:19

THE Savior had just returned from his baptism and consecration to his great mission. Entering into the synagogue at Nazareth, there was given unto him the roll of Isaiah, from which he read a portion of that prophecy, "The Spirit of the Lord is upon me," &c., Isa. 61:1, &c. This beautiful passage was appropriated to himself, and therein he taught the people, that he was in truth the long-predicted and long-expected Messiah. The last sentence of the scripture which he quoted, evidently refers to the year of jubilee, and thus he gives to the era of the gospel the direct application of that celebrated and joyous season. Let us contemplate the year of jubilee, so that we may discover the most striking typical features which it presented.

I. The Year of Jubilee was appointed as a period of Mercy and Joy to the Afflicted and Poor of the People of Israel.

This was evidently its broad and comprehensive character. Such evidently is the gospel era, a period of the full revelation of the mercy and love of God to our world. A year of glad tidings, and of great joy to all people. Its great design and end, is the well-being and happiness of the human race.

II. The Year of Jubilee was a Period fixed and appointed by God.

God directed that they "should hallow the fiftieth year and proclaim liberty throughout all the land, unto all the inhabitants thereof; it shall be a jubilee to you," Lev. 25:10, &c. Thus God fixed and appointed the gospel dispensation, and to it the prophets bare witness; to this day of salvation Abraham looked, and for it kings waited; and John at length, as the immediate herald of Christ, announced the approach of the jubilee, or gracious reign of the Son of God.

III. The Year of Jubilee was ushered in on the great Day of Atonement.

This was the most sacred day in the Jewish calendar. On this day a bullock was slain as a sin-offering, a ram as a burnt-offering, and the scapegoat symbolically bare away the sins of the people On this day the mercy-seat was sprinkled And the priest in the holiest place inter ceded for the people, and then came forth to bless them in the name of the Lord. Now the whole of these services had a distinct reference to the death and sacrifice of Jesus Christ. They had no virtue or value but as they typified the atonement made by Christ. And that atonement is the basis of the gospel dispensation. There can be no tidings of mercy and salvation to the sinner but through the death of the Lord Jesus Christ. "Thus it was written and thus it behooved Christ to suffer," &c., Luke 24:46.

IV. The Jubilee was announced with Trumpets and with Acclamations of great Joy.

The trumpet was to sound to all the people throughout the land. To this doubtless the psalmist refers, when he says, "Blessed is the people that know the joyful sound," Ps. 89:15. Thus was the gospel introduced into our world. Angels from heaven sang with rapture, while they announced the birth of the Savior of man. Jesus and his disciples went everywhere through the land, proclaiming peace and joy to the people. And the Christian ministry is designed to convey the lifegiving sound through all the world, and to every creature.

V. The Jubilee conferred great Privileges and Blessings on the People.

1. It was associated with abundant provision.

The promise was, "that the land should bear fruit," and that they should "eat their fill, and dwell in safety," Lev. 25:19. Now the gospel era is one of overflowing plenty. It is compared to a great supper. To a royal feast. See Isa. 26:6-8; Matt. 22:1-4.

2. It proclaimed liberty to captives and the opening of the prison doors to those that were bound.

The bond-servant was now free, and universal liberty prevailed through all the land, Lev. 25:39. The gospel also makes known to the slaves of sin and the captives of the wicked one, emancipation and freedom. O yes, Jesus frees all who come to him from the galling yoke of hellish bondage, and introduces them into the liberty of the sons of God. Whom the Son makes free, they are free indeed. See Rom. 6:22.

3. It provided for the remission of debts.

Those who were waxen poor, and could not pay their creditors, were on this year, to be discharged from the obligation. Now his is the great blessing announced in the gospel, "Forgiveness of sin." Jesus came to forgive sin. He freely forgave every earnest applicant in the days of his flesh And he is exalted a Prince and a Savior, to give repentance and remission of sin Acts 13:38; Luke 24:47.

4. It restored forfeited possessions.

Estates and possessions mortgaged now returned to their original owners. See Lev. 25:23, 24. Here again we behold the clear application to the design and spirit of the gospel. It announces to us the restoration of all we have lost through the introduction of sin into our world. Or rather it gives us more precious and abiding blessings in their place.

"In Christ the tribes of Adam boast,
More blessings than their father lost."

We regain the love and favor of God, the fountain of every other blessing. We regain our sonship and likeness to God. We regain a heavenly renewed nature. We regain a title to glory, and honor, and riches, and dominion, in the heavenly paradise. We become "heirs of God, and joint heirs with Christ," Rom. 8:17. Oh the grandeur, the sublimity, the eternity of the inheritance which is made known to us in the gospel!

5. The year of jubilee was one of freedom from toil.

It was a year of festivity and rest, Lev. 25:11, 12. The land overflowed with plenty, and richly spread its fulness before all the people. Such is the gospel dispensation. A period wherein the graciousness of God is richly seen, in the fulness and freeness of the promises of his love. No painful rites, no tedious ablutions, no expensive sacrifices, no heavy yoke of observances, all the institutions of the gospel are easy, simple, gratuitous, and gracious. "The law (with all its ceremonies) was given by Moses," but "grace and truth came by Jesus Christ."

Application

1. Learn the privileges and blessings of that dispensation under which we live.

2. The importance of a personal and practical improvement of them.

3. Despisers must necessarily be miserable, and finally perish.

29. GOD THE FATHER OF HIS PEOPLE

"Will be a Father unto you." —2 Cor 6:18.

JEHOVAH is the author or fountain of all things. All creatures derived their existence from him, and "for his pleasure and glory they were created. He is the father of the Savior. The father of angels. The father of the whole human family. But our text refers to him as the spiritual father of his people. As the father of our natural being, we are brought under his government, become the subjects of his providential care, and are amenable to his righteous laws. But in our unrenewed state he cannot behold us with delight. The carnal mind is enmity to him, our wills and hearts and lives are opposed to his will and equitable authority, and by disobedience we yield ourselves to Satan, so as to become the children of the father of lies. It is when we return to God by genuine repentance and faith in his word and Son, that he says, "I will be a Father unto you." As a Father,

I. He is the Author of their spiritual Being.

He by his Holy Spirit quickens those who were dead in trespasses and sins. He imparts the principle of spiritual existence, and raises from the death of sin, to newness of spiritual life. And as father, he not only gives life, but he imparts his *own nature*. His spiritual children are made to partake of the divine nature, 2 Pet. 1:4. Hence it is said they are "born again of the incorruptible seed of the word of God, which abideth forever," 1 Pet. 1:23. "Born not of blood, nor of the will of the flesh, nor of the will of man, but of God," John 1:13. So as God imparts his own nature to his spiritual children, so he also impresses his own image and likeness. Thus the new man is said to be "renewed in knowledge, after the image of him that created him," Col. 3:10. See also Eph. 4:23, 24. In connection with the divine nature and image, the children of God also possess his Spirit. Of such it is said, "The Spirit of God dwelleth in you." Thus God said, "I will give them one heart, and I will put a new spirit within you," &c., Ezek. 11:19. As father,

II. God supplies all the Need if his Children,

In this respect, infants are not more helpless and dependent than the children of God. They are without strength and without resources. All their springs art in God. As an affectionate father, he does not allow them to lack any good thing. He supplies "all their need." He spreads before them a table in he wilderness. He gives them the bread and the water of life. His grace is freely bestowed to help them in every time of need. They have food to eat, of which the world knows nothing. His promises are like milk, and honey, and manna, as well as containing strong meat for the more mature and strong of his household. He also *clothes* them with the best robe, the garments of joy and salvation. He provides also for all their sicknesses, removes all their infirmities, and heals all their diseases. His supplies to his children are rich and abundant, varied and ever new, free and gratuitous, overflowing, satisfying, and everlasting. His mercies never fail, and his paternal care abideth forever and ever. As father,

III. He provides them with a suitable Home and Habitation.

In some respects God himself is the habitation or dwelling-place of his saints. But he has provided for his spiritual family, the tabernacle of his church on earth. Here they dwell in the bonds of fraternal love, united in the fellowship of the saints, having God their father with them, to do them good. The church is the dwelling-place, the home of God's children. Here they have the shelter, the repose, the solace of home. Here they have the interchange of thought, and feeling, and conversation, of kindred spirits. Here is the social board, the family table, &c. Then the Lord has prepared for their future residence and dwelling, the temple of his glory above. In the wilderness, the tabernacle, as a moveable tent, is most suited to them as sojourners, &c. The church beneath is their residence during their minority. But when of full age, they are received to their father's residence on high. That house, not made with hands, eternal in the heavens. This is the saints' everlasting home, where the united family of God shall be forever with the Lord. See Heb 11:16. As father,

IV. He secures the Instruction of his Children.

For the soul to be without knowledge is not good. Knowledge is one of the distinguishing traits in the children of God. They are children of the light and of the day. They have the excellency of the knowledge of Christ Jesus their Lord. The heaven to which they are destined and journeying, is the region of mind, the world of cloudless day. For the education of his children, he spreads before them *his marvelous works*. He has written for them the *volume* of life, the *scriptures* of eternal truth. He has appointed for them *teachers,*—pastors, to feed them with knowledge and understanding. In addition to these, he sends into their hearts his Holy Spirit, to lead them into all truth, to guide them by his counsel, that afterwards they may be received to glory. As father,

V. He guards and protects his Children.

As spiritual, they are exposed to innumerable perils and enemies. The world hateth them. Satan seeks to destroy them. They are encompassed with adversaries. Without God's gracious help and protection, they would necessarily perish. God however is their shield and defense. He is their fortress and high tower. He is round them as the walls were round about Jerusalem. He secures them from all evil, and keeps them night and day. Holding them in his hand, "they shall never perish," &c. "Kept by the power of God," &c. As father,

VI. He gives them a Glorious and everlasting Portion.

None can tell the reward and the riches of the inheritance which God has laid up for them that love him. Now, they have the unsearchable riches of grace; and hereafter, the unfading glories and riches of eternity. He gives each of his children a kingdom, a throne, a crown, and bliss, and joy for evermore.

Application

1. Learn the happiness and blessedness of those who are the children of God. What honor, what joy, what security, they possess! Consider,

2. The high claims which God has upon his children. How they should reverence and fear him. Love and delight in him. Follow and obey him.

3. The misery of the children of the wicked one. Dark, wretched, enslaved miserable and perishing.

4. Urge upon such to turn unto God, and to seek his pardoning mercy, that they may live.

30. THE ROYAL CHARACTER OF GOD

"A great King above all gods." —Ps. 95:3

THE greatness of God is unsearchable. None can fully find him out, or know him to perfection. He is the one infinite, self-existent, and ever-blessed potentate, who hath immortality in himself, the same yesterday, today, and forever. Among the various representations of the divine being, is that wherein he is exhibited as the great ruler of the universe, as the supreme monarch of heaven and earth. Often is he spoken of as king—"King over all the earth." As "clothed with majesty." As "an everlasting King," whose throne is "in the heavens," and whose "kingdom ruleth over all." As king, the blessed God,

I. Has his Dominions.

These embrace the whole universe. He rules over all. He reigns over heaven and earth, and in hell he sways the scepter of his righteous judgments and holy displeasure Within his dominions, we must include all the material parts of the universe. All existence, whether merely animal, or rational, or angelic. All worlds, and all things, are within the range of his rule and dominion. Or we may view the kingdom of God as comprising, 1. The kingdom of nature, wherein he rules over the whole material universe. 2. The kingdom of providence, wherein he superintends and directs all events to the effectual accomplishment of all his holy, wise, and benevolent purposes. 3. The kingdom of his grace, or the administration of his love and mercy to a sinful race, through the mediation of his Son, our Savior Jesus Christ. 4. The kingdom of his glory, where he more fully and immediately diffuses abroad the rays of his divine splendor, and where, among angels and happy spirits, he especially dwells, and where there is "fulness of joy and pleasures for evermore." As king,

II. He has his Throne and Scepter

The throne of God is in the highest heaven, and Job describes it as being so elevated that its splendor is beyond created vision. "He holdeth back the face of his throne, and spreadeth his cloud upon it" Job 26:9. It. is described as the "throne of his holiness," Ps. 47:8. Daniel beheld Jehovah's throne in a vision, and likens it to "the fiery flame," and says, "A fiery stream issued and came forth from before him," &c., Dan. 7:9. See also Ezekiel's vision, 1:26, 27, &c. Now the scepter of God is a scepter of righteousness. He reigneth and ruleth in righteousness. In all his administrations "just and right is he." As a king,

III. He has Laws and Statutes.

Now these laws are the established principles for the regulation of all things pertaining to his wide and glorious dominions. He has physical laws for the material works of his hands. And moral laws for the direction of intelligent and responsible beings. These laws are the reflection of his own wise, and righteous, and benevolent mind. They are just and good. Those laws which relate to mankind, are revealed and published in the holy scriptures. Here we have the will of God written under the infallible direction of the Holy Spirit. These laws are clear, impartial, full, and are sanctioned by the most awful penalties and glorious rewards. As a king,

IV. He has his royal Guards and Army.

In Daniel it is written, "He doeth according to his will in the army of heaven." Elisha's servant, after his eyes were opened, beheld the mountain was full of horses and chariots of fire round about, 2 Kings 6:17. The psalmist says, "The chariots of God are twenty thousand, even thousands of angels," Ps. 68:17. Myriads of exalted creatures vested with power, and swifter than the winds, are ever ready to do his will and execute his pleasure. As king,

V. He has magnificent Palaces and Dwellings.

His presence fills all space. He is everywhere, beholding all things, and upholding all things by the word of his power. But he has his especial dwelling-places. He dwells, 1. In the hearts of his humble saints. He says, I dwell with "him that is of a contrite and humble spirit," &c., Isaiah 57:15. "I will dwell in them," &c., 2 Cor. 6:16. 2. He dwells in the midst of his church. As he dwelt in ancient times in Zion, and displayed his presence from between the cherubim, so he is in the midst of his spiritual sanctuary, and in the plenitude of his Spirit, he makes the church his holy and delightful habitation. The apostle says, "In whom ye also are builded together, for an habitation of God through the Spirit," Eph. 2:22. 3. He has his august and most glorious dwelling on high. He says, "I dwell in the high and holy place." The poet had this passage in view when he sang:—

"Eternal power whose high abode,
Becomes the grandeur of a God,
Infinite lengths, beyond the bounds,
Where stars revolve their little rounds"

Application

If Jehovah be invested with supreme and universal dominion and majesty, then learn,

1. The reverence and humility which we should exhibit before him.

How we should hallow his name, and fear, when we contemplate his holiness and glory.

2. As king he demands our loyal homage and constant obedience.

His claims are founded on his right to have dominion, and on our duty to yield him our willing and cheerful service.

3. As a king his wrath will be fearful and overwhelming.

His holiness and truth will not allow him to connive at iniquity. All sin is treason against his majesty, rebellion against his government. Let disobedient sinners forsake their evil ways and live. He will freely exercise mercy towards those who repent, and come to him through the mediation of his beloved Son.

4. How happy are his loyal subjects.

He enriches, dignifies, and makes supremely happy those who trust in him and love him. "Happy art thou, O Israel," &c. "Let the children of Zion be joyful," &c.

5. His incorrigible foes he will cast down into the abodes of darkness and misery forever and ever.

31. GOD THE REFUGE OF HIS PEOPLE

"God is a refuge for us." —Psa. 62:8

THE life of the godly man is one of exposedness to sorrow and peril. He participates in that trouble which is the common portion of all men. He with all others is liable to sickness, adversity, bereavements, and death. Born to trouble, as the sparks fly upward. But in addition to these, he is in an enemy's country. He is passing through a dreary wilderness, a wilderness of storms and dangers, where hostile hosts are leagued against him. Strengthless and insufficient of himself, this is his comfort and safety,—God is his refuge, a present help in every time of trouble. We ask,

I. When is God a Refuge to his People?

He is so,

1. In the period of temptation When Satan comes in like a flood, &c. When he would sift as wheat. When his fiery darts are directed in fearful volleys against the people of God. These seasons are perilous, and would be fearfully fatal, were not God a refuge for us.

2. In the day of adversity.

When earthly good seems to forsake us. When our enjoyments fail. When providence seems adverse to us. When all appears to be against us. When created resources are dried up. To Jacob, to Job, to David, and to thousands, he has been their help and refuge.

3. In the night of affliction.

When health has been exchanged for sickness, strength for weakness, ease for pain, joy and gladness for weariness and decay,—when wearisome days, &c., are appointed, when heart and flesh fail. None but his arm can then sustain, his presence cheer, his love console. He is the sick man's refuge, when compelled to retire to his solitary chamber, a I lie upon the couch of pain.

4. In the solemnities of death.

Whence shall the spirit fly when chased out of her old habitation and abode? when she is no longer surrounded by the tabernacle of the body? Then the bosom of God is the refuge. The house not made with hands is the abode; the heavenly mansion, the dwelling, forever and ever. We inquire,

II. What sort of a Refuge God is to his People?

1. He is invulnerable.

In God is absolute security. A far more secure defense than the munition of rocks. "If God be for us." &c. "Who is he that shall harm us," &c. "In the Lord Jehovah is everlasting strength."

2. He is a refuge ever near.

His omnipresence ever surrounds us Wherever we are, God is near at hand, and not afar off. No difficulty in coming to the refuge. Indeed, we cannot flee from him. We cannot go from the presence of his Spirit. See Ps. 139:7, 12.

3. Always accessible.

Not only near to us, but open to receive. Ready to shelter and to screen us. His eyes are ever upon the righteous, and his ears always open to their cry. In the day of trouble, he hears the prayer of the distressed, and sends deliverance, and enables them to glorify him.

4. Unchanging and eternal.

A refuge to his people in all countries, and ages, and generations. A refuge now, and always, and evermore. A refuge that never fails. A refuge in time and through all eternity. If God be such a refuge, then we infer, 1. The absolute security of his people. Amidst all the changes and revolutions around them, though the earth be removed, and though the mountains be carried into the midst of the sea, &c., "God is their refuge, a very present help in trouble." 2. The confidence they should feel towards God. Trust in him at all times and forever. Commit all to his care and keeping. 3. The course they should pursue in all their troubles. Flee to God. Seek his almighty help and succor. Fervently call upon his holy and gracious name. 4. Let the sinner flee by faith in Christ to this refuge, that he may escape the storms of unending wrath in the world to come.

32. GOD THE GUIDE OF HIS PEOPLE

"He will be our guide even unto death." —Ps. 48:14.

THE people of God are pilgrims and strangers on the earth; they seek a better country, that is to say, a heavenly one. A life of piety supposes the affections and desires of the heart to be in heaven. This is not the good man's rest, for it is polluted. Like the children of Israel, he is journeying to the place which the Lord said he would give unto him, and, as the tribes who went up to Jerusalem, he goes forth from strength to strength, until he appears before God in Zion. But he is a creature of wants in all his pilgrimage. He wants necessary food, and raiment, and rest. But he also requires constant direction,—he needs a constant guide. His path is one he has never before traversed. He is ignorant of the way, and without a guide, his course would be uncertain, and very probably his end unattained. God graciously engages to conduct him. To be to him as the pillar of cloud and fire was to Israel. So that with joyous rapture he exclaims, This God shall be my God forever and ever. He will be my "guide even unto death." Observe,

I. The good Man's Need of a Guide.

And this necessarily arises,

1. From his ignorance.

He is not in darkness, but he is at present the child of the dawn. His knowledge is so limited, that he cannot trust to it. He only knows the first elements of truth. He has entered on the path of life, but he feels it needful to seek direction and guidance every step. He prays, "Lead me into a plain path," &c. "Lead me in the way everlasting," &c.

2. From the diversified paths which surround him.

Now there are many paths which seem right to men, and which are called good and excellent by men of the world, and which notwithstanding lead from the right way. Sin has a thousand treacherous paths, many of them apparently good, and most of them fascinating, &c. There are paths of mere morality, of self-righteousness, of spiritual apathy, of carnal security, &c. How necessary then to have a guide.

3. From the temptations to which he is subject.

It is the work of Satan to allure and deceive, that he may ruin and destroy. He lays snares for the travelers' feet. He tries to turn them aside, from the way of duty and safety. Or to suggest that the way is tedious, embarrassing, and uncomfortable. Then,

4. There is the tendency of their own hearts to evil.

The heart within them is only partially sanctified. Liable to err. Often willing to be deceived. Apt to turn aside. Hence the caution of the apostle, "Take heed lest there be in any of you an evil heart of unbelieving, in departing from the living God," Heb. 3:12. The child of God often prays,

"Let thy grace, Lord, like a fetter,
Bind my wandering heart to thee."

Let us inquire,

II. How God guides his People.

1. By the counsels of his truth.

"Thou shalt guide me by thy counsel." God has given his holy word to be the guide of our steps. Here is plainly and distinctively marked out the way we should go. How often the psalmist refers to it. "O that my ways were directed to keep thy statutes," Ps. 119:5. "Wherewithal shall a young man," &c., ver. 9. "I will run in the way of thy commandments," &c., ver. 32. See also verses 35, 59, 104.

2. By the ministry of his servants.

Of old he raised up Moses, and Joshua, and Caleb. Afterwards Samuel and the prophets. He also came to minister and to teach mankind in the person of his Son. Heb. 1:2, &c. He has established the ministry of the word with the Christian dispensation. "He gave some apostles, and some prophets, and some evangelists," &c., Eph. 4:11. See also 1 Cor. 12:28

3. By the teaching of his Spirit.

"And I will pray the Father, and he shall give you another comforter," &c. "He shall teach you all things." "He will guide you into all truth," John 14:16-26, 16:13. Let us ascertain,

III. What kind of a Guide God is to his People.

1. He is an infallible guide.

He is incapable of error. He knows everything connected both with the travelers, the way, and the perils to which they are exposed. He knows all things even from the beginning.

2. He is patient and forbearing.

He remembers that his people are but dust. His long suffering is greatly displayed in enduring their provocations, in not wearying with their slow advances and patiently sustaining them amidst all their unworthiness.

3. He is affectionate and tender.

As the shepherd kindly leads his flock. As the mother aids her infant child to walk. His lovingkindness is perpetually displayed. He breaks not the bruised reed, &c. He carries in his arms, shelters beneath his wings, guides with his eye, and preserves in the hollow of his hand.

4. He is constant and unfailing.

He never leaves, nor ever forsakes. He guides their youth to mature years, and, casts not off in the time of old age, nor forsakes when their strength fails. He guides even to death. He conducts his people to glory

Application

1. Are we under the guidance of God?

Have we yielded ourselves to him? Do we hear his voice and obey it? Read his word and follow it? Meditate on his example and imitate it? Pray for his Spirit, and attend to the holy suggestions which he imparts?

2. Let such cherish a spirit suited to their character and condition.

Reverence and holy fear. Confidence in God. Adherence to the truth. Fervent prayer and earnest activity of mind. Self-denial and glowing ardor after the heavenly state.

3. Urge sinners to turn from the way of death, and live.

In the way of darkness, under the guidance of the prince of darkness, you must inevitably sink into the abyss of darkness forever. "Thus saith the Lord Ask for the old paths," &c.

33. GOD THE SHIELD OF THE RIGHTEOUS

"I am thy shield." —Gen. 15:1.

To Abraham these gracious words were spoken. Spoken unto him in a vision, spoken by the Lord of hosts. Spoken by him who is faithful and true, and who never failed in aught that he promised to his people. Abraham's history verified the promise. God was indeed his shield; no evil came near him; and after having enjoyed the protection of the divine presence, and the favor of the divine friendship, doubtless God became his heavenly and exceeding great reward. But the text need not be limited to Abraham. The promise is equally the property of all his spiritual seed. God is the seed of all the righteous, Observe,

I. The Righteous require a Shield.

They have enemies. Wicked men are such. Evil spirits are such. Against the righteous these are combined under one mighty, malevolent, persevering, and potent adversary, the devil. He is represented as a roaring lion. As a powerful prince. As an enemy who throws his fiery darts to destroy them. Of themselves they are not sufficient to oppose his diabolical power, consequently they are in a position of imminent peril. Under these circumstances they would necessarily perish, it God did not graciously interpose and engage to be their shield. Consider,

II. In what respects God is their shield.

A shield is that piece of defensive armor by which the arrows or strokes of the adversary are warded off. Now God is the shield of his people in a variety of respects.

1. He is the shield of their substance.

He puts a hedge around all that they have. Satan could not injure the property of Job until God said, "Behold, all that he hath is in thy power," Job 1:12. God says that no plague shall come nigh their dwelling, Ps. 91:10.

2. He is the shield of their bodies.

He holds the lives and breath of his saints in his hand. He gives his angels charge concerning them, &c., Ps. 91:11. See also Isaiah 33:16. The Lord will preserve and keep them alive, &c., Ps 33:16, 19.

3. He is the shield of their souls.

He guides, he keeps, and upholds the souls of his people. He watches for their safety. He preserves from Satan's attacks, from the world's snares, and from the frailties arising from the infirmities of the flesh. Thus God is the shield of the righteous, in all they are, and have. Notice,

III. The peculiar Excellencies of this Shield.

1. It is omnipotent.

The mighty power of God is the shield and defense of the righteous. "Kept by the power of God." A shield all-sufficient. Never failed.

2. It is a perpetual shield.

At all times and in all places. In every age and season. Throughout life, and in the valley and shadow of death.

3. A universal shield.

Of the whole collective church, and of each member in particular. Not one of God's spiritual family is overlooked or left exposed to peril. He is the shield of each one, and of all who trust in him.

4. The only shield.

Nothing would avail. Human policy, wisdom power, combination, all unavailing without God. He only is the sure invincible, and everlasting defense and shield of the righteous.

Application

1. Let saints cleave to the Lord, and thus avail themselves of this invaluable shield. Faith and prayer encircle us with God's protecting and preserving power.

2. Be grateful for it. How we ought to exult in it, and give God constant and hearty thanks for it.

3. How awful is the condition of the sinner. Not only without this shield, but in opposition to God, and exposed to his divine power and wrath. O let such flee to the Mediator, and lay hold of God's strength and be at peace.

34. JEHOVAH LIKENED TO A HUSBANDMAN

"My Father is the husbandman." —John 15:1.

RURAL and agricultural figures are often made use of to express the relationship between God and his people. The church is sometimes represented as the garden of the Lord, the Lord's plantation, or the field of grain, ripening for a joyous and an abundant harvest. The figure of a vineyard is very often employed by the ancient prophets. Isaiah says, "My well-beloved hath a vineyard in a very fruitful hill," &c., Isaiah 5:1; and see also, Jer. 2:21, &c.; Ezek. 19:10; and Joel 1:7. The Savior adopts the same emblem, and says, I am the true vine and "my Father is the husbandman," or the proprietor and dresser of the vine. As a husbandman let us consider,

I. Jehovah's Vineyard.

This is his church. And this vineyard of the Lord,

1. Was originally a waste.

Sin blighted both the powers and condition of man. Robbed him of his righteousness and bliss, and also his dominion and estate. Left him barren of true good. Now God by his providence and grace, transforms this sterile waste and makes it a delightful vineyard to himself. Thus, the prophet speaks of him, "gathering out the stones," &c., Isaiah 5:2. He makes all things new. This vineyard,

2. Became the object of his choice and care.

He fixed his gracious regards upon it. He resolved to form a people for himself To bring out of sterility a vineyard, to yield abundantly its cheering and refreshing fruit. To this end he planted it with plants of righteousness. He walls it round with the protecting fence of his presence and love. He raises up men to attend to its cultivation. He employs laborers to work in it.

3. On this vineyard he communicates the means of fruitfulness.

The vine-owner must depend upon the benign blessings of heaven. He must rest on his goodness who sends the fruitful shower, the genial beams of the sun, and favorable seasons of increase. Jehovah has all these resources within himself. He gives to his spiritual vineyard, the teeming rains, the enriching dews. The cheering rays of light and heat. He gives his word, his ordinances, his spiritual influences, and causes his favors there to descend, even life for evermore.

4. From this vineyard he expects an adequate return of fruit.

The end of a vineyard is the obtaining of fruit. The husbandman expects this, reasonably looks for it; and looks for it in proportion to the means expended, and the favorable situation the vineyard occupies. Thus, God expects a return of fruit from his church. He blesses them that they maybe manifest blessings. He enlightens that they may shine, &c. He expects from them a return of *heart fruit*—holy dispositions, desires, tempers, thoughts, &c.; *lip fruit*—a wise and edifying conversation; *life fruit*—a constant regard to himself, by reverence, fear, grateful acknowledgments, supreme love, &c. And towards man, equity, truth, benevolence, and mercy. Over ourselves, vigilance, self-government, self-denial, &c. And God expects this fruit from all. But, from all, in proportion to their privileges and blessings. This fruit honors and pleases God; and is the best evidences that we can have, of our regeneration and acceptance with God. "He that is righteous doeth righteousness."

From the connective passage of our text, Jesus clearly teaches that union—vital union to him is essential to fruitfulness That all believers are branches of him, who is God's precious vine. And severed from him, we could yield no fruit. God has given him to be head over all things to his church. He is the great and only medium of life and salvation, Let us consider.

II. The Characteristics of Jehovah as the Husbandman of his Church.

Consider,

1. His infinite knowledge and wisdom.

All his plans and arrangements are grounded on wisdom that never errs. He adapts all means to their right and proper and. He knows all concerning his vineyard. What is best for it, &c.

2. His unbounded resources.

He has all things within the limit of his power. All events he can control. All kinds of seasons he can command. All evil he can avert. And all that is good and benign he can effect.

3. His unfailing fidelity.

He has made many gracious engagements with his people. Has given them many precious promises. But he never fails in executing his plans, and accomplishing his purposes. He forsakes not the work of his hands. And he will finally make all things to redound to the eternal honor and glory of his name.

Application

1. Learn the happiness and safety of God's people.

2. The righteous claims which God has upon them.

35. GOD THE PORTION OF HIS SAINTS

"The Lord is the portion of mine inheritance." —Psa. 16:5.

THE wicked have their portion in this life. They seek after earthly good, on it they place their affections, and they are indifferent to the spiritual necessities of their undying souls. How insufficient, fleeting, and worthless is such a portion. Without satisfaction now, the mind in a state of restless anxiety, and as death approaches, nothing in prospect but a dark and dreadful eternity. Well might the preacher exclaim, "vanity of vanities." Well was the man, who made his barn and goods his portion, denominated "a fool." And wisely indeed does the psalmist pray, "Deliver my soul from the wicked, thy sword: from men which are thy hand, O Lord, from men of the world, which have their portion in this life," Psa. 17:13, 14. What a delightful contrast does the experience of the godly man present. He can rejoice, exclaiming in the language of the text, "The Lord is the portion of mine inheritance." Notice,

I. How God becomes the Portion of his Saints.

He does this by munificently, according to the riches of his grace, giving himself to his people. He says, "I will be your God." And this he does through the person and work of Jesus. He embodied the fulness of his love in Christ. And Christ came to reveal and to convey to every believer the favor and love of God. In Christ he exhibited his overflowing mercy, and made himself over as the portion and inheritance of all his saints. As God gives himself in Christ Jesus, so he is received and enjoyed as such, when faith is exercised in Christ. To as many as receive Christ, that is, believe on his name, he gives the privilege to become the sons of God, John 1:12. We become children and heirs of God by faith. In God, grace only is seen; and in man, faith only required for the possession of this divine portion, Eph. 2:8; Gal. 4:4-7. Consider,

II. The Characteristics of this Portion.

1. God is an infinite portion.

Every good is included in the enjoyment of God. Good equal to our need, and beyond all we can ask or conceive. Good beyond the need of all the intelligences he has created. Yea, infinitely beyond all this. All the attributes of God are infinite. Infinity is the region in which he dwells. And all that can be comprehended in the infinitude of God's riches and fulness, becomes the portion of the saint, Eph. 3:20

2. God is a satisfying portion.

He who made the soul can till it, and with such blessings and enjoyments which are suited to its capacities and desires. Now this is what the whole world could not do. The spirit of man must have spiritual good, and this is found in God alone. O yes, God can fill, and overflow the heart with ineffable joy and delight, 1 Peter 1:8.

3. God is a present portion.

He is not a good in prospect merely, but in possession. He dwells in the soul, and is hiss present bliss and consolation. "O God, thou art my God," &c., Psa. 63:1

4. God is a sure portion Other portions may be exhausted, God cannot fail. Other portions may be lost or transferred, but God is the abiding, unchanging treasure of his saints. Sure to them in all countries, at all times, and under all circumstances. Sure in youth and old age. In prosperity and adversity. In health and sickness. In life and death. In time and eternity.

5. God is an eternal portion.

A portion for the world to come. A portion of "life everlasting," infinitude of joy, and "pleasures for evermore." And it is not too much to hope, a portion which will be increasingly blissful and precious forever and ever. "An eternal weight of glory." "A crown that fadeth not away."

III. What is the right Application of this Portion.

1. We should enjoy it.

God desires that we should enjoy his light, his love, his peace; in one word, his divine nature.

2. That we should be grateful for it.

So we ought for every blessing. For existence, health, food, &c. Much more, for God as our portion. Our thanks should be sincere, fervent, constant, as they will finally be everlasting.

> "Eternity will be too short,
>   To utter all his praise."

3. We should be improved by it.

In purity of nature, in dignity of character, in expansion of soul, in usefulness of life, and in fitness for heaven.

4. We should recommend it.

How many are poor, and wretched, and dying. Far from God. Without God, and without hope in the world. O tell them of God's love. Of his mercy. Of the way to his favor. Of his readiness to bless and save

Application

1. Consider the present and eternal advantages of piety.

2. The misery of men who know not the love of God. However learned, or dignified, or rich.

3. Advise every sinner to seek the Lord, and live.

36. GOD COMPARED TO A FOUNTAIN

"The fountain of living waters." —Jer. 2:13.

WATER is one of the essential things of life. As such it is often made the emblem of spiritual blessings. Jehovah is appealing in the text to the Jews who had given themselves up to idolatry, and he calls upon the heavens to be astonished at the twofold evil of which they were guilty. They had forsaken him, "the fountain of living waters;" and they had hewn out "cisterns, broken cisterns that could hold no water." A fountain is that which has a spring within itself, and thus supplies from its own source what may be taken from it. A cistern only holds that conveyed into it, may be drained, and has no source of supply in itself. A cistern broken is still more useless, and only tantalizes those who may approach it to obtain water. God is the great source of all the good man needs, or can possibly enjoy, in the present life, or in that which is to come.

I. God is the Fountain of all Existence.

All creatures have their being in him. He is the God of life. He gives life. Sustains and preserves life. In him, angels and men, with every animated creature, live, and move, and have their being All the gods of the heathen never gave existence to one creature. All the idols of the world never perpetuated for a moment the life of one devotee. God is the fountain of universal existence and being.

II. God is the Fountain of all Enjoyment.

All creatures are happy as they answer the end of their being. God designed that every order should have enjoyment in proportion to their instincts, capacities, and powers.

Thus the mere animal creatures enjoy life and the provision needful for their wants. Thus rational beings and celestial spirits enjoy existence, and are happy as they move in the spheres appointed them, and exercise to the glory of the Creator the powers they possess. But this enjoyment is from God. It proceeds from his goodness and benignity, and his wisdom is manifested in the medium of imparting i unto them which he has devised and appointed. But all enjoyment is from God All that is real, and solid, and valuable All that is suitable and abiding.

III. God is the Fountain of Salvation.

1. The author of salvation came forth from him.

He gave his Son, sent him forth, anointed him, delivered him up, accepted his sacrifice. Attested to his divinity and glory. "God so loved," &c. "Herein is love, not that we loved God," &c.

2. The gospel of salvation emanates from him.

It is the "glorious gospel of the blessed God." It publishes God's love, and mercy, and grace, to a lost world. Message of God to man. The stream of gospel invitation takes its rise in the fountain of Jehovah's compassion.

3. The spirit of salvation flows from him.

"If any man thirst," &c. This Jesus spoke of the Holy Spirit. The Spirit proceeds from the Father. He pours it out from on high. He gives his Holy Spirit to them who ask it.

4. The blessings of salvation are the streams issuing from the fountain.

Of these there are several, all precious, sweet, and essential to the well-being of man.

1. There is the stream of remission of ins and justifying grace.

2. There is the stream of adopting love.

3. The stream of sanctifying influence.

4. The stream of holy peace.

5. The stream of heavenly joy.

6. The stream of communion with God.

And all these streams flow to us in one great channel, "the unsearchable riches of his grace."

IV. God is the Fountain of Glory.

All the dignity and bliss of heaven flows from him. He is the sun of heaven. His throne is surrounded by "a pure river of life, clear as crystal," &c., Rev. 22:1, &c.

In his presence is "fulness of joy," and at his right hand "pleasures for evermore." He gives immortality and eternal life to all he saved in glory.

Application

Learn,

1. How vain to seek bliss except in God. it cannot be,—myriads have tried to obtain it, irrespective of God, but all of them have failed.

2. How sufficient God is for the perfect happiness of all his creatures.

In him is infinite good. Fulness of all benignity and love. Fulness which cannot be diminished.

3. How accessible is this fountain through Jesus Christ.

A way opened to it. All invited. All made welcome. And faith in Christ the only prerequisite. O come and drink of these living waters. Abide by this four tain, forsake it not, and live forever

37. GOD THE HUSBAND OF THE CHURCH

"Thy Maker is thy husband." —Isa. 54:5.

How unsearchable is the greatness and glory of God. He is the high and lofty one, who inhabits eternity, who fills heaven and earth with his presence, and before whom unnumbered myriads of bright intelligences worship and adore. Yet notwithstanding his supreme majesty and glory, he condescends not only to behold the things done upon the earth, but to visit sinful man with his favor, and to exalt him to dignity, happiness, and heaven. In exhibiting his wonderful grace to man, he stoops and assumes the most close and endearing relationship to him. How surprising that the monarch of the skies should condescend to represent himself as the "husband" of his people. Yet he did so to wayward rebellious Israel, and he does so to all who constitute his church or people now. Each believer may consider the text as addressed to him, "Thy Maker is thy husband." Observe,

I. The Union specified.

"Thy husband." The union when rightly formed is,

1. Grounded in love.

God loved the church, and fixed his gracious affections upon it. The height, and depth, and length, and breadth, of this love, are immeasurable; they surpass all created understanding. It is a union,

2. Most intimate and endearing.

In this union there is a community of interests, and the connection is one of the most close that can be formed. The apostle refers to this in several passages. Such, (and in some respects still more intimate,) is the union between God and his church. By faith we are made recipients of the divine promises, and through them of the divine nature. Believers are said to dwell in God, and God dwells in them

3. It is a union most abiding.

It endures until the death of one of the parties. It is very different to a mere friendly compact, or commercial treaty. Such also is the union between God and his people Believers yield themselves to be his for over in a perpetual covenant never to be broken off again. God engages to be their present salvation, and everlasting portion and reward.

4. It is a union entirely mutual.

Personal interest is lost, and the mutual interests of both is the professed end of this union. The husband cares for the things of his wife, and the wife for the things of her husband. Thus God manifests his sympathy, love, and care, for his church. And the church professes in all things to show forth the glory of God. She engages to hallow his name, to revere his laws, to maintain his ordinances, and to show forth everywhere his praises, by devout and fervent thanksgiving to his name. Consider,

II. The Formation of this Union.

1. It originated in God's amazing love.

God fixed his compassionate regards on fallen, sinful man. He purposed his restoration to himself. He determined to raise him to dignity and bliss, and this through the conjugal union with himself.

2. It was rendered possible by the work of Jesus Christ.

God as the fountain of light, and purity, and love, could not be closely and complacently united to ignorance, impiety, and sin. He therefore sent forth his Son in our nature, to magnify his law, to atone for sin by his death, and as mediator, to be the reconciler and the medium of union between God and man. "God was in Christ reconciling the world unto himself," &c., 2 Cor. 5:19.

3. To this union God invites sinners in his blessed gospel.

He compares the provision of the gospel to a nuptial feast. He represents his spiritual kingdom as being like unto "A certain king who made a marriage for his son," &c., Matt. 22:1-13. The great end of the gospel is to bring men to a state of gracious and saving union with God.

4. This union is consummated on the *day* when the believer yields himself to God.

Faith in God's word brings our souls into gracious and acceptable contact with Deity. To those who receive his gracious overtures of mercy, he gives the privilege of adoption, of union to himself, and of hope as to the bestowment of eternal life.

III. The Advantages of this Union to Believers

1. It is their exaltation How mean and low and wretched in their natural state. How dignified and exalted when the bride of Jehovah. This is rank and elevation above that of angels. Dignity which human language cannot express.

2. It is their unspeakable riches.

Poor and insolvent, by this union they become enriched with the unsearchable riches of his grace. The blessed God, in all his attributes and glories, is their portion, and present and eternal reward. "All are yours," &c. "Heirs of God."

3. It is their present blessedness.

Union with God is associated with comfort, peace, and joy in the Holy Spirit. The love of God is shed abroad in their hearts. They rejoice too with joy unspeakable and full of glory. God's favor is their constant enjoyment, and in the radiant beams of his smiling countenance, they have overflowing bliss.

4. It will be their everlasting salvation.

Salvation intrinsically consists in the soul's union with God. And this union, which in heaven will be immediate, fill, and unceasing, will be the very essence of that glory and happiness which the redeemed will enjoy forever and ever. This will annihilate all sources of evil, and be the blissful river of endless life.

Application

1. From this union diversified duties and obligations arise. From this union God claims supreme love, reverence, subjection, and obedience. He requires unfailing fidelity, confidence, and dependence. He requires zeal for his glory. Jealousy of his honor. Activity in his service, and entire devotedness to his cause.

2. Urge upon sinners immediate self-dedication to God. Every possible reason and motive should induce them so to do. "Seek first the kingdom of God," &c. This is the basis of all good, both for body and soul, earth and heaven, time and eternity.

38. NO ROCK LIKE THE GOD OF ISRAEL

"For their rock is not as our rock; even our enemies themselves being judges." —Deut. 32:31.

GOD is a spirit, and therefore he cannot possibly come under the observation of our senses. We cannot see him. There is considerable difficulty too in enabling us to understand rightly a spiritual being. To effect this the sacred writers have generally presented him to our view in the language of figure. Thus we often read of him as though he possessed bodily senses and parts, as eyes and mouth, and feet and hands. Sometimes too the inanimate creation is made use of to give us clear and striking views of his character and perfections. He is the sun of the universe. He is the breath or wind of the world. He is the fountain of living waters. He is the rock or foundation of all things. Now this last was a very favorite metaphor with the sacred writers. Hence we read of the rock of Israel. The rock of our refuge. The rock of salvation. Now in considering the blessed Jehovah under this figurative distinction, we will endeavor,

I. To illustrate the Metaphor.

In this text the metaphor refers to what God is in himself and what he is to his people.

1. When we speak of God as a rock in reference to himself, the ideas are such as these.

1. Strength. The rock is the emblem of strength. The mighty tree appears strong, but the wind roots it up,—the storm levels it in its fury. Not so the rock, the tempest passes over it in vain. The foaming waters of the ocean dash upon it in vain. God is the perfection of strength. All power belongs unto God. His word is omnipotent He speaks and it is done: he wills and it stands fast.

2. Stability. The rock is the emblem of stability. The traveler in visiting ancient cities, is directed to the relics of former grandeur. The work of science and art cannot stand against the effacing influence of age. The ancient cities, and temples, and palaces, and monuments, have in many cases passed away. Not so the rock,— the rock of Horeb, the scene of such ancient miracles and grandeur, remains unto this day. Now God is distinguished for his stability. He is of one mind. He changes not. He is the same yesterday, today, and forever.

3. Perpetuity. The rock is a striking emblem of perpetuity, a faint representation of eternity. Other things move and change. The heavenly bodies, the waters of the sea, &c. But the rock reminds us of that great being who is from everlasting to everlasting—God. Now these ideas serve to show us the propriety of the metaphor as it respects what God is in himself. Let us consider the metaphor in reference,

2. To what God is to his believing children.

111

1. As such he is the rock of their defense. Jerusalem was thus considered impregnable. Of all sources of security the rock seems to yield the surest. Now the Lord is the sure defense of them that trust in him. "Trust in the Lord Jehovah," &c. He is the munition of rocks to all his saints. "If God be for us," &c. Who can curse if God blesses?

2. He is the rock of their foundation. Every man is building a structure for the future. Christ beautifully illustrated this in the two builders, &c. Now God is the basis of all the hopes, &c., of the Christian. They rely on him. Trust in him He is their sure foundation, elect, precious, and eternal.

3. He is their rock of shelter and shade. When storms arise, they flee unto him. He is their immutable security. Hiding-place from the storm. He is the cooling, refreshing shade of his people, from the scorching heat, &c. The Christian is a pilgrim, and in going through the desert, he meets with terrible storms and sultry heat. God is both his shelter and his shade, Isa. 25:4, 32:2.

4. He is the rock of their supplies. You remember that the people of Israel were ready to perish. See Numb. 22:11; Deut. 32:13. Now the writers here refer to the wild honey which was collected from the fissures of the rocks, the oil of olives too which was collected from the same place. Now God is the fountain of all our supplies. He yields all we need for body, soul, time, and eternity. All our springs are in him. "Every good gift and perfect," &c. Such then is the character of our rock. Observe,

II. The triumphant Comparison which is instituted.

"Their rock," &c. Now whatever we depend upon and trust in is our rock. The pagan trusts in his idols. The infidel in his skepticism. The miser in his riches. The sensualist in his pleasures. The Pharisee in his works. Now to all of these we say, your rock is not as our rock. You have not the security, the sensible enjoyments, the supplies,—in one word, the happiness which the people of God possess. Now we will not allow our opinions to decide, but, even ye yourselves being judges,

1. We appeal to your experience.

This testifies that your rock, &c. What changes do you profess to have experienced? What evils removed? What principles implanted?

2. We appeal to your enjoyments.

What peace,—what comfort,—what hope,—what real bliss!

3. We appeal to your practice.

From what follies and sins have you been delivered. Are your principles more pure? Spirit, conversation, temper, &c.

4. We appeal to our advantages in sickness and death.

What security,—what ecstasies,—what clear enrapturing prospects! You know that your rock is not, &c.

Application

1. Invite the shiner to choose the Lord for the rock of his salvation. Flee to him by repentance. Build on him by faith in Christ Jesus.

2. Let the Christian be *satisfied* with his choice. The everlasting God is his refuge.

39. GOD THE FATHER OF LIGHTS

"Do not err, my beloved brethren. Every good gift and every perfect gift is from above, and cometh down from the Father of lights, with whom is no variableness, neither shadow of turning." —James 1:16-17

THE text was evidently designed to counteract and overthrow a very dangerous sentiment which has prevailed in every age of the world. The error was this,—that all good and evil emanated from God;—that God was the fountain of both good and evil. This seems to have entered into the spirit of Adam. The same evil seems to have prevailed in the days of the apostles. Doubtless this opinion was that which the apostle referred to in ver. 13,—"Let no man say when he is tempted, I am tempted of God, for God cannot be tempted of evil, neither can he tempt any man." Let us observe,

I. Presents us with a sublime Representation of Deity.

1. He is the father of lights.

By father is meant source, &c. In this sense he is the father of the universe—men, angels, &c. But the text refers to lights. Light is the emblem of goodness, and God is the father of all good

> 1) *There is in nature the creature light.* That which shines and makes manifest, this was the direct offspring of Deity. There was a period when the eye of Deity rested on nothing but one chaotic mass. There was the almighty pleased to say, "Let there be light: and there was light."

> 2) *There are the orbs of light.* The sun, moon, planets, and fixed stars. God is said to have created all these. The psalmist hath said in the language of inspiration, "He made the sun to rule by day, the moon and stars to rule by night." Ps. 136:8.

> 3) *There are minds of light.* Mental light. God gave Adam an extensive capacity of knowledge, which he showed in giving proper names to all the beasts, birds, &c. When we look abroad on human nature, we see some minds of mighty intellect. A Newton, Locke, and Milton, &c., but there never was one ray of light, but what was derived from God. He is the father of lights.

> 4) *There are angels of light.* And he is the father of these Angels are styled morning stars. The angel who rolled away the stone from the sepulcher is thus described: "His countenance was like lightning, and his raiment white as snow. They dwell in the presence of God, &c. God is the father of lights.

5) *There is the Savior of light.* —And he is the father of him. In him dwells all the fulness of the Godhead. God filled him with his glory, so that he was the express image of the effulgence of the Deity. God is the father of the Messiah—he is the father of lights. But in the sublime representation of Deity in the text we are referred,

2. To the unchangeableness of his nature.

With whom is no variableness, &c. He does not—he cannot—alter or change. He is unchangeable. The heavenly bodies perform their revolutions. Day is exchanged for night, light for darkness, &c. But God alters not. God the fountain of all light and purity is ever the same. Even the angels fell from their first estate, and the sons of light became messengers of darkness,—but God, the great father of light, is without the shadow of turning. His nature is absolutely so. His perfections and attributes are so. His purposes and mind are so, &c. It is the prerogative of Deity to say, "I am the Lord, beside me there is none else." God is to his creatures the father of lights.

II. God is exhibited as the Source of all possible Good.

All that is really good proceeds from God. The text gives us a distinction. Every good and every perfect gift. Let us look at these two kinds of gifts.

1. Good gifts. Among the blessings to which we refer, are, existence, health, reason, all temporal blessings. Food, raiment, and all our providential mercies. God is the father of every good gift. This is a thing which we should never lose sight of. We have not a single good which is not the blessing of a good God.

2. Perfect gifts are those which emanate directly from Deity; they are sent to prepare us for eternity. The chief of these gifts are,

1) The gift of the only-begotten Son of God. Jesus is the perfect Savior. In him dwells all the fulness of the Father. God's great gift. God's holy, perfect Son, &c. His delight. This perfect gift proceeded from the father of lights.

2) The gift of the Spirit. The comforter and sanctifier of the church of God. He came down from above, &c.

3) Gift of the glorious gospel. God's news from heaven. The message of life, &c. Perfect good.

4) The gift of a full pardon. Thy sins are forgiven. God gives remission of sin. He justifies, &c.

5) Gift of a new nature. Renewed into the image of God. A new heart. Partakers of God's nature.

6) The gift of sufficient grace. The enjoyment of God's constant favor. Perfect grace &c. Every good and perfect gift proceeds from the father of lights. We have now noticed good and perfect gifts. Observe,

III. The Caution which the Text contains.

Do not err, &c.

1. Do not attribute any moral evil or darkness to God It makes the Lord of glory worse than Beelzebub, &c. It attributes all wicked and impious thoughts to Deity. It makes the blessed Lord, who is the father of lights the fountain of darkness. No darkness or evil can proceed from him.

2. Do not attribute any good to any other being but Deity.

Whatever blessing you have received, it has all come from God, &c. All our influences proceed from God. This is an important truth. We never had one happy thought, but what proceeded from the father of lights—the Deity.

3. Do not err in restricting the benevolence of Deity.

It is a blessed truth that the bounties of nature are free to all. God is not partial, nor a respecter of persons. There is no man that cannot be perfectly happy if he choose God for his portion.

4. Do not err in respect to your own nature.

Every good and every perfect gift cometh from God, and not from yourselves Within much evil remains, and there are many things which you have not yet obtained: you are not to be satisfied with those blessings which you already possess, but strive to possess still more.

5. We ought to be thankful to God for the blessings we enjoy.

Our blessings are more numerous than the stars of the firmament, or the sand on the sea shore. We ought to know them. Be thankful for them. What are we to return to God? We are to return a grateful heart, &c. And even then, as the poet hath said,—

> "Eternity's too short,
> To utter all his praise."

To him be glory and honor forever and ever. Amen.

40. CHRIST AN ADVOCATE

"An advocate with the Father." —1 John 2:1

THE epistles of John are eminently of a practical and experimental character. They are designed to illustrate and enforce the true spirit and practice of godliness. Especially we have presented to us the supreme importance of love. Love to God and love to the saints, and love to all men He does not, however lose sight of the frailties of human nature, and the imperfections of the best of saints. See ver. 8, If we say," &c. And he directs how to obtain its pardon and removal from the soul. "If we confess," &c., ver. 9. He then enforces holy vigilance and avoidance of evil, ch. 2:1,—"My little children." And then that the mind may not be involved in despair by contracted guilt, he presents the delightful truth of the text "And if any man sin," &c. Observe.

I. The Case supposed.

"If any man sin," &c. Sin is the transgression of the law. The law of God relates both to evils, which must be avoided, and to duties which must be performed. Now we may sin by omission of duty, or by violation of positive commands. The text, however, is addressed to the people of God, and it supposes that they may sin, yea, that if we say that we have no sin, he truth is not in us. Now this,

> 1. Is a universal fact.

"In many things we all offend." There is not a just man that does not sin. We are taught continually to pray for mercy. And to go to the throne of grace for mercy, &c. There are sins of life, and how often we do what we ought not, &c. Sins of word, and how often the tongue offends. Sins of thought, secret sins of the heart, and how often these lead us from God, &c.

> 2. This is a most humbling fact.

We ought to repeat it with sorrow. With shame. With contrition. Our sins ought to abase and fill us with real sorrow. It is not a trifle to disobey God. To grieve our heavenly Father. To do despite to the Spirit of grace.

> 3. This is a fact which should not sink us in despair.

Our sins might justly bring down God's avenging wrath. "It is of the Lord's mercy," &c. Yet there is hope for the frail and erring followers of Jesus. There is a remedy for them. A door of hope. "A fountain opened for sin," &c. Then while they cannot be indifferent, and careless, and presumptuous, yet they need not despair. For observe, IT. *The Remedy provided.*

"We have an advocate," &c. An advocate is a patron or friend, who exerts his influence for another. In a court of justice, the advocate vindicates and pleads for his client. Now sin would expose the believer to eternal death. There is infinite evil in sin—in his sin. He has no liberty or charter to do evil. Therefore God's justice might righteously condemn him. But Christ is his advocate. He stands forth to avert the wrath he deserves, and, in doing this,

1. He does not plead our innocence.

2. He does not deny the charges brought forth.

3. He does not vindicate our conduct. But he advocates the *bestowment of mercy,* and the communication of *renewing grace.* And he does this on the ground of out union to him. Faith unites the Christian to Jesus. He is in Christ. One with Christ. Christ pleads therefore his cause on the ground of his own perfect obedience to the law of God. And the sacrifice he has offered for sin. A sacrifice possessing infinite and eternal merit and efficacy.

II. Observe then the qualifications which at our advocate Christ possesses.

1. He possesses the most exalted purity.

He stands before God, reflecting every ray of divine holiness. God beholds him with ineffable delight and approbation. This is expressed in the text, "The righteous." Not only so, but he exhibited his supreme love to his Father's honor in magnifying the law, &c. Finishing all the work the Father gave him to do.

2. He possesses infinite knowledge.

He knows all things, wherein the honor of his saints is concerned. He sees their circumstances, perils, and enemies. He knows what is best for them. We know not what to pray for, &c. Jesus cannot err, nor omit any thing through ignorance, which is for our welfare. He knows all the mind of God, and all the need of the Christian.

3. He possesses unbounded tenderness and love.

He loveth his people with inconceivable affection. He laid down his life for them. He is the gentle and good Shepherd, who carries his lambs, &c. He breaks not the bruised reed, &c. What compassion he displayed to the woman who was a sinner, to backsliding Peter, &c. How secure then our interests in his advocacy. He will not, he cannot forget, &c. "Can a woman," &c.

4. His advocacy is most prevalent and effectual.

Him the Father ever hears. He presents that to God more effectual than words. He appears as the lamb slain.

119

"Five bleeding wounds he bears,
Received on Calvary;
They pour effectual prayers,
They strongly plead for me.
Forgive, forgive, they ever cry,
Nor let that ransomed sinner die."

5. His advocacy is limited to believers.

For these only he intercedes: unbelief refuses Christ, and therefore necessarily excludes from his intercession. Faith puts the sinners' cause into his hands. And living by faith on him, and in him, it keeps it there.

Application

1. Let the Christian rejoice and trust in the advocacy of Christ. Let him rejoice in its gratuitousness, freeness, &c.

2. We must constantly avail ourselves of it. Without it our best deeds will be rejected. And our sins separate us from God. In all things let Christ be our living advocate with the Father.

3. We invite the sinner to place his cause in Christ's hands. Such as come unto him by faith he will in no wise cast out.

41. CHRIST THE REFINER

"And he shall sit as a refiner." —Mal. 3:3.

CHRIST is obviously intended in this prophecy, and it quite accords with the apostle's description of the end of Christ's coming: "Who gave himself that he might redeem us from all iniquity, and purify unto himself a peculiar people, zealous of good works," Tit. 2:14. Christ's refining is the purifying of his people, the removal of all dross and alloy, and imparting unto hem those holy qualities which will render them fit for the most honorable purposes on earth, and finally meet for the inheritance of the saints in light. The gold of Christ's church is not pure, until he hath sat, and brought it through the refining process.

I. How then does he do this, in what Way does he act as the Refiner of his People?

1. His truth is refining.

The words of his mouth are pure words, and they enlighten the eyes, and exert a cleansing power over the heart and life. Hence he prayed to his Father, and said, "Sanctify them through thy truth, thy word is truth."

2. His Spirit is refining.

Hence that blessed agent is called the Holy Spirit, not only because he is essentially holy, but also because all holiness is the result of his influences. The Spirit refines by leading the mind into all truth, and by applying the blood of Jesus to the conscience, which cleanses from all sin. Hence in reference both to the truth and the Spirit conjointly, the apostle says, "Ye have purified your souls in obeying the truth through the Spirit," 1 Pet. 1:22.

3. Christ refines by affliction.

He brings his people into the furnace, and by causing them to pass through the fires, he makes them to lose the dross and tin of sin. He himself is said to have been made perfect through sufferings, and though no chastening for the present is joyous, but grievous, yet afterwards it yields the peaceable fruits of righteousness to them who are exercised thereby. It is by afflictions, that many of the graces are matured, and that the soul is conformed to the suffering Redeemer. Hence it is written, "Tribulation worketh patience, and patience experience, and experience hope; and hope maketh not ashamed." And again, "If children, then heirs; heirs of God, and joint heirs with Christ; if so be that we suffer with him, that we may be also glorified together."

II. The Qualifications of Christ as a Refiner.

As the refiner, Christ possesses every qualification necessary for the work.

1. His skill is infinite.

He knows the nature of his materials. What they should lose, in what they are deficient, and what is requisite for their complete salvation.

2. Then his experience is extensive.

He has suffered, and knows the nature of every variety of affliction to which we are exposed. Poverty, reproach, tribulation, anguish, and death itself, were all endured by himself.

3. Then his tenderness is unbounded.

He not only knows the true nature of our sorrows, but he is "touched with the feeling of our infirmities." The attack of Saul upon the primitive Christians was felt by Jesus, when he said, "Saul, Saul, why persecutest thou me?" His tenderness being such, he will not allow our sufferings to be injurious, nor our temptations to be stronger than we are able to bear, nor will he ever leave us to the scorching influences of the fires, but when we are tried, bring us forth as gold. It is said, "he shall *sit* as a refiner;" that is, he shall watch the whole process; he shall heat or cool the furnace as circumstances require, and when he beholds the design accomplished, and his own image clearly reflected, he will then bestow the crown of glory that fades not away.

42. CHRIST THE LIGHT OF THE WORLD

"The light of men." —John 1:4.

ONE of the most wonderful and beautiful creatures in the world is light. It is one of the most striking emblems of the Deity. "God is light," &c. He is described as the father of lights. From him all light emanates. He is the light both of heaven and earth. The great moral sun of the universe, whose radiant beams fill heaven with glory, and earth with his benignity and love. Jesus, in whom dwelt all the fulness of the Godhead bodily, is represented in the text as "the light of men," and in another place, he spoke of himself as "the light of the world." It is the province of light to illumine and thus make manifest, and it is doubtless in this sense that Jesus is spoken of as "the light of men." Consider,

I. The Subjects which Jesus has made manifest.

Some things were accessible to human investigation, irrespective of Christ's advent and mission. Such were the works of nature, the wonderful phenomena of the material world. These were studied by men who had no written revelation, and therefore were not directly enlightened by the Savior. So it is still; many laborious and successful philosophers have been unfavorably disposed towards the Christian religion, and it is obvious that a man may be a student of the works of nature, and yet ignorant of the doctrines of the gospel. Neither did Jesus shed any light on literature, or the arts; on jurisprudence, or political economy. He pronounced no opinion as to forms of governments, but declared that his kingdom or administration was "not of this world."

1. Jesus made manifest the true character of God.

"No man hath seen God at any time the only-begotten Son, which is in the bosom of the Father, he hath declared him," John 1:18. Moses and the prophets had given men revelations of the divine character. But theirs was exceedingly limited, only partial manifestation of God. Jesus shed his illustrious beams over all the perfections of the divine nature. He placed Deity before men in all his graciousness, and greatness, and glory. He placed the Father before men, in the boundlessness of his mercy, and in the unspeakable depths of his goodness and compassion. He also gave brighter views of his purity, justice, and truth, than had ever been revealed before. He made known his heavenly Father, as reconciled to the world, and as the friend of the guilty and perishing sinner. See John 3:14-18.

2. Jesus made manifest the true condition of the sinner.

He shed light over the dreary valley of dry bones, and opened to observation the miserable state of a world without God. He revealed the depravity of human nature, the deceitfulness of the human heart. The extreme evil of sin. The helplessness of man. And the wrath to which his sins had justly exposed him. He gave a full and searching view of man's lost estate and miserable condition.

3. He made manifest the way of man's recovery and salvation.

He revealed himself as the way to heaven. He declared that he came expressly to seek and to save that which was lost. That he came to give his life for the world. That his sufferings, and death, and resurrection, were necessary to the remission of sins and acceptance with God. He repeatedly set himself forth as the one object of saving faith, and the only mediator or advocate with the Father.

4. He made manifest the nature and necessity of holiness.

He laid the basis of holiness in the regeneration of the soul. "Ye must be born again." "Except a man be born of water and the Spirit," &c. He demanded for God supreme love and obedience, and universal righteousness, goodness, and mercy, towards mankind. And he exhibited the gracious truths of his word, and the influences of the Spirit, as the divine means of renewing, sanctifying, and keeping the heart. He insisted on holiness as essential to the enjoyment of the glory and face of God in heaven.

5. He made manifest the high calling and glorious privileges of his disciples.

He spoke of them as the sons of God. The objects of the Father's peculiar love. As his own friends. And as co-sharers in all the blessings and immunities of his kingdom. He made over to them the rich bequests of unspeakable peace. He gave them as their guide and comforter, the Holy Spirit. And he left all the promises of his love to be the solace of their souls, and the rejoicings of their hearts.

6. He made manifest their future blessedness and glory.

He brought life and immortality to light. He described heaven as his Father's house, and promised to receive them into those mansions of light and felicity, that they might be with him forever and ever. He engaged the bestowment to his disciples of a crown and kingdom that should never pass away. "Fear not, little flock," &c. Then shall the king say, "Come ye blessed," &c. Such are the subjects which Jesus made manifest as "the light of men." Observe,

II. How he communicates himself as the Light of Men.

He does so,

1. By the radiant beams of his word.

His glory gilds the hallowed pages of revelation. He is the light of the glorious gospel of the blessed God. His divine mind and will are revealed in and by the oracles of truth. The scriptures are full of the knowledge of Jesus, and they testify of him,

2. By the brightness of his divine example.

He arose upon our world as the sun of righteousness, and in his spirit and conversation, and in his holy and benevolent life, he gave mankind an exhibition of heavenly goodness and purity, and left an illuminated path to glory and eternal life. "He hath left us an example," &c. Practical godliness consists in hearing his voice and following him.

3. By the illuminating rays of his Spirit.

The Holy Spirit takes of the things of Jesus, and applies them to the mind. He is the spirit of light, and sheds abroad the beams of day and joy in the soul. Thus, Jesus is the light of men. He is too the light of the world by his gospel. The light of the church by his spiritual residence in it. The light of the believer's soul, as the hope of glory. The light of heaven by the resplendent beams of his divine countenance.

Application

1. Have we all partaken of that spiritual and gracious light which he diffuses? Are we the children of the light and the day? If so we shall reflect the light we have received, and diffuse it abroad to others.

2. Invite the benighted sinner to receive Christ and to walk in him.

43. CHRIST THE HEAD OF THE CHURCH

"The head of the body, the church." —Col. 1:18.

THE church of the Redeemer is beautifully likened to the human body. Like the human body, it is composed of various parts and members. Some of these resemble the hands, others the feet, all of which united, make one compact body. Of this body, Jesus is the head.

I. He is the Head exclusively.

Angels may minister to it, and highly gifted and holy men may have official stations, but there is but one head, that is Christ. The pope therefore may be the head of the church of Rome, but not of the church of Jesus. Kings, and ecclesiastical powers, may form the headship of religious communities, but Jesus only is the head of his body, the church. "One is your master, even Christ," and all ye are brethren.

II. As the Head. Christ is the Source of Vitality

From him, existence and energy are diffused through the whole system. There may be life without some of the inferior members, but separation from the head is immediate death Thus we have life from and by Christ. Out of him we are dead in him we are new-born creatures, and alive from the dead.

III. As the Head, Christ is the Source of Knowledge and Wisdom.

The head thinks, and devises, and plans for the body. The head is the seat of understanding and judgment. Thus, Jesus is made unto his people *wisdom,* as well as sanctification and redemption. In Christ dwells all the fulness of wisdom and knowledge, and from this boundless source all the need of his people is supplied.

IV. As the Head, Christ is the Source of all Authority and Power.

The head directs and governs the body. All the members are subordinate to the head. As the head is the residence of the mind, and as the material man is influenced by the spiritual, so with Jesus only, is the right to exert power, and to rule over every believer, being head over all things to his church.

V. In reflecting on the Headship of the Church, we must be struck with its Dignity.

How glorious—how illustrious—how divine is the church's head.

VI. We are reminded also of its All-sufficiency.

There can be no lack with such a head—no perplexity nor imbecility: the head of the church is emphatically *full* of grace and truth.

VII. Neither ought we to forget the efficient Sympathy of this Head.

Jesus, as the head of the body, feels all that his members suffer. He is touched with a feeling of all their infirmities, and he knows well how to succor and to support in temptations and trials,

"For he hath felt the same."

In all their afflictions he is afflicted, and whatever is done to them he considers it as done to himself: the most insignificant member cannot suffer without the sympathizing consciousness of the head.

Application

The duties which devolve upon the members of the body to the head, obviously include,

1. *Sacred reverence:* to him belongs all honor and glory: we are to revere and honor him even as we revere and honor the Father: his glory we are to seek in all things, and whatever we do, we are to do it in his name 2. As the head, he also demands our *subjection* and *obedience:* we are his disciples only if we follow and obey him; if his grace influences our hearts, and if we rejoice to keep his commandments.

3. There must likewise be *conformity* and *resemblance* between the members and their head: as members of Jesus, we are partakers of his divine nature; "beholding as in a glass the glory of the Lord, we are changed into the same image from glory unto glory, even by the Spirit of the Lord." As we once possessed the image of the earthy, by grace we are renewed, and bear the image of the heavenly. How endearing, interesting, precious, and everlastingly momentous, is the union between Christ and his church!

4. How presumptuous for any to *arrogate power* and *authority* over the church of Jesus. "One is your master, even Christ," &c.

44. CHRIST THE BRIDEGROOM OF HIS CHURCH

"He that hath the bride is the bridegroom." —John 3:29.

THE Baptist was bearing testimony to Christ when he made use of the language of the text. And similar representations are given of the Redeemer in various parts of the holy scriptures. The parable of the Virgins evidently refers to the coming of Christ as the bridegroom. The apostle in speaking to the church at Corinth, remarks, "I have espoused you to one husband, that I may present you as a chaste virgin to Christ," 2 Cor. 11:2. And John, in the visions of the Apocalypse, was invited by one of the seven angels to behold the bride, the Lamb's wife, Rev. 21:9. One of the most rich and striking parables of Jesus contains the same implied truth, where the gospel provision is represented as a feast, which a certain king made it the marriage of his son, Matt. 22:1, &c. We just premise, that the bride of Jesus is his church, composed of all renewed spiritual persons. That in conversion they are espoused to Christ, and that the marriage ceremony will be consummated with his perfected and glorious bride, when he shall come the second time, without a sin-offering, to the salvation of his people Let us notice, then,

I. How Jesus became the Bridegroom of his Church.

Now he did so, both as the gift of the Father and as the voluntary act and choice of his infinitely blessed and benevolent mind. It was his own unbounded mercy and pity to man, which induced him to present himself as the bridegroom of his church. He so loved the church as to give himself up for its redemption, and to purchase it by the shedding of his precious blood. In accomplishing this great act of grace it behooved him,

1. To assume the nature of the intended bride.

Thus he became wedded to our humanity. He became of one flesh and blood with us, in being made of a woman, and in becoming in reality a child of man, and, according to the promise, of the seed of Abraham. "And the word was made flesh," &c.

2. To remove all difficulties to the union.

These were of a threefold kind. There was guilt, pollution, and the curse. Each and all of these prevented the union of the holy and blessed Son of God with mankind. These he effectually took out of the way. He became our substituted sacrifice. He bare our sins. Became a curse for us. And opened a fountain for sin and uncleanness. He opened a clear and honorable channel for the remission of sin, the sanctification of the sinner, and thus his elevation to a dignity, worthy of being united to the Son of God. O how great the cost of the union to Jesus! He had to redeem his bride from misery, pollution, and death. And he did this by the voluntary sacrifice of himself. "And thus it was written, and thus it behooved Christ to suffer," &c. Well may the ransomed church in rapturous songs exclaim, Unto him that loved us and washed us from our sins," &c., Rev. 1:5. Notice,

II. What sort of Bridegroom Jesus is.

He is one,

1. Of peerless dignity.

The Son of the most high God. The Lord of life and glory. The prince of the kings of the earth. The eternal Word, of light and being, John 1:1-14. The prince of the kings of the earth. The joy of angels, and the Lord of all. God's equal fellow and eternal delight. The governor of the universe, and proprietor of all things. Words utterly fail to describe his dignity or to reveal his glory.

2. Of matchless beauty.

All that is fair, and bright, and beautiful, as employed to show forth his loveliness. "Fairer than the children of men." "The desire of all nations." "Who is the brightness of the Father's glory, and the express image of his person." He is likened to the "rose of Sharon," and to the "bright and morning star."

3. Of boundless riches.

He is heir of all things. "The Father loveth the Son, and hath given all things into his hands." The treasures of nature, of grace, and glory, are all his. His riches are spread through immensity; they are infinite, exhaustless, and eternal

4. Of perfect goodness.

Every excellency is concentrated in him. His love passes understanding. His tenderness is inexpressible. His compassion does not fail, and his mercy and loving-kindness endure forever and ever.

5. Of inviolable faithfulness.

Truth is the girdle of his reins. He is faithful and true. All his excellencies are, like his divine nature, immutable; "the same yesterday," &c. His mind alters not. His heart knows no change.

> "His love is as great as his power,
> And neither knows measure nor end"

Such is the character of Christ as the bridegroom of his church. We observe, that he also does for his people what no other bridegroom can do. He removes all her diseases, purifies her from all her impurities, transforms her into all the beauties of his own holy image, preserves from all enemies and perils, and saves unto all the glories of a blissful immortality and eternal life.

Application

1. Let the church see its high and distinguished exaltation, and walk worthily before him. Let his love, and truth, and fidelity, be reciprocated. How believers should love, serve, and honor him!

2. Let sinners listen to the gracious invitations of the Savior, and accept of his love. He invites them to be married to him. To partake of his grace, of his divine nature, of his immeasurable riches, and of his eternal glory. To this end, he has sent his word and his ministers to beseech and entreat them to be reconciled unto him.

3. None but those who have Christ as their bridegroom shall enter his kingdom or enjoy his salvation.

4. Let backsliders return to Christ, their "first husband," for then it was better with them than now.

45. CHRIST A PHYSICIAN

"They that be whole need not a physician, but they that are sick." —Matt. 9:12.

IN the application of this proverb to himself, Jesus evidently professed to be a physician, and his whole ministerial career will establish that profession. Christ proved himself to be a physician of the body. He cured all sorts of diseases;—dropsies, fevers, palsies, blindness, deafness, leprosies, bloody issues, and dumbness, all fled before his healing power. It mattered not how deep, how complicated, how universal, or of how long standing, he never failed in restoring to perfect health and soundness. Many cases which were humanly speaking hopeless, he restored by he word of his power. His power was so extensive, that even death was forced to yield his prey at his command. One he brought to life from the bed on which she had just expired—a second as they were bearing him to the place of burial—and a third, after he had been entombed, heard his voice, and lived, and came forth. Jesus does not now employ his miraculous influence in healing the diseases of the body, but still his ability is the same. And though we are not called to expect his supernatural interposition in curing our bodily diseases, yet all human means will fail without his blessing.

We have seen that Jesus was a celebrated physician of the body, but he was equally successful in healing the maladies of the *mind.* In the wonder-working days of his flesh, he healed all sorts and degrees of mental and moral diseases. He cured the lunatic boy—he cured the demoniac, who dwelt among the tombs, and brought him to sit at his feet clothed, and in his right mind. But he also proved himself the physician of the *soul.*

I. The Soul of Man is the Subject of Disease.

Every faculty is impaired; every power disordered; the plague spot is upon it; the leprosy defiles it; the fever consumes it; it is affected with the torpid paralysis. The eyes of the mind are blinded, the ears stopped, and the tongue is speechless. The afflictions of the soul are hereditary,—complicated,—deep seated,—universally prevalent,—painful,—and absolutely fatal. They never exhaust their strength, or cure themselves,—neither are they curable by any human agency whatever. Now, of these otherwise incurable maladies,

II. Jesus is the efficient Physician.

1. His knowledge is infinite.

He knows the cause, the progress, and the precise state of the disease of the human heart.

2. His power is almighty.

There is nothing too hard for him to effect—he can eradicate the most virulent and confirmed disorders of the soul.

3. His tenderness is inexpressible.

He deeply commiserates the misery of sinsick souls,—his bowels yearn over them,—his heart is full of tenderness towards them,—he does not want an application from them, but he seeks to heal, and says, "Wilt thou be made whole?"

4. His terms are astonishing.

He heals without money, and without price,—all he desires is the use of his medicines, and humble attention to the prescriptions he gives.

5. His success is infallible.

He never fails to effect a cure,—none ever sought his aid in vain. Though death had already commenced its ruinous work upon the dying malefactor, yet one word of his healed the malady of his soul, and saved him from the jaws of eternal death, and made him meet for the healthy abodes of the heavenly paradise.

6. As a physician, Christ's invitations are universal.

He does not confine his practice to any grade or class of society: the world is his hospital; and all mankind may become his patients: the poor are alike welcome with the rich: he heals all who come unto him. Notice,

III. The Method of Healing which he adopts.

In curing the diseases of the soul,

1. He employs the agency of his word.

It is said he sent his word, and healed them: the word contains a revelation both of the disease and mode of cure: the word is emphatically the word of salvation—the word of life. He also employs,

2. The catholicon of his blood.

The blood of Jesus is the true balm of Gilead—that in which alone we have redemption, even the forgiveness of sin. It is this which speaks peace to the guilty mind, and which cleanses from all unrighteousness.

3. By the power of his Spirit.

The Spirit applies the precious blood of Christ to the heart, and thus the malady of sin is removed, and the soul is made whole.

Application

1. The cure which Christ imparts to the sinsick soul is radical, universal, and abiding. He heals every wound, and restores every faculty: he gives beauty for deformity; strength for weakness; and blooming health for sickness and decay.

2. How important that we ascertain our true state and condition. Hath he healed us? have we been convicted of sin—have we loathed it—and have we been delivered from it? Have we the signs of spiritual health upon us? do we live in the exercise of godliness? is the pain and smart, arising from consciousness of sin, removed? have we the indwelling of the Spirit testifying that we are the sons of God?

3. Let spiritual health be carefully cultivated. Avoid all that is pernicious to the soul. Cherish the influences of the Spirit, and thus grow in grace, and in the knowledge of the Lord Jesus Christ.

4. The spiritually sick, who despise this physician, must inevitably perish. There is no other balm in Gilead, nor any other physician there.

46. CHRIST THE CAPTAIN OF SALVATION

"And commander to the people." —Isa. 55:4.

SIN commenced by the revolt of God's creatures from their allegiance and obedience to him. Angels thus fell, and kept not their first estate. Thus too did man unite himself to the fallen spirits of darkness, by yielding to Satan's temptation, and transgressing the laws of God. The honor of God, and the safety of holy beings, required that God should not allow sin to reign with impunity. He graciously compassionated the state of mankind, and by giving Christ, his beloved Son, as a sacrifice for guilt, has redeemed our fallen and helpless species unto himself. In carrying out this salvation, Jesus not only had to expire as the great sacrificial lamb, but to exert his almighty power, in destroying the works of the devil. In this great arduous work, Christ appears as a man of war. As the Bozrah conqueror—as the captain of salvation. The phrase commander, in the text evidently signifies a general, one who leads on the army—who goes forth at the head of his troops to conflict with an opposing foe; such is the character and work of Jesus, as the "commander to the people." Observe,

I. The Cause in which Christ is engaged.

It is,

1. The cause of holiness against sin.

Christ came to vanquish the powers of wickedness. He came to overthrow ignorance and error, crime and pollution, prejudice and unbelief. He came to put down rebellion, treason, and disloyalty towards God, and to establish truth, and righteousness, and love and peace, throughout the earth. He designs the moral restoration of man to the holy image and Spirit of God.

2. The cause of happiness against misery.

A sinful state is one of wretchedness and misery. Jesus came to remove the cause, that the effects of depravity and guilt might ccasc. He designs the blessedness and consolation of man, by his emancipation from the yoke and service of the devil. Jesus scatters every kind of blessing in his course. He confers freedom and rest,—peace and joy in the Holy Spirit.

3. The cause of heaven against hell.

He is engaged to destroy the works of the devil. His kingdom is to overthrow it. Against his church the gates of hell are not to prevail. The power and authority of Satan and sin are to be overturned, and the reign of heaven to be established throughout the earth. All nations are to be blessed in him, and to call him blessed.

134

II. The Qualifications which, as Captain, Christ possesses.

1. Infinite knowledge and skill.

He knows everything which concerns either his own troops or those of the enemy. His wisdom and skill embrace every subject, so that he cannot err, he never fails in his plans, nor is necessitated to alter his arrangements. He is never baffled, nor perplexed, nor confused. He discerns all things and knows all things, past, present, and future, as though they were directly before him. How surely then will all the guilt and craftiness of wicked men or their subtle leader Satan, be put to naught

2. Omnific energy and power.

His wisdom is associated with irresistible power. Power which can do every thing that is worthy of a holy and righteous being. In the days of his flesh he often manifested it in curing diseases, stilling the tempest, raising the dead, and expelling devils. The energy of Christ's power is diffused everywhere, sustaining and preserving that which is good and conformable to his will, and in overwhelming his foes with confusion and dismay.

3. Undaunted courage and valor.

He displayed these during the whole of his suffering life. He never turned aside from his holy purposes, nor ever feared what men or devils could do against him. He feared not Jewish conspirators, nor the Roman soldiery. He feared not Pilate, nor Herod and his men of war. He feared not, and his courage never failed amid the pressure of thorns on his temples, the scourging of his back, the nailing of his hands and feet, or the piercing of his side. He did once indeed fear, but it was not the power of earth or hell; when he feared, it was when the cup of expiation was presented, and then he prayed, and was delivered from that fear, Heb. 5:7. As commander, he was distinguished 4. For unbounded tenderness and love.

Towards his ransomed devoted troops, he displays the greatest and most ardent affection. He bears with their frailties. Never withdraws his compassionate regards. Amply provides for their comfort and well-being. Never forsakes nor leaves them to their own resources, but causes his lovingkindness to surround them continually. "A bruised reed," &c., Heb. 4:14, 15. Observe then,

III. The Spirit and Practice which his Soldiers should evince.

1. Affectionate confidence and trust.

Of this he is most worthy. This he requires. To feel this and to exercise it constantly, is both for the happiness and welfare of his troops. "Trust in the Lord Jehovah," &c.

A. firm relying persuasion of his skill, and power, and faithfulness, and love, will cheer and animate the Christian, amid all the struggles of the arduous warfare.

2. Devoted obedience and attention.

Christ must be the model, the object of the Christian soldier's constant study and imitation. Jesus must bo followed. We must walk in his steps. Hear and obey his words. Imbibe his spirit. And walk even as he walked.

3. Unshaken and persevering activity.

The Christian's life is one, not only of professed, but real active conflict and warfare. The soldiers of Christ, therefore, must fight and struggle, till every foe is vanquished, and every enemy destroyed. They must go forth with Christ from conquering to conquest. Fight the good fight, until they receive the crown of life.

Application

We notice,

1. The warfare of the Christian is one of certain victory and triumph.

2. Invite men to fight under the standard of Jesus.

3. The enemies of Christ shall be confounded and covered with everlasting shame.

47. CHRIST THE WAY TO HEAVEN

"I am the way." —John 14:6.

THE Christian is professedly a pilgrim, a pilgrim on his way to glory. He is seeking a better country, that is to say, a heavenly one. He looks upward beyond the glittering starry skies, and sings,

> "There is my house and portion fair,
> My treasure and my heart are there,
>   And my abiding home."

To this world of happiness and rest, Jesus is the way,

I. By the revelation he gave of it.

A clear description of that blessed world was never given until Jesus was manifested in the flesh, and brought life and immortality to light by his gospel. He spoke of it in the most plain and familiar terms, called it his "father's house," the place of many mansions. And on some occasions he referred to its purity, and its celestial glory. How splendid must the imperial palace of Jehovah be!—the seat of his heavenly court, the residence of his spiritual and glorious hosts, where he is seated on his high and lofty throne, in overwhelming splendor of eternal light. To dwell in the presence of God, is supreme felicity and eternal life. Here is fulness of joy, and pleasures for evermore.

II. Christ is the Way also, because he only can confer the Title to the Possession of Heaven.

Heaven is the inheritance, and we become heirs through the justifying grace of Jesus. By faith in his mediatorial work, we become the sons of God, and joint heirs with Jesus Christ.

III. Jesus also imparts the Meetness necessary to its Enjoyment.

Before it can be enjoyed, we must be made meet; this he effects by the cleansing power of his blood, as communicated by the sanctifying influences of the Holy Spirit. Thus he makes us partakers of his own nature, and renders us capable of participating in his glory.

IV. Then he is the Way, as he is our glorious Leader and Example.

He is the guide of his people, and he hath left us an example, that we should follow his steps. O yes, he, as our forerunner, has gone before, and has opened a new and living way into the holiest place, and hath consecrated it for us, by his precious blood. No man can come to the possession of the Father's favor on earth, or the possession of the glory he bestows in heaven, but through him.

V. Jesus is the only Way to eternal Glory.

There is but one mediator between God and man, the man Christ Jesus. He is the one immutable foundation, the rock of ages, and other foundation can no man lay, than that is laid, which is Christ. To him, as the way, all the prophets testified; and John, as his illustrious harbinger and herald, proclaimed him as the Lamb of God, who taketh away the sins of the world. It is the especial work of the ministry, to point inquiring penitent souls to Jesus, as the only refuge and Savior from the wrath to come. And in doing this, the distinguishing features of this way must be specified.

1. Its *freeness* must be proclaimed; that it is not restricted to a select few of mankind, but that Christ is the Savior of all men, especially of them that believe. That there is no condition, natural or moral, which can exclude from Jesus and his salvation, but the self-willed and persevering exercise of unbelief. He hath declared that whosoever cometh unto him he will in no wise cast out.

2. Then its *gratuitousness* must be announced. As it is free to all, so it is free to all on he most gracious terms; there is no moral fitness required. No meritorious service is demanded. Unworthy, wretched, and truly despicable, rebellious sinners may approach Jesus as they are, for

> "All the fitness he requireth,
> Is to feel their need of him."

3. Then it is a way of *sure* and *certain blessedness.* All who have received Jesus and walk in him, possess peace and joy in the Holy Spirit. Their course infallibly tends to eternal life. No evil can come near them, no mischief can befall them; abiding in him they cannot perish, neither can any pluck them out of his hands. They go from strength to strength,— every one of them at last appears before God in the celestial Zion.

> "Jesus, my Lord, thou only art
>   Salvation's blessed way,
> Oh, cheer my heart, and keep my feet
>   Unto eternal day."

48. CHRIST THE WONDERFUL

"And his name shall be called Wonderful." —Isa. 9:6.

WHEN the angel of the Lord (doubtless none other than the Son of God) appeared to Manoah, and was asked his name, he said, "Why askest thou thus after my name, seeing it is *secret* or *wonderful,"* Judges 3:18. Now this is the very title the evangelical prophet is here applying to the Redeemer: his name, he says, shall be called Wonderful. How truly applicable is this title to Christ! He is wonderful in every respect in which he can be contemplated. As the Deity, he must of course be past finding out. But he is wonderful in all that relates to his mediatorial person, offices, and work.

I. Consider the wonderful Constitution of his Person.

Jehovah-Jesus, God manifest in the flesh Eternity united to a span of human existence. Omnipotence dwelling in the weakness of our manhood. The great and most high God assuming human form, and really allied, by the most mysterious of all unions, to a nature which had become degraded and worthless, by reason of transgression Then, too, how wonderful, that not withstanding that union, his own purity and dignity remained unaffected; he partook not of one feature of our depravity, or of one sinful infirmity. How marvelous indeed that the glory of Jehovah of hosts should be enshrined in a tabernacle of flesh And dwell amongst us, that the splendor of his divinity should be beheld, as the glory of the only-begotten of the Father, full of grace and truth. In the mysterious formation of Christ's human nature, the Holy Spirit employed his miraculous influence in a way unknown before, and thus produced a divinely glorious personage, who is the wonder both of heaven and earth. O let us contemplate the character of our adorable and wonderful Jesus. Here our thoughts may be employed to our real profit and abiding welfare. Here is a mystery, which prophets and apostles, yea, and angels, have endeavored to explore, but in vain.

> "'Tis mystery all, let men adore,
> And angel minds inquire no more."

II. Wonderful in the Offices which he assumed.

In previous ages, God had separated his servants to various duties and pursuits. Some had filled the prophetical, others the priestly, and others the kingly office. Some were rulers over the people, others teachers, and others the generals, or leaders of their armies. In Christ all these offices centered, on him all these duties devolved. He was emphatically the prophet of the most high God, the priest after the order of Melchizedek, and Zion's great and glorious king. He came to rule over his people, to instruct the ignorant, and to be the illustrious captain of salvation. And he possessed all the requisites for these various offices, and that in the most perfect degree. He was copiously anointed with the spirit of prophecy, and knew all things. The sacred unction rested on his priestly head in all its sanctifying plenitude. Wisdom, power, and essential dignity contributed to elevate him as the King of kings, and Lord of lords. His rule was associated with perfect and infallible knowledge, and spotless justice and equity. As a teacher, he spoke and taught as no man ever else did; he spoke with divine authority and power, so that the people were astonished at his doctrine, and exclaimed, "Never man spoke like this man." And as the captain of God's sacred host, he went forth to conflict, and spoiled all his foes, and returned to his throne, as the Bozrah conqueror, terrible to his adversaries, yet mighty to save. Oh the amazing combination of qualities in our wonderful Redeemer! Greatness and humility, courage and meekness, power and voluntarily assumed weakness, glory and abasement, riches and poverty, holy, wise, omnipotent, and eternal, yet accounted base, utterly worthless, and at last actually despised, and put to death.

III. He is also wonderful in the Titles by which he is set forth.

He is the great, mighty, and only true and wise God. He is the prince of the kings of the earth—the Lord of armies—the only living and true potentate—king of kings—governor of the nations—and proprietor of the universe. Before him the loftiest seraphs bend, and all the angels of God worship him. The Father speaks of him as his fellow, his eternal delight, and says unto him, "Thy throne, O God, is forever and ever." All ascriptions of praise, and blessing, and honor, and power, and glory, and rule, and dominion, are presented to him by the intellectual hosts of glory, incessantly:

> "Before his feet the countless hosts
>   Of seraphim do fall,
> And, with profoundest awe, unite
>   To crown him Lord of all."

IV. He is wonderful in all his Works.

His works are those of true and essential divinity. He has created all things by the energy of his omnific voice, and he upholds all things by the word of his power. Here then Christ appears before us in all the inconceivable greatness and grandeur of his boundless operations and works. Who then can understand his wonderful character, or by searching, find him out to perfection? Oh the depths of the riches, both of the wisdom and knowledge of God! And yet in redemption it appears that he has exceeded all his other works, that here has been a mightier and grander display of his essential and infinite perfections; hence, says the poet,

> "Our thoughts are lost in reverend awe,
>   We love and we adore;
> The first archangel never saw,

So much of God before"

O yes, in redemption we have not the hidings, but the manifestations of his glory and power; here is not a partial, but a full display of the glories of the divine nature

"Here the whole Deity is known,
Nor dares the creature guess,
Which of the glories brightest shone,
The justice or the grace."

V. Christ's Love is wonderful.

If we consider the objects of his love, now sinful, wretched, and unworthy they were of the least favorable regard. Yet he pitied, and had compassion even on the ungodly. And the intensity of his love towards us is wonderful. He loved us with a love altogether unparalleled and unknown. He loved us so much as to yield himself a free atoning sacrifice for our guilt. Loved us more than he loved the dignities and joys of his glorious and imperial palace. Herein is love; love setting all description and all human conception utterly at defiance,—love that passes all understanding.

VI. His sufferings were wonderful.

Well might he be called, "A man of sorrows and acquainted with griefs." How varied, yet how deeply intense were his sufferings! He suffered poverty, calumny, and hatred; he was bitterly persecuted, falsely charged, unjustly tried, and wickedly condemned to die. He was scourged, buffeted, spit upon, and nailed to the cross. In dying, he was ridiculed, taunted, and mocked. Earth and heaven seemed combined to cause the waters of affliction to cover his sacred spirit, and the waves of trouble, in successive rolling billows, went over his blessed head.

"Oh, Lamb of God! was ever love,
Was ever grief like thine?"

His life in all its stages was wonderful. From the announcement of his incarnation, to his last shout upon the cross, there was one continued series of great and astonishing events. He spoke as never man spoke; he lived, and prayed, and blessed men, in a way peculiar to himself. He arose upon our world, as the great and wonderful orb of spiritual day; and in a sky of sable blackness—except as it was streaked with the crimson of his precious blood—he set on Calvary's elevated and solemn summit Christ is,

VII. Wonderful in his Triumphs.

He triumphed over all his adversaries. Over sin and Satan. Over death and the grave. He is the Bozrah conqueror, "Mighty to save."

Application

1. How worthy is Jesus of our highest admiration.

2. How deserving of our most exalted praises.

3. How suitable as the foundation of our peace, and hope, and salvation.

4. How supremely should we love and serve him.

49. CHRIST A COUNSELOR

"Counselor." —Isa. 9:6.

WE now have to consider the second illustrious title of the Messiah, of whom it is said, "The government shall be on his shoulders." The spirit of prophecy testified of Christ as the "Counselor," Prov. 8:14; and Isa. 2:2. Let us ascertain,

I. Wherein he has exhibited himself as our Counselor.

He did so,

1. In the council regarding the redemption of our world.

With us there is time past, present, &c.; with Jehovah all things, as it were, are before him. Now, it is clear that God foresaw the entrance of sin and ruin into our world. It is clear also that he benevolently contemplated its deliverance from sin, and the power of the evil one. Now this is often spoken of as the council wherein the agreement was formed and the covenant made, None in heaven could be found sufficient for the undertaking, until Jesus, one of the council, said, "Lo I come," &c. This council seems clearly intimated in Isa. 53, where both the sufferings and reward of the Messiah seem determined.

2. In the council respecting the creation of our world.

This event, and especially that of forming man, seem to have been decided in council. The language found in the book of Proverbs, 8:22, is generally ascribed to the Son of God. And here Christ was appointed to have creative power and universal authority, &c. Now there are four places in the holy scriptures where the plural number is used in respect to Deity, and which implies council, Gen. 1:26, 3:22, 11:7; Isa. 6:8.

3. In his actual work when he brought life and immortality to light by the gospel He came to give counsel to a lost world He came to make known the way of peace, the way of salvation and eternal life. Wherever he went he appeared as a Counselor from heaven. And he was such to all persons. He counselled both the Pharisees and the publicans, the religious and the profane.

4. In his especial counsels to his believing disciples.

How often he conversed, &c. with these, with all affection, with all tenderness and simplicity. He spoke to them what he did not to the world. For them he had especial instruction. So also now he manifests, &c. He anointed them with the holy unction, &c. So the Asiatic churches, Rev. 3:18.

5. In his personal counsels and pleadings with his Father on our behalf.

That solemn prayer, which is recorded throughout the seventeenth chapter of John, is a striking evidence of this. So also he says again, John 14:15, "I will pray the Father," &c. So says the same apostle, "If any man sin," &c. See also Rom. 8:33.

II. The peculiar Characteristics of Christ as our Counselor.

Now,

1. He possesses infallible knowledge.

Of the mind of God and the heart of man. Of all that relates to us, both as it regards time and eternity. In him dwelt all the treasures of wisdom and knowledge.

2. He possesses immutable rectitude.

Justice, purity, and truth, are the perfections of his nature.

3. He possesses unbounded influence.

Him the Father always hears. In pleading with God for us, he has the firmest grounds of appeal to the Father,—his office,—his merits,—his glory, &c.

4. He is distinguished for his unfailing tenderness and compassion.

He makes the case of every disciple his own. "In all their afflictions," &c. He sympathizes in all their distresses, and bears all their sicknesses. And he never tires, never is wearied, and never forsakes his people.

Application

Learn,

1. The privilege of the true Christian. Christ the Counselor is his Lord and friend. Now we must use him as such or we dishonor him. In difficulty. In temptation. In sorrow. When the enemy has injured you. In despondency, &c. Go to him. Go humbly believing, confiding

2. Let the backslider regard his counsels. How unwilling he is to give you up &c.

3. Let the sinner also hearken. "Come unto me," &c.

4. Let the incorrigible enemy tremble Hear the voice of God respecting his anointed, Ps. 2:10, &c.

50. CHRIST THE FOUNDATION

"For a foundation." —Isa. 28:16.

THE prophet is clearly referring to the Messiah in the text. The apostle Paul, speaking of the believer, likens him "to a house, and as a habitation of God through the Spirit." He is also likened to a temple, "know ye not that ye are the temple of God." Now these metaphorical statements show the connection and propriety of Christ being set forth as a foundation, see 1 Cor. 3:11.

I. Let us then notice of what Christ is the Foundation.

1. Now Christ is the foundation of the sinner's acceptance with God.

God cannot be merciful to man, consistently with the demands of his holiness justice, and truth, except in and through Jesus Christ. Christ's holiness, obedience, and merits, are the only grounds on which God is propitious to the sinner: so that Jesus is the only foundation of pardoning mercy, and justifying grace.

2. Christ is the foundation of the believer's peace.

Hence he is called, "Our peace," Eph. 2:14. Jesus came and preached peace. When he arose from the dead, he imparted peace to his disciples. "And being justified by faith, we have *peace* with God, through our Lord Jesus Christ." He is the foundation of all sorts of peace. By him, angels are at peace with us. God is at peace with us. And we have peace with conscience, the peace of God within us, which passes all understanding.

3. Christ is the foundation of hope.

We are begotten again to a lively hope by the resurrection of Christ from the dead. Christ's blessed gospel has brought life and immortality to light. Christ's merits have laid a solid and honorable basis for their bestowment. And his great and precious promises respecting them, give the believer a hope unspeakably bright, and full of glory.

4. Christ is the foundation of eternal life.

He died, rose again and ascended into heaven, that we might obtain eternal life. He gives unto his sheep eternal life. We have eternal life in his name. "And this is the record that God hath given unto us eternal life, and this life is in his Son."

5. He is also the foundation of his collective and universal church.

The church is likened to a temple and to a city, of which Jesus is the glorious basis. He is the rock on which his church is built, and against which the gates of hell shall never prevail. Holy men, and prophets, and apostles, are all stones in this superstructure, but Christ alone is laid, as the foundation, who bears all its massy weight,—on which it entirely rests. And whether we consider the church, in its militant state on earth, or in its glorified and triumphant state in heaven, Christ is the basis of the whole. Each and all of God's spiritual family, from the new-born babe on earth, to the most exalted beatific spirit in glory, rest wholly upon Christ as the foundation.

II. What are the distinguishing Characters of this Foundation?

1. Christ is God's elect and precious foundation.

He is the select and chosen of God; and he is essentially and infinitely precious.

2. He is a strong foundation.

Omnipotence is one of his attributes. He is the Almighty: both the wisdom and power of God. So strong that it is probable that myriads of worlds are upheld by him. He is a suitable foundation. In him God is glorified, and the sinner honorably saved. He is high enough to shed eternal lustre on all the perfections of the Deity, and low enough to meet the sinner's state, and amply to supply all his exigencies.

3. He is a universal foundation.

Hence a guilty world is to be directed to him, and every creature invited to build upon him.

4. He is a perpetual foundation.

In all ages believers have rested upon him. Our parents were directed to him in he first promise; Abel built upon it, and lied a martyr for his faith in him. Abraham built upon him, and seeing his day, though afar off, rejoiced and was glad. Prophets and all the holy men of old rested their hopes on him, who in the fulness of the times should come, who is the Chris of God, blessed for evermore. And through all the ages which have passed since his actual appearance to the present, and through all the periods which shall elapse, to the grand and final consummation, he is, and shall be, the one great, and only foundation. As a foundation Christ comes to us,

5. As having been tried, and as always sufficient.

How many have built upon mere *doctrines* and *sentiments,* upon *creeds* and *systems;* but in the day of distress, when they wanted comfort, their foundation being only nominal, merely theoretical, they have been left in wretchedness and despondency. How many have built on the *abstract mercy* of *God,* but when their foundation was tested, they have found out that Jehovah is just as well as merciful, and he will by no mean, clear the

146

guilty. How many have built upon their own *works,* upon their *self-righteousness,* and have only been awakened time enough to discover, that all their goodness is as filthy rags. But all who have tried Jesus have found him a sufficient foundation. And how extensively has he been tried. In all ages thousands have rested all their hopes upon him. He has been tried by all classes and grades of men. By the rich, and by the poor; by the learned, and by the illiterate; by the savage, and by the refined; by the moralist, and by the profligate; and they have all realized in him, an all-sufficient foundation. He has proved all-sufficient, for all times, and places, and occurrences, —he has been tried in prosperity, and in adversity,—he has been tried in youth, and in old age,—he has been tried in health, and in sickness,—he has been tried in life, and in death. And in all diversities of state, they who have trusted in him have never been confounded. His sufficiency has been tested, under reproach, persecution, distress, at the stake, and at the block; and so strong has it been, that pain has been found as ease, and death in its most terrific forms embraced, in the hope of a better resurrection

Application

1. Let the Christian abide on this foundation; be not moved from the hope of the gospel.

2. The sinner's peace, happiness, and sternal well-being depend upon the acceptance or rejection of this foundation.

51. CHRIST A KING

"There is another king, one Jesus." —Acts 17:7.

THE kingship of Jesus was both extensively typified and predicted in the old testament scriptures. Melchizedek was an eminent type of Jesus, combining in himself both the office of priest and king. David and Solomon too were both types of the royalty of Jesus. The prophets also predicted of him as the "King of glory," Ps. 24:8; "King of Zion," Jer. 8:19; "A mighty king," xi. 3. He is called, "David their king," Hosea 3:5. And "King over all the earth," Zech. 14:9. Christ also confessed to Pilate, that he was a king, but that his kingdom was not of this world.

I. Consider the kingly Character of Jesus.

Considered in the divinity of his person, He is universal king. King of kings and Lord of lords. In this sense, his empire extends to heaven, and earth, and hell. All creatures, and all worlds belong to his illimitable empire, and of his dominion there is no end. But we now especially consider him in his mediatorial office, as feigning in the midst of the Zion of his church.

1. His kingdom consists of two branches; that of the *spirits* of the just in heaven, and that of all true believers on earth.

2. His palace is in glory, where he has his great and exalted throne, where the homage of countless attendants is constantly paid to him.

3. His laws and statutes are revealed in his word, and the gospel is his royal scepter, the rod of his strength.

4. The officers of his kingdom are the pastors and teachers of his church, who are to publish his laws, and to enforce the discipline of his kingdom.

5. All who truly believe in him, and unfeignedly love him, are his subjects; on the throne of their willing hearts he sits, and sways the scepter of his grace. It will thus appear, that his kingdom is not confined by local bounds, or geographical limits, but in whatever nation or country, or of whatever people, or clime, or color believers are found there is his spiritual empire, there he reigns as King of his universal Zion. Notice,

II. The Characteristics of Christ's kingly Office.

Jesus Christ as a king is possessed of the most illustrious distinctions and titles

1. He is the king immortal.

He has life in himself—he ever lives—he had no beginning of years, or end of days—he claims the prerogative of absolute immortality and self-existence—he is the "I am,"—the "Jehovah of hosts," and besides him there is none else

2. He is the king invisible.

He once appeared in our world and tabernacled amongst us, and his glory was beheld, the glory as of the only-begotten of the Father, full of grace and truth, but now he is removed from our mortal vision, having entered into the holiest place of all, where he ever appears in the presence of God for us.

3. He is the king eternal.

His reign shall be everlasting, and of his dominion there shall be no end.

4. He is the king of kings.

His providence extends to all the affairs of earth. By him kings reign. By him all the complex machinery of governments is overruled and directed.

5. He is the king of glory.

He dwells in glory. His throne is in the highest heaven. All the glorious hosts adore before him. All the angels of heaven worship him. For this king we should cultivate feelings of profoundest reverence and veneration. To him in all things we should be subject. His will is supreme and unchangeably binding in its obligations on all his disciples.

6. He is a righteous and equitable king.

He is the holy and just one. He reigns not as a usurper, his dominion is not based on iniquity, but in eternal righteousness and truth. His name is the "Lord out righteousness." "A scepter of righteousness is the scepter of his kingdom." "Righteousness is the girdle of his loins."

7. He is a bountiful and benevolent king.

His goodness is associated with all his acts, and all his engagements,—his goodness is over all his works. He reigns to diffuse his goodness—

"Blessings abound where'er he reigns,
The pris'ner leaps to lose his chains,
The weary find eternal rest,
And all the sons of want are blest"

149

8. He is also a gracious and merciful king.

Grace is poured into his lips,—he is full of grace and truth,—the scepter be sways is a scepter of mercy,—he delights in mercy,—his mercy extends to his greatest enemies. It abounded to Saul of Tarsus as a pattern or example of what it could effect, and to whom it could extend. Those whom we should have supposed had totally excluded themselves from the possibility of his favor, were the first to whom the gospel message of mercy and grace was sent. Remission of sins was to be preached to all nations, but first of all, "beginning at Jerusalem."

Application

1. The throne he now occupies is one of grace, to which the vilest may have access by repentance and faith, and obtain mercy and grace to help them in time of need.

2. Let the children of Zion be joyful in their king.

3. Let the sinner be exhorted to "kiss the Son lest he be angry, and he perish from the way, when his anger is kindled but a little," Ps. 2:11.

52. CHRIST A TEACHER

"And seeing the multitudes, he went up into a mountain, and when he was set, his disciples came unto him, and he opened his mouth and taught them." —Matt. 5:1, 2.

ONE great end of Christ's coming into our world was to illuminate it with the light of life, and to show unto men the way of salvation. As such, his appearing had been predicted. Moses had said, 1400 years before, "the Lord thy God will raise unto thee a prophet from the midst of thee, of thy brethren like unto me, unto him shall ye hearken." Thus, too the apostle prefaces his epistle to the Hebrew believers, "God who at sundry times and in divers manners spoke," &c., Hebrews 1:1, 2. Let us then consider,

I. The Character of Jesus as a Teacher.

Now as a teacher he has been properly styled the great Teacher. Greater than the prophets. Greater and higher than the angels.

1. He possessed infinite knowledge and wisdom.

The knowledge of all created beings must be limited. His was unbounded He knew all things, nothing could be hid from him. As the creator of worlds, the universe was all as transparent light before him. He knew all the mind of God. He knew all concerning the heavenly world. He knew all concerning man—concerning death. As such he is styled "God only wise." In him was hidden all the treasures of knowledge and wisdom. The wisest of prophets only had knowledge revealed unto them in small portions, but he had the fountain within himself.

2. He was possessed of infinite holiness and truth.

Not only was he so in essence, but in spirit, conversation, and practice. Moses was a good man, but by anger he disgraced his office, and excluded himself from the promised land. So Elijah and the whole of the prophets were fallible, erring men. But he embodied his own religion. He lived and exhibited every precept. His character was blameless. He was pure and holy, undefiled and separate from sinners. He reflected the spotless purity of the Godhead.

3. He was distinguished for unbounded goodness and love.

His errand, his whole work, was one of love. It was this that brought him to seek and to save, &c. He went about doing good. His design was to bless, to make men wise, and holy, and happy. He came to open a pathway to the heavenly world. He had nothing in his heart but pure, disinterested, and universal love. Hence when he began his work, he stated the nature of his mission. "The Spirit of the Lord is upon me," &c., Luke 4:18.

4. He displayed the greatest condescension and patience.

He became the teacher both of the people and the rabbis. He stooped down to their residences, occupations, and capacities. He went to the sea-side and taught fishermen, laborers in the field, beggars on the highway. A poor Samaritan woman at the well. His discourses were always suited to the people—plain, simple, &c. He did not upbraid. He did not exhibit any pomp. He did not break the bruised reed, &c.

5. He enforced and ratified all by divine power and authority.

He taught in his own name. He spoke as one having authority, &c. He said, "I say unto you." He assumed the supremacy, and enforced all by unparalleled signs and miracles. Prodigies and wonders attended his steps. He healed the sick, cured lepers, restored the paralytic, expelled devils, awed the elements, and raised the dead. The people often were overwhelmed, and exclaimed, "What manner of man is this," &c. His promises too were more splendid, and his threatenings more terrific, than those of any other teacher. Heaven he opened to his disciples, and showed the gates of hell to obstinate unbelievers. Consider,

II. The Subjects of his Instructions.

1. His instructions were all-important.

Nothing trifling, nothing of a secondary kind. He taught great truths, relating to the soul and to eternity. His subjects were chiefly heavenly and eternal. He left nature, science, politics, and commerce, to others. He revealed the glories of the heavenly world, and showed how we might make them our own forever.

2. His instructions were chiefly practical.

He stated some few points of doctrine, out how seldom were those introduced. His truths were not ceremonial but practical. He told men how to live. How to act towards his Father, towards himself, and towards each other. He spoke of the spirit we possess, the tempers we should cherish, the conversation we should cultivate, and the actions we should practice.

3. His subjects were perfect and abiding.

He introduced no temporary customs. No mutable ordinances. No local institutions. He was to be the last, and therefore the perfection, of all that teachers had revealed from God. His truths were to abide forever. So his morals—so his worship—so his ordinances,—baptism, Lord's supper, &c. Nothing deficient—nothing misplaced—nothing redundant in all he taught. He introduced the perfect day, and nothing shall be brighter but the light of heaven. Consider,

III. The Claims of Christ as a Teacher.

1. Profound reverence.

This a prophet would deserve—an angel more. How much more then God's Son,—his equal—his fellow; especially when we remember he is the appointed judge of quick and dead; his voice will decide the destiny of every creature.

2. Peculiar and intense attention.

Our every interest is at stake; our peace—comfort—life—salvation. If we neglect him it will be our everlasting loss. On his lips hang life—death—heaven—and hell.

3. The highest gratitude.

His love, his kindness, his mercy—all claim this. Our interests he ever consulted, not his own; for us he said and suffered all things.

4. Prompt obedience.

This is the end of all. To obey him—always—in all things—from the heart—with the whole life. To know, in order to do his will.

Application

1. Address disciples.

2. Inquirers draw near.

3. Unbelievers tremble.

4. Hear Christ on all subjects and at all times.

53. CHRIST THE SUN OF RIGHTEOUSNESS

"But unto you that fear my name shall the Sun of righteousness arise with healing in his wings."
—Mal. 4:2.

THE sacred waters, in exhibiting the character and work of Jesus, are compelled to adopt the language of metaphor, and by referring to the various objects of nature, faintly to set forth his beauties and glory. The earth, and sea, and sky, are exhausted of their wonders, to accomplish this great design. The rock exhibits his stability and strength. The vine his fruitfulness and the lily rose his purity and beauty He is the pearl of great price. The fountain of living water. He is the morning star; and the true light—the light of the world. In the text, the prophet Malachi exhibits him as the sun of righteousness &c. Notice,

I. The Metaphor.

"The sun of righteousness." Jesus may be fitly likened to the sun,

1. On account of his unity.

In creation we have many stars—many seas—many trees and flowers; but there is only one sun. He has no comparison,—no rival or assistant illuminator. So in the celestial world there are many angels, seraphim and cherubim, of various ranks, and orders, and offices, but there is only one essential Son of God,—one Jesus,—one mediator between God and man,—the man Christ Jesus.

2. On account of his greatness and magnificence.

The accounts given by astronomers of the orb of day, as to his size, are sublime and overwhelming. The center of the solar system, he appears the monarch of the whole, diffusing his glories around. Now Christ is most emphatically the Most High. Higher than the sons of men. His greatness is unsearchable. His nature is above the nature of angels. His name is greater than theirs. His throne is the most exalted, and around him move all the shining ranks of glory, and his brightness fills heaven with joy and gladness.

3. On account of the universality of his influences.

The beams of the sun are common to every part of our world, and there is nothing hid from the heat thereof. He shines upon the mountain and the valley. Upon the sterile desert and the fruitful vineyard. Upon the monarch's palace and the peasant's cottage. How applicable to the sun of righteousness! He is God's great gift to the whole world. Designed for the benefit of the universal family of man. The Savior of all men, but especially of them that believe. He has shone upon every part of our earth. Asia, Africa, Europe, and America, have alike enjoyed his gladsome rays. He shines on men irrespective of their earthly distinctions; the beggar is free to enjoy his light, while kings come to the brightness of his rising.

4. On account of the nature of his benefits.

> 1) He is the fountain of light. Clouds, and darkness, and night, are chased before him. He introduces light and day. So, also, the sun of righteousness, he banishes the shades of night, and introduces the moral and spiritual day. To him we are indebted for the light of knowledge, the light of happiness, the light of holiness, and the light of heaven.

> 2) He is the source of beauty. The various hues and tints of flowers and plants, are owing to their absorbing, in different quantities, the peculiar properties of light Without his rays, nature would be one vast and gloomy blank. So Christ is the source of all moral and spiritual beauty. He transforms the mind into the divine image. He arrays the soul in all the celestial beauties of holiness.

> 3) He is the cause of vegetation. The light and rays of the sun are necessary for the fruitfulness of the earth. He removes the dreary, barren appearance of winter, and produces the enlivening spring, the fruitful summer, and the gathering of autumn. All the fruits of righteousness are produced by Christ. "Without me ye can do nothing." Hence, he is not only called the sun of righteousness, because of his essential purity, but also because he makes his people righteous. He is made unto them "wisdom, righteousness," &c. He makes the stony heart soft and fertile, until it brings forth fruit as the garden of the Lord. Observe,

II. The Declaration.

"The sun of righteousness shall," &c. Now, as the sun of righteousness,

> 1. He arose upon our world in the day of his nativity.

The hemisphere had been faintly illumined by the stars of types, sacrifices, and prophecies, all of which were precursors of approaching day, the day of the world's light and redemption. At last the eventful period arrived, the fulness of the times when God sent his Son, &c. Then Zacharias sang, "Through the tender mercy of our God," &c., Luke 1:78. Thus he brought life and immortality into light, &c.

> 2. He arises upon the benighted mind in the day of conversion.

He opens the eyes of blind sinners. When they feel their misery, and cry to him, &c. Night ends, darkness is dispelled, and the day of grace begins in the soul, 2 Cor. 4:6.

> 3. He will arise upon the world in the day of his second advent.

Hence, we read of the brightness of his coming. His glorious appearance. "Behold, he cometh with clouds," &c. Then will be the morning of the saints' coronation. His rays will enter every grave, and irradiate every sepulcher. Then he will come to be glorified in his saints, and admired by all them that believe Notice,

III. Those who will be benefited by the Savior's Rising.

"That fear his name." Now, the fear referred to is a holy filial fear, which produces a regard for his authority and laws. Such a fear as is associated with love and obedience. Like Noah's. Where this is not, Christ will be rejected, and his benefits despised. Not to fear him, is a sign of an unbelieving and rebellious mind. This fear the penitent has, and is tremblingly alive to his safety. This fear the believer has, and he cherishes it, and ever keeps it in his heart.

Application

1. Are you the characters?

2. Has Christ arisen upon you?

3. There is no saving light but that which he communicates.

54. CHRIST THE BEST FRIEND

"A friend that sticketh closer than a brother" —Prov. 18:24.

To none can these words be so truly applicable as to Jesus. His conduct was so gracious, and his Spirit so benign and condescending, that his enemies proclaimed him "A friend of publicans and sinners." In this they rightly set him forth—it was his delight; the joy of his heart, to exhibit the fulness of his love to the wretched worthless children of men. Nothing has more frequently been the topic of conversation, the subject of eulogium, and the theme of song, than friendship. Striking instances have been recorded on the pages of history, and handed down for the admiration of posterity. Friendship has been represented under the idea of one heart and spirit animating and influencing two bodies. An appropriate illustration of true affection and kindredness of soul which forms the very essence of true friendship. Let us,

I. Take a view of the Evidences of the Friendship of Christ to Man.

This was seen,

1. In the compassion and pity which he felt towards our apostatizing race.

He saw man guilty, self-ruined, ungodly, perishing. Without a plea of self-vindication. Without one redeeming trait of character, or one reason why the displeasure of his affronted Lord, should not descend upon him But even then Christ's heart moved with compassion, and his bowels yearned in mercy over his guilty creatures

2. In the purposes which he formed for his redemption.

All his thoughts, and purposes, and counsels, were fraught with friendliness and love. He saw his misery, and contemplated and purposed his recovery. He committed himself to his rescue and salvation. He resolved to pass by all his repulsive foulness and pollution, and to adopt an expedient for his purification and help.

3. In the means he employed for his salvation.

He became surety for him. He engaged to be his Redeemer. He clothed himself with our nature, and thus became our true brother. Then he gave himself as the voluntary victim to bear, in his own body, our sins upon the tree. He left glory, and riches, and praises, and honor, and divine blessedness, and became abased, and vilified, and poor, and the subject of scorn, and malice, and hatred, and, above all, died a malefactor's death, to secure riches, and bliss, and honor, and eternal life, for mankind.

4. In the blessings which he obtained for his enjoyment.

These are various, and include all good both for body and soul. They comprehend the unsearchable riches of his grace, and the boundless and everlasting riches of glory. By these he is the recipient of pardon, adoption, holiness, and eternal life:

> "Slaves are made partners of his throne,
> Deck'd with a never-fading crown."

II. The peculiar Features by which Christ's Friendship is distinguished.

1. Entire disinterestedness.

It is not possible that Jesus, who is Lord of all things, could be profited by his dependent creature man. Oh no, he had his good, his real and eternal good only at heart. He sought not his, for what had he which Christ had not bestowed?

2. Amazing condescension.

It is wonderful condescension in our divine Lord to behold the things which are upon earth; but how much more marvelous, that he should visit man, become his kinsman, live with him, and die for him

3. Unshaken constancy.

Having undertaken to be the friend of men, he carried out his design to the utmost. With the cost and sacrifice before him, his pity never failed, his good will abated not, his dying prayer attested his unfailing and devoted regard for our well-being and salvation. And although eighteen centuries have rolled since his resurrection and ascension to his Father's right hand, his gracious attachment to the interests of sinners is as ardent and tender as ever. Still it is true of him,

> "His bowels melt with tenderness,
> His heart is full of love."

4. Unlimited ability.

As his heart is full of immutable love, so his power to help is equal to the infinity of his grace.

1) He is never far from us A friend near to us at all times and in all places.

2) His resources are inexhaustible. He possesses every good we can need, and he is disposed every moment to impart it to us.

3) He can ward off all evils, silence the tongues of all adversaries, and deliver us from all our enemies. He is every day and hour the help and shield of his people. He gives grace, &c.

4) Having immortality and life in himself, those interested in his regards will never be deprived of his mercy and love. He will be our guide unto life's termination, our solace in death, and our portion forever. Notice,

III. The Duties which Christ's Friendship involves.

His friendship,

1. Should be reciprocated.

He calls us to be his friend, and tells us how we may exhibit our friendship towards him. We cannot be Christ's friends if we are in league with his enemies,—with sin and Satan. He requires us to abandon these. Then we must also exhibit our love to him and our confidence in him, by receiving his words, embracing his truth, imbibing his spirit, following his steps, and keeping his commandments. "Ye are my friends if ye do," &c. His friendship,

2. Should be gratefully acknowledged.

Our mouths and hearts should extol it.

We should celebrate it from day to day,—

> "Praise should employ our highest powers,
> While life or thought or being last,
> Or immortality endures."

3. It should be ardently cherished.

How careful we should be not to grieve, act to displease him. How solicitous to please him and honor him. How deeply we should value his friendship, and how ready to relinquish everything incompatible with it. By constant intercourse, and frequent visits to his palace and throne, should the friendly spirit be cultivated, and its ardor excited. It should indeed be a growing friendship, deepening and enlarging through all time and through all eternity.

4. It should be universally recommended

"Should we not tell to sinners round,
What a dear Savior we have found?"

Oh yes, everywhere should we speak of the preciousness of Christ. The love of Christ. The graciousness of Christ.

Application

1. Are we Christ's friends? If not, how wicked and ungrateful. If we are such let humble gratitude celebrate it day by day.

2. Urge the sinner full, of enmity now to be reconciled to him.

3. The doom of his adversaries will be fearfully terrible.

55. CHRIST THE DOOR

"I am the door." —John 10:7

JESUS has a peculiar claim to the metaphorical title here expressed. In reference to every thing that relates to the happiness and dignity of man here, or to his advancement in felicity and glory to come, he is the door, the only way of access. Consider man as an alien or outcast, a wandering, dying rebel against his God, and then,

I. Jesus is the only Door, or Way of Access, to the Divine Favor and Family.

It is when we come to God, exercising faith in his Son, that we are accepted of him, are freely justified, and have the privilege of becoming his adopted sons. To his spiritual house Jesus is the only door. God will not, and, by reason of his eternal spotlessness, cannot treat with us but through the person of the Lord Jesus Christ,

II. Jesus is also the Door to all the Privileges of his Church.

By union to the head only can we derive that spiritual nourishment which the members of the mystical body require. By faith in Jesus, we have an evangelical right to all the privileges and immunities of his people. Then all is ours,—the word, the gospel preached, the promises recorded, the precious ordinances, and the all-essential influences of the Spirit, are all ours. Then may we dwell in his banqueting-house. and sit down at his table with great delight.

III. Jesus is also the Door to Communion with the Father.

To God, there is but the way of access, and that is by his Son Whether it be by prayer, or meditation, or praise, we only can approach Jehovah, and hold intercourse with him by coming through this door.

IV. Jesus, too, is the only Door to eternal Glory.

He is the way into the holiest place of all. By him we come to God graciously now, and by him we shall enter into the paradise above, for, as our forerunner, he hath passed before us, taken possession of heaven for his people, and waits to receive them unto himself, that where he is, there they may be also. Now in all these respects,

> 1. Jesus is a constantly open door.

> He became the door from the instant the first promise was announced, and he has been the open door from that period to the present time. The way to God has not been closed for a single moment. During the thousands of years that have rolled onwards in their changing course, he has remained fixed in his mediatorial office, and has changed not.

How blessed is the consideration that, whether by day or night, the seeking sinner can never find this door of hope closed against him.

2. Then he is also a door for all.

None have been excluded from God's compassionate regards, for he hath loved the world, and Jesus is the propitiation for the sins of the whole world, and the gospel freely invites all, without respect to country, age, or character, to come unto God by him. There never was, nor is, nor ever will be, any other exclusion than that of the sinner's impenitency and unbelief. We remark,

3. That Jesus is the only door.

There is but one mediator between God and us. There is but one name given, one Savior found, one sacrifice offered, one gospel preached—that name and Savior is Jesus—that sacrifice, the blood of his cross—and that gospel, the gospel of Christ. There is but one door for the profligate and the moral, the profane and the professor, the publican and the Pharisee. There is but one door for the rich and the poor, the learned and the illiterate, the aged and the young, the monarch and the slave. In short, there is but this door for the whole of our guilty world. He is the door, and whosoever refuses or neglects him must be excluded from heaven, but whoever enters in by him shall obtain eternal life

Application

1. If Christ be the only door, then how desirable is it that we see how we stand connected with him.

Let us inquire, then as to our *knowledge* of Christ as the door. Have we right views of our necessity of such a door? Have we felt our distance from God, and have we perceived the glorious adaptation of Jesus in his person and work to bring us nigh to him? Have we beheld in Jesus the very object adapted to our spiritual need, in whom there is a fulness of grace to meet all our exigencies and supply all our wants? Jesus cannot be the door to us unless we know him, for this is life eternal, to know the true God and Jesus Christ whom he hath sent.

2. Let us also ascertain as to our *approach* to God by this door.

Have we come to him and believed in him, availed ourselves of his merits, trusted in his mediation, and thus obtained forgiveness of sins and peace with God? If we have used Christ as the door, then are we no longer without, no longer at a distance, no longer condemned; but now are we reconciled to God, and by the testimony of the Holy Spirit to our spirits, we know that we are the sons of God.

3. Then, let us ascertain also as to our estimate of this door.

Do we value it above all things? for to them that believe Christ is precious, precious always, yea, superlatively precious. If we value this door, we shall extol it by lips of sanctified praise, and by lives of ardent love and holy obedience to Christ.

4. How necessary it is that we constantly avail ourselves of this door.

We cannot hold intercourse with God for a moment but through Christ, and God cannot behold us with complacency except when he beholds us in the face of his anointed One. Then Christ is emphatically our life and salvation, and the life that we live must be a life of faith in who Son of God, who loved as and gave himself for us.

56. CHRIST THE LIVING AND PRECIOUS STONE

"To whom coming, as unto a living stone, disallowed indeed of men, but chosen of God, and precious." –1 Pet. 2:4.

THIS passage evidently refers to Christ. And is quite similar language to that employed by the psalmist more than a thousand years before, when he sang of Messiah in Ps. 118:22. The verses following the text refer to a passage in the prophecy of Isaiah 28:16. Let us notice,

I. The Description given of Christ.

A living stone, &c. Often represented as a stone.

    1. A stone.

        1) As expressive of the strength and power of Christ. Created things are like the sand,—fleeting,—gliding,—uncertain. Christ possesses all power. "All power is given," &c. He gave repeated displays of it on earth. He exerted it on obstinate diseases,—on the furious storm,—on the dead,—and also on devils, &c. "He is able to save to the uttermost," &c.

        2) Expressive of his *firmness* and *durability.* Stone is not like corruptible things, as hay, straw, or stubble. He is a rock—the rock of ages. Nothing can affect him; no change or commotion. Time has worn down the marble column, and undermined the foundations of Babylon and Nineveh, &c.

    2. Living stone

        1) He has life in himself. He is the source of life. All life emanates from him. He is the true and living God. The being in whom we live, &c. All nature lives in him, &c. Especially spiritual life. Only source of spiritual life. "I am the way;" &c.

        2) It denotes the feeling of Christ. He is not insensible. He is not unconscious, &c. No. He feels for *us*—knows our wretchedness,—sees our misery—can hear our groans, &c. He is alive to all the circumstances connected with our state Notice,

II. Men's Rejection of this Stone.

"Disallowed of men." This refers to the Jews. They would not receive him. Denied his *Messiahship,* and despised his miracles. Rejected his doctrines, and put him to death, Matt. 21:42; Acts 4:11.

Why did they reject him? For want or evidence? No. Never man did what he did. He appeared the very person, &c. described in their scriptures, &c. It was pride, producing unbelief, and then malice, &c. He did not appear as they desired. *He* did not *preach* as they *desired. He* did not *promise* as they *desired.* Therefore they would not allow him or approve of him, &c. *But* Christ is still *disallowed* of men,—still of the Jews, Mahomedans, infidels,—still by all *unbelievers,*—lovers of the world. They do not admire his *doctrines,*—are offended at the *sacrifice* he requires, &c.

III. God's respect to this Stone.

1. Chosen of God.

1) Originally selected. Originally selected for the great enterprise. God fixed upon his Son—called him forth, as the only fit personage for the stupendous undertaking.

2) God was pleased with him. He answered his expectations. He told the multitude this at Jordan; the disciples this, at the mount of transfiguration, &c.

3) When he had finished his work, he was accepted of God; he raised him from the dead, &c.

2. Precious.

This also refers to God. He was always precious in his Father's eyes. His eternal delight, &c. But expressly as Mediator.

1) His name was precious. God exalted it above every name, &c.

2) His doctrines. "Hear ye him."

3) His sacrifices. It met all the in finite claims of justice and purity.

4) His person. Hence, he says, "Let all the angels of God worship him," and "Sit thou on my right hand," &c. Observe,

IV. The Sinner's Duty and Interest.

To whom coming. This implies

1. Scriptural knowledge of Christ.

We must know him, as scripturally revealed. Have we proper views of his person and of his work, &c.

2. A feeling sense of our need of Christ.

That we are at a distance, and that as such we are unhappy, unsafe; that we have destroyed ourselves, and in Christ alone is our help.

3. A sincere and hearty approval of Christ.

Receiving his doctrines as the word of life. His blood as the meritorious cause of salvation. Leaving every other source, and trusting all with Christ. "To whom should we go but unto thee," &c.

4. A perpetual resting on and cleaving to Christ.

He is laid as the foundation. We must not only come and see and admire him,—but build on him, cleave to him, and abide on him. "This God is my God," &c. This is the sinner's duty and interest. Christ is the only stone. This the only way to enjoy his benefits.

Application

1. To disallowers. Rejectors of Christ. How foolish. How infatuated. How ruinous, &c. It is to reject pardon, happiness, salvation.

2. To believers. O value this stone. Rest constantly upon it. All here is secure. Secure in time, in death, and forever.

3. To inquirers. Those who are coming to it, we say, be decided, exercise faith in it. Cast all upon it, and live forever.

57. METAPHORICAL REPRESENTATIONS OF THE HOLY SPIRIT

"The supply of the Spirit of Jesus Christ" —Phil. 1:19

IF we are to know anything clearly of Deity, it must be from his word. Especially from the statements and declaration of the only-begotten of the Father, who came to manifest the glory of the Godhead, and to bring life and immortality to light by the gospel. By referring to this we discover the unity of the Godhead, and the spirituality of his nature. But we also have presented to us the personal distinction of Father, Son, and Spirit. The same terms are applied to each, and each is clothed in the glorious attributes of the Godhead. Doubtless this is one of the profound mysteries of our religion. What shall we do,—shall we reject the truths stated, on the ground of mystery? If so we might reject many of the palpable facts connected with nature. Is it not rather then our wisdom to receive the truths of revelation, and to use the phraseology of the scriptures, and not to attempt to explain, and define what God has not defined in his word. Let us at this time attend to the great and interesting theme presented in the text. "The supply of the Spirit of Jesus Christ." We shall,

I. Offer some Remarks on the Holy Spirit.

We notice,

1. The Spirit bears the essential titles of Deity.

He is frequently styled the Spirit of God. "Know ye not that the Spirit of God dwelleth in you." "Grieve not the Spirit of God." By comparing Ex. 34:34, 2 Cor. 3:15-17. And also Ex. 17:7; Heb. 3:7-9. See also Acts 5:1-4.

2. The Spirit is represented as possessing the attributes of Deity.

1) Eternity. "How much more shall the blood of Christ, who through the eternal Spirit offered himself without spot to God, purge your consciences from dead works to serve the living God," Heb. 9:14.

2) Infinity and omnipresence, Psa. 139:7, 8.

3) All knowledge and omniscience. "But God hath revealed them unto us by his Spirit, for the Spirit searcheth all things; yea, the deep things of God. For what man knoweth the things of a man, save the spirit of man, which is in him? even so the things of God knoweth no man, but the Spirit of God," 1 Cor. 2:10, 11.

4) Holiness. "The Spirit of holiness," Rom. 1:4. "Grieve not the Holy Spirit of God," &c.

3. The Spirit is connected with the glorious works of God.

1) In creation. It is said, "the Spirit of God moved upon the face of the waters." It is also said, "God by his Spirit garnished the heavens." See Job 33:4

2) The renovation of the soul, the new creation of man, is the work of the Spirit "Born of the Spirit." "It is the Spirit that quickeneth." That gives liberty. That transforms into the divine likeness. That seals, sanctifies, keeps, &c.

3) The resurrection of the body is to be effected by his power. This is most beautifully and forcibly illustrated in Ezekiel's vision of dry bones. "Then said he unto me, Prophesy unto the wind, prophesy, son of man, and say to the wind, Thus saith the Lord God, Come from the four winds, O breath, and breathe upon these slain, that they may live," Ezek. 37:9. See Rom. 8:11. "But if the Spirit of him that raised up Jesus from the dead, dwell in you, he that raised up Christ from the dead shall also quicken your mortal bodies by his Spirit that dwelleth in you." Observe,

4) Some of the emblems by which the Spirit is presented to our minds in the holy scriptures.

Of these we select the following.

1. He is likened to wind or air. This was the figure used by the Redeemer with Nicodemus. "The wind bloweth where it listeth," &c., John 3:8. So also when it descended on the disciples at the day of Pentecost, there was heard as it were, "a sound from heaven as of a mighty," &c., Acts 2:1, 2. Now this emblem teaches as the invisibility of the Spirit. Its universal pervading presence encircling all things. Its mighty power.

2. He is likened to water. "In the last great day of the feast, Jesus stood up and cried," &c. Hence, in prophecy we read of it being poured out,—of floods,—of streams,—of the wells of salvation. Now this emblem denotes the freeness, the abundance, or plenteousness of the Spirit. It teaches us also its vegetating and refreshing influence. Its cleansing and purifying power.

3. He is likened to fire. So John spoke of the baptism of the Holy Spirit. "I indeed baptize you with water unto repentance," &c., Matt. 2. See Acts 2:3, 4.

And there appeared unto them cloven tongues, like as of fire," &c. Thus "we are not to quench the Holy Spirit," &c. Now this emblem denotes the penetrating nature of the Spirit. Its illuminating power. Its refining influence.

168

4. He is compared to oil. Hence all the passages which speak of its anointing, imply this figure. This includes its softening, healing, comforting, and beautifying influences. Hence, we read in that striking prophecy of Christ, "Wherefore God, thy God, hath anointed thee with the oil of gladness above thy fellows," Psa. 45:7

II. The characteristic Appellation by which the Spirit is presented to us in the Text.

"Spirit of Jesus Christ."

1. The Spirit which was essentially connected with his person and work

1) His conception was by the Spirit.

2) He was anointed with it at his baptism. The visible emblem of the dove descending, &c. It rested in all its fulness, and was not given by measure unto him.

3) He did all his works by it. In its fulness he went forth to preach, to suffer, to work miracles, &c. See Heb. 9:14. "Who through the eternal Spirit offered himself," &c.

4) It raised him from the dead, Rom 8:11.

2. The Spirit which he obtained for his church.

"And when he is come, he will reprove," &c., John 16:8. "But. the Comforter, which is the Holy Spirit, whom the Father will send," &c., John 14:26.

3. The Spirit which Christ confers on all believers.

All things are in Christ's hands. "He hath ascended on high," &c. Hence the Spirit, in all his saving influences, he sheds down upon his believing people. Faith in Christ only can realize his blessed operations.

Application

1. How desirable to have clear views of the Spirit of God.

2. How necessary to fear and reverence before him.

3. How anxious we should be to be filled with his influences.

4. How may we obtain them? "If ye being evil," &c.

58. THE CHURCH OF CHRIST A FLOCK

"The flock of God." —1 Pet. 5:2.

THE text is found in the midst of an exhortation given by the apostle Peter to the bishops and elders who had been appointed to the oversight of the churches of Christ. As such the apostle urges upon them to "feed the flock of God," and to take the pastoral care without constraint, "willingly; not for filthy lucre, but of a ready mind." The figure employed by the apostle, in reference to Christian pastors, is that of a shepherd, and in the fourth verse he announces the delightful promise, that when the chief, or great shepherd shall appear, they shall receive the crown of glory that does not fade. Let us then consider the church under the metaphorical representation of a flock. The primary idea is that of believers as sheep. Christ thus speaks of them as his sheep, and of himself as their good shepherd. In their collective capacity they are a flock.

I. Notice the Flock itself.

It is composed of all renewed, converted persons. It supposes they have been brought from their wanderings on the mountains of sin, to the pastoral care of Jesus, the shepherd and bishop of souls, 1 Pet. 2:25; Isa. 53. Believers only are the sheep of Christ. Those who have been brought nigh to him by saving grace and the power of his truth. Docility, meekness, and usefulness, are the invariable characteristics of those who belong to the flock of Christ. Among these are young converts, mature believers, and saints, who have borne fruit even to old age.

II. The Flock of God have one chief Shepherd.

Redeemed by his precious blood they are the especial property of Christ. He laid down his life for them. They are given to him as his seed, and reward. They form the joy of his heart. He loves them with inexpressible tenderness and affection. He watches over them with constant solicitude. He never leaves nor forsakes them. He provides them with under-shepherds, men whom he qualifies and appoints to feed them with spiritual knowledge and understanding. But these are all subordinate to Jesus who is the great shepherd of the sheep, and head over all things to his church.

III. The Flock of God have rich and verdant Pastures

Thus the psalmist sang, "He leadeth me into green pastures," &c. There are the pastures of his holy word. And the pastures of his refreshing ordinances. In these they are amply provided with necessary provision. Here they enjoy the adapted, rich, and overflowing blessings of heavenly grace. Here they have food and enjoyments of which the world know nothing. And these pastures are ever fresh and green. Made verdant by the copious showers of holy influences, and through which ever flow the waters of the river of life. To these all the flock have constant access. Here they lie down and rest in safety.

IV. The Flock of God have one Fold in Heaven.

Here they are one in nature, all renewed and partakers of the divine nature. One in spirit,—one in union with Jesus,—one in the privileges and blessings of salvation. But they are scattered over the face of the earth. Dwelling remotely from each other. Have lived too in various ages of the world. Been partially separated by language, denominational distinctions, &c., &c. But there is one great and blessed fold for the flock of God. One celestial Eden, one heavenly paradise. It will be their unspeakable privilege to be with their divine shepherd, and dwell in perfect unity and delight on the glorious plains of light forever and ever.

Application

1. A variety of duties devolve upon the flock of God. Submission to the authority of the great Shepherd. Cultivation of docility, meekness, and love. Affectionate attachment to everyone belonging to Christ's spiritual flock. Supreme regard for the honor of Jesus, and the prosperity of his cause in the earth.

2. A variety of blessings their present portion. An interest in the rich covenant of divine love. A gracious right to the riches of heavenly grace. Exceedingly great and precious promises. The holy comforting influences of the Spirit of God The sweet joys of Christian fellowship Invulnerable protection and security from all their enemies, and every possible peril.

3. Urge wandering sinners to listen, and obey the voice of the compassionate Jesus and live.

4. How wretched and miserable are those who have forsaken Christ. O return that he may heal your backslidings, &c.

59. THE CHURCH A HABITATION FOR GOD

"An habitation of God through the Spirit." —Eph. 2:22.

GOD in a variety of forms expresses his complacent regards and delights in his church. He loves the church with the devotedness which a mother feels to her only son. He values it as his peculiar treasure, and as such he exercises his care constantly for its preservation. He maketh his church his especial dwelling, and fixes his gracious residence within it. He has chosen it for his hallowed rest, and there he has said, his eyes and his heart shall be continually. As such the apostle represents the church of Christ in our text. It is a building fitly framed and united together. For "an habitation of God through the Spirit."

I. As a Building it has a strong and immoveable Foundation.

That foundation is the Lord Jesus Christ. A foundation "elect," "precious." A foundation stronger than the pillars of heaven, against which the gates of hell can never prevail. On Jesus all the interests of the church rest. He sustains the whole weight of the massive structure, and upholds all by the word of his power. From this foundation we may conclude as to the strength, immoveableness, and perpetuity of the building itself, 1 Cor. 3:11, &c.

II. As a Building it is formed of various and many Materials.

These materials were originally unfit, and in their natural state adapted only to the purposes of the wicked one. Divine truth and grace brought them out of the quarry of nature; gave them their suitable shape and character; chiseled them, and gave them polish and fitness for this spiritual erection. And this applies to all the materials. For in the true and spiritual church of Christ, there are none but real converts, those who have become spiritual persons. Of these there is great diversity of character, and condition, and extent of intellectual and moral worth. The number of these is only known to God, as they are scattered in all Christian congregations over the face of the whole earth, and have been added to this holy structure in every age of the history of our world.

III. This Building includes the Union of these Materials with each other.

"Fitly framed together." "Builded together. Hence the term church signifies congregated persons. Persons united and associated with each other. Grace unites men to God, and also the good and excellent together. Those who believed on the day of Pentecost "were together." In this way the *safety* of all is contemplated. Separated, they would indeed be feeble; united, they are as a wall of adamant. In this way the *comfort* of all is promoted. The social feelings are sanctified and cherished, and they feel that many are better and happier than one alone. In this way the *usefulness* of all is increased. In serving Christ we are also to serve one another. The foot and the hand both serve the body, and also each other. In this way the *welfare* and *prosperity* of all are advanced. Christian virtues are exercised, Christian graces cherished, Christian feelings excited, and Christian prosperity thus very materially extended. The church, as a building, unites the holy to God and to one another.

IV. As a Building it is devoted to the most hallowed and glorious Purpose.

"A habitation for God." What a sublime thought! God dwells in the highest heaven. The heaven of heavens cannot contain him. His presence fills the universe. He is everywhere by the immensity of his omnipresent Spirit. Yet he dwells in the midst of his church, as its glory and blessedness.

"He makes the churches his abode,
His most delightful seat."

Here he sanctifies unto himself a palace. Here he has a glorious high throne of holiness. Here he holds audience, and scatters amply around the blessings of his grace. Here makes the place of his feet glorious. Here has the attendance of his holy angels, those ministers of his who do his pleasure. Here he manifests himself as he doth not unto the world.

V. This Building is erected and prepared as an Habitation for God through the Spirit.

The Holy Spirit of God is the efficient agent in all the gracious change effected in the souls of believers, and by which they are sanctified to the hallowed service of God. The Spirit of God illumines the soul and fits it to be a palace of holy light. The Spirit purifies the soul and fits it for the enthronement of the immaculate Deity The Holy Spirit furnishes the soul with all those graces and qualities, by which it secures the approbation and complacent smiles of the divine countenance. Through the Spirit the means of the church of Christ are blest to the real growth and welfare of its members. The Spirit counteracts and overthrows the Satanic powers, which would overwhelm the believer, or, if possible, raze the kingdom of Christ. "When the enemy comes in like a flood," &c.

All that purity with which the church is beautified, and is rendered meet for the residence of Jehovah, is through the Spirit. Of the church as the habitation for God we notice,

1. It is the habitation of his choice.

He fixed his delights upon it, and chose it as his residence on earth. He passes by the palaces of the great and the mansions of the noble, and dwells with his afflicted and persecuted saints.

2. It is the habitation of his love.

173

How much he loves what seraph can tell? Let the amazing gift of his Son, and the scenes of Gethsemane and Calvary, declare it. Let the history of providence attest his unchanging regards towards it.

3. It is the habitation of his care.

He ever watches over it. He keeps it continually. His everlasting arms encompass it. His angels minister to it. All his perfections are pledged for its security.

4. It is distinguished for its antiquity.

It has been God's habitation for nearly six thousand years.

5. For its vast extent.

It is now so enlarged as to embrace many lands, and shall ultimately reach from the rivers to the ends of the earth—be the glory and joy of the whole world.

Application

1. Do we form a part of this holy structure?

2. Does the God of love dwell within us, and reign over us?

3. What sacredness, what purity, what dignity, is associated with this representation of the church.

4. With what wisdom, veneration, and lowliness of mind, should every member of the church be clothed.

60. THE CHURCH THE GARDEN OF THE LORD

"As a watered garden." —Jer. 31:12.

THE world is a dreary, sterile wilderness. Here nothing spiritual and holy thrives or flourishes. Under the curse, it yields briers, and thorns, and noxious weeds. Sin blighted the moral creation of God, and turned the Eden of the Lord into a barren desert. Through the intervention of divine mercy, God has set on foot a scheme of merciful renovation. He has sent down the riches of his grace, that earth might again become the paradise of holiness and bliss. His kingdom set up in the world, is the separation to himself of the called and regenerated children of men. United in the fellowship of the gospel, they constitute his spiritual church, and appeal in our wilderness world as the "watered garden" of the Lord.

I. As a Garden the Church is separated from the World.

Originally like the waste, howling wilderness; now distinct and separated, called out of the world as to spirit and character. The church is in the world, but not of it Not like it. Separated by a prominent line of demarcation. This separation is to be manifest, as unlike the world as the garden is unlike the barren heath.

II. As a Garden the Church is surrounded by a protective Fence.

Otherwise it would be a prey to wild beasts. It would be a thoroughfare for every rude foot. It would become a waste, a desolation. The church of Christ is fenced round, as with a wall of adamant. God is its keeper and defense. He is round about in the energy of his omnific power, and by the omnipresence of his irresistible Spirit. "As the mountains are round about Jerusalem," &c., Psa. 125:2.

III. As a Garden the Church is in a state of Cultivation and Improvement.

The association of believers as the church of Christ, is for their edification and advancement in knowledge and holiness. Besides, the church itself under every dispensation is in a state of progress until it shall reach millennial glory and perfection. For the church's cultivation he sends his word, his messengers, and the benign influences of his benevolent providential administrations.

IV. As a Garden it is distinguished by its Trees and Plants.

The good man is likened to a lofty cedar, the useful olive, the fruitful vine, the fragrant myrtle, the thriving willow, the refreshing pomegranate, &c. Believers may be compared to beautiful flowers. Adorned with the graces of the Spirit, they are indeed flowers of loveliness pleasing and acceptable to God, and ornamental to the world in which they live. These plants are said to be the Lord's planting, Matt. 15:13. To be planted in the house of the Lord, &c. Psa. 92:12-14.

175

V. As a Garden it is richly watered by the Blessings of Heaven.

Water is indispensable to fertility and growth. Without, nature is scorched up, and vegetation languishes. The Spirit of God is often presented to us under this figure. Isaiah prophesied that in the wilderness "waters should break out," &c., ch. 35:6, 7. So Jesus in the last great day of the feast "stood up and cried," &c., John 7:37. See also Isaiah 44:3, 60:1; and in reference to his vineyard the Lord says, "I will water it every moment," &c., Isa. 27:3. These holy and spiritual communications are essential to our comfort, well-being, fruitfulness, &c. They keep the garden of the Lord ever verdant, and produce from the trees of the Lord an abundant increase.

VI. As a Garden the Lord expects a Return of Fruit from it.

All the labor and outlay of God's goodness is to produce to the glory of his name the fruits of holiness. He expects holy graces to be manifested. Holy virtues to be exercised. A holy Spirit to be displayed. Holy conversation to be exemplified. That spiritual fruitfulness which will render fit for transplanting to the pure and blissful regions of the Eden above. And how reasonable is this expectation. And how important to us. Let us inquire if we render to the Lord the fruits of righteousness, and show forth his praises who hath called us out of darkness, &c.

Application

1. Do we form a part of the Lord's garden?

2. Are we the plants of his right-hand planting?

3 Are we flourishing? Retaining our verdure, growing as the fir-tree or the cedar. Yielding fruit to God.

4. The impenitent wicked, as briers and thorns, he will consume in the day of his fiery indignation.

61. CHRISTIAN CHURCHES LIKENED TO GOLDEN CANDLESTICKS

"I saw seven golden candlesticks." —Rev. 1:12.

OUR text relates to the visions of Patmos. Here the servant of God was shown wonderful things in reference to the kingdom and reign of Jesus. He was allowed to see through the vista of succeeding generations, until he beheld the termination of time, the conflagration of the earth, the erection of the judgment, and the everlasting destiny of the universal family of man. Thus was the banishment of God's servant to a dreary island overruled for the glory of God, and for affording those revelations by which the canon of the scriptures should be completed. It appears that the things which were first presented to the mind of John, were the seven Asiatic churches, unto whom the mind of the Spirit and the word of God were to be first sent. The representation under which these churches were brought before him was that of a golden candlestick, having seven branches, in the midst of which appeared the "Son of man, clothed with a garment down to the foot," &c. This representation equally applies to all the churches of the Savior throughout the world. The seven candlesticks would doubtless be better rendered lamps; but the spirit and signification of the metaphor is in both cases the same. Observe, then,

I. The Metaphor employed.

"A candlestick." That is, an instrument of light. That by which light is lifted up and made manifest. "Ye are the light of the world." "A city set upon a hill," &c. Every Christian church is elevated above the world to give light to it To shine forth," &c. "Holding forth he word of life," &c. Now the church of Christ is to diffuse abroad,

1. The light of knowledge.

They know the truth, and have it richly deposited with them. Pillar and ground of truth. Gospel of light is with them, &c. And herein they know God, and his holy and blessed will, and Jesus Christ the blessed mediator whom he hath sent, and this light of the knowledge of the glory of God they are to diffuse abroad, even to the ends of the earth.

2. The light of holiness.

That which is the opposite of the darkness of depravity and sin. The light of the divine image. "The glory of the Lord hath risen," &c. The light of the new moral creation, &c.

3. The light of benevolence.

Darkness is the fit emblem of the vicious and malevolent. Light the emblem of goodness. God is love. And this love is the distinguishing feature of renewed minds, and of his sanctified church. This good will is to be prominent and distinctly evidenced towards all men, but especially to the household of faith.

Thus the church is to shine forth in truth, in beauty, and goodness. And this they are to do in their individual character, each one as the servant of God. And in their collective character all united in effort to show forth his praises and to advance the divine glory in the world. The church is to do this,

1) By maintaining the ordinances of the gospel in their purity.—Word, baptism, Lord's supper, &c.

2) By enforcing spiritual discipline and order.

3) By vigorous exertions to extend the Kingdom of Jesus. Observe,

II. The Material of which it is composed.

"Gold." A golden candlestick. Indicating,

1. The purity of the church.

Formed of the most holy and excellent materials.

2. The splendor of the church.

Arrayed in moral beauty, in spiritual splendor. "All glorious within." "Beauty of the Lord upon them," &c. "Changed into the same glory," &c.

3. The preciousness of the church.

Intrinsically valuable. The purchase of precious blood, &c. Compared to Jehovah's diadem. His jewels. His treasures His delight.

4. The perpetuity of the church.

Durable. Not corruptible or evanescent Firm, abiding, in all countries, ages, &c. Unconsumed in fire, purified in flames and preserved always. Notice,

III. The Source of its Light and Splendor.

The Son of man in the midst. What a sublime and glorious description is presented of him. His eternity—"Hairs white." &c. His purity—sacerdotal "garment," &c. His knowledge—"His eyes like a flame," &c. His strength and power—"Feet as brass," &c. His sublime majesty—"His voice as the sound of many waters," &c. His station is in the midst of his churches. Accessible to all. Near to all. The glory of all.

1. He is the source of the church knowledge.

The truth. The light. The depository of all wisdom.

2. Of her purity.

His blood, righteousness, Spirit.

3. Of her benevolence.

His love imparted produces it. It if his love, operative, constraining, &c.

4. Of her perpetuity.

Because he is in the midst she is not destroyed. He lives, and *therefore* his church lives also. He is the Alpha and Omega of the church, its glory, and all in all.

Application

1. How differently God and the world estimate the church. To one the object of scorn and contempt, to the other glorious and exalted.

2. The true design of Christ. To give light. To shine. To show forth the glory of God.

3. What will be its splendor and magnificence in heaven.

4. If the omniscient Jesus is in the midst, how holy and spiritually minded should his members be.

62. CHRIST'S CHURCH A FAMILY

"The whole family in heaven and earth." —Eph. 3:15.

IT is the very nature of sin to di vide and to destroy. Sin sowed the seeds of anarchy and rebellion in heaven, and thus separated the sinning angels from those who retained their original holiness and glory. Sin separated the first of our race from God, and expelled the transgressors from the peaceful abode of the earthly paradise. Sin separated the hearts of the first brethren, and having filled the breast of Cain with hate and envy, caused him to slay his brother. From that period to the present, sin has been separating men from God, and from each other. Religion is designed to counteract this evil, malevolent work of sin. It brings together, reconciles, unites in bonds of amity and love. It reconciles earth and heaven, man and God, and man with man. It has one anthem which it sings, "Glory to God in the highest, and peace on earth," &c. Our subject leads us to contemplate one scene wherein this is exhibited, and that is in the church below, which is likened in the text to one family. "The whole family in earth." Let us consider,

I. Who constitute the Divine Family on Earth.

Now it appears that there is one text that clearly settles this point,—John 1:12.

1. Faith then is the first evidence.

"For we are all the children of God by faith," Gal. 3:26.

2. Regeneration is the second evidence.

"To as many as received him he gave power," &c. "Blessed be the God and Father," &c. "Except a man be born again," &c. "If any man be in Christ," &c.

3. Obedience is a third evidence.

"For as many as are led by the Spirit of God," &c. "For whosoever shall do the will of God, the same is my brother, and sister, and mother."

4. Love is the fourth evidence.

"We know that we have passed," &c. "Everyone that loveth is born of God," &c., 1 John 3:16.

These are essential evidences, nothing can make up for the want of these, and they will always go together. We shall see then that this family may include,

1. Persons of all countries.

2. Of different parties and sects.

3. Of various creeds.

4. Of all classes, rich and poor, learned and illiterate. Diversity of opinions seem the necessary result of the present state of things. Such as, (i.) Different grades of mental powers, (ii.) Different amount of knowledge, (iii.) Different mode of education, (iv.) Different media of receiving our ideas and religious impressions.

II. That which forms the Bond of Unity so as to constitute Believers one Family.

1. They have one common Father, 5:14.

In prayer they all address the same Being, and by the same appellation, "Father"—"Our," not mine merely.

2. They have one common nature.

This does not render absolute likeness necessary any more than the resemblance of all of the same species. New nature The spiritual principle—that which is from heaven—heavenly.

3. They have one common Savior.

Jesus Christ. "No other name given," &c. His merits only avail. He is the sacrifice. The one intercessor. One mediator, &c., 1 Tim. 2:3-6, and iv. 10.

4. They have one common spirit.

There is only one spirit to dwell in them to guide—cheer—comfort—sanctify, &c.

5. They have one common revelation.

The scriptures are the gift of Christ to his church. As such they are common property. Belong to all, both ministers and people. They have each and all a right to read, and study, and judge for themselves. All the same right of appeal "To the law," &c.

6. They have one common treasury.

The inexhaustible mine of the precious promises; every promise is the common portion of every child of God.

7. They have one common home.

All sailing to the same haven. All bound for the same Canaan. Hence Christ said, "They shall come from the east," &c., Rev. 7:9.

But this would encroach on the other part of the text.

Application

1. In contemplating the whole family of God upon earth we are called to mourn over its imperfections, and its divisions, yet it is clear it will only be in the millennial state of things when these will be removed.

2. We learn the great necessity of Christian forbearance and love. This does not imply indifference to any truth, or that we shut our eyes against error. But let us always distinguish between the person. and the error. And let us rejoice with men for the truth they hold, and always be found speaking the truth in love.

3. Mutual kindness and sympathy should distinguish the same family, "Love as brethren," &c. "Bear ye one another's burdens," &c.

4. Let it lead us to personal examination. Are we members of this family, &c.

63. BELIEVERS SERVANTS OF GOD

"Become servants to God." —Rom. 6:22.

THE apostle is contrasting the believer's past with his present condition. Once, he reminds the converted Romans, they were strangers to righteousness and the servants of sin. A state of debasement, and of the fruit of which they were now sincerely ashamed. A state too, which would have terminated in death: "For the end of those things is death." But by the saving grace of God they had been emancipated from sin and its degrading vassalage, and were now "become the servants of God." What kind of service is that which the Christian yields to God?

I. It is voluntary Service.

In the day when sin is abandoned, and the gospel of salvation is cordially embraced, the soul, and heart, and mind, are yielded to God. As a living sacrifice they lay themselves on God's holy altar. They cheerfully devote themselves to the service and glory of God. God has displayed his willingness to engage us in his service by removing every impediment out of the way; by redeeming us from the curse of the law and the dominion of the devil; by sending us his gracious and tender invitations full of mercy and compassion; by tendering to us the richest promises in entering on his holy service. To these by cordial faith the believer assents, and freely engages to serve the Lord Christ. As it begins voluntarily, so also is it thus continued. Nothing else would please God. Nothing else would indicate a state of grace, or evidence the love of God shed abroad in the soul.

II. It is comprehensive Service.

As comprehensive as the revealed will of God. A service which includes the supreme love and veneration of God; the constant exercise of the devotional services of the heart; an unwavering regard to the glory of God in all things; personal advancement in knowledge and true holiness; a scriptural regard to the relative duties of life; a fervent employment of all our powers, talents, and means for the prosperity of Zion, and the diffusion of the gospel of Christ. In one word, seeking the honor and approbation of God in all things—"Living to the Lord"—embodying his commandments in our hearts and lives, and laboring to do "whatsoever he has commanded."

III. It is arduous Service.

Requiring the giving up to it the whole soul. Cannot be performed acceptably in a listless, supine state of mind. A service which calls for incessant zeal, for continuous fervor. A service involving life, energy, and resolution. It is arduous because of the internal dislike which the natural man has to it,—because of the temptations by which it is assailed,—because of the crosses and trials often connected with it. And,

IV. It is highly responsible Service.

For which an account will be demanded, and which must be given. He says, "Occupy" this sphere "until I come." He giveth talents and opportunities, &c., and will return and reckon with his servants This responsibility is personal,—solemn, and connected with consequences most momentous and everlasting. Glory, honor, bliss, and immortality, to those who do well. Shame, misery, and ruin, to those who are unfaithful and do evil. Yet,

V. It is delightful Service.

"Her ways are ways of pleasantness." There is nothing grievous to the rightly regulated mind in all the commandments or ordinances of the Lord.

On the other hand, the service of the Lord is connected,

> 1. With intellectual dignity.

> It includes a sound mind. It is the glory of reason to be employed for God. It elevates all the powers of the soul. Expands the feelings of the heart, and capacitates the imagination for the loftiest and most sublime contemplations. To serve God is the glory of angels, the highest dignity of cherubim and seraphim. It gives to the soul both intellectual and moral elevation

> 2. With real enjoyment.

> The enjoyment of a pacific conscience towards God. The enjoyment of inward heavenly peace. The enjoyment of God's gracious smile. The enjoyment of the Holy Spirit, as the earnest or pledge of the future inheritance. The possession of a good hope, and joy unspeakable and full of glory.

> 3 With great profit.

> Service of God is profitable to all things. To body and mind. To ourselves and others. To the life that now is, and that which is to come. The profit is real,—great,—invaluable,— and everlasting.

VI. It is a Service which will be gloriously recompensed.

Beyond mere right. Not according to our imperfect part, and almost valueless services, but according to the exceeding riches of the goodness and grace of God. There will be dominion, triumph, joy, a crown, a throne, and a kingdom. Honor, riches, and glory. Exalted dignity and eternal life. What a reward! How vast and inconceivably glorious. How infinitely transcending all our desires and thoughts. Worthy of boundless love and immeasurable grace

Application

1. On the servants of God we urge great lowliness of mind. Watchfulness. Diligence and perseverance. "Be faithful unto death."

2. To the servants of God we present the promises of sufficient grace here, and eternal life in the world to come.

3. We invite the servants of sin to forsake the work of evil and death, and to take Christ's yoke, &c.

4. The day of reckoning for all is at hand.

64. SAINTS PILGRIMS ON THE EARTH

"And pilgrims on the earth." —Heb. 11:13.

THE text relates to believers of Old Testament times, to whose history the apostle had been referring in the previous verses. He had spoken of Abel the first martyr. Of Enoch who was translated and did not see death. Of Noah who built the ark for the saving of his house. Of Abraham who went out, not knowing whither he went. Of Isaac and Jacob, heirs with him of the same promise. He then gives the delightful summary, "These all died in faith, not having received the promises, but having seen them afar off and were persuaded of them, and embraced them, and confessed that they were strangers and pilgrims on the earth." But equally true is it of all the people of God in every age of the world. This state is the house of the godly man's pilgrimage. To us then do the words equally refer. Let us ascertain,

I. What is included in the Metaphor.

A pilgrim is one without a fixed habitation, and who is journeying through a strange and foreign land. See verses 14, 15.

1. The pilgrim's original home was in the city of destruction.

In this he was born and educated. Here he lived and dwelt. Here he followed the carnal employments of the citizens. In this state he was far from God. Far from peace. Far from safety. He was an alien without God, without Christ, without hope. A child of wrath even as others.

2. His pilgrimage commenced through the influence of the gospel on his heart.

The truth came unto him. His misery and peril were depicted. His condition of ruin was declared. Escape and instant flight were urged upon him. A better land was revealed. Gospel salvation, including present rest and future glory, were published. Receiving the truth of the gospel, he abandoned the city of guilt and death, and fled for refuge to the hope set before him.

3. By faith in Gods testimony he set his face towards the heavenly Zion.

He believed God, and therefore set his heart to seek

"A city out of sight,
A city in the skies."

A city whose builder and founder is God. The city of the new and heavenly Jerusalem. The inheritance of light.

4. As a pilgrim he claims no possession in the country through which he passes.

His good is not here. His affections are placed on high. He lays not up treasures on the earth. He considers all around him as mutable, and therefore he buys as through he bought not, rejoices as though he rejoiced not &c. He considers the world as the desert in the way to Canaan,—the sea over which he crosses to the shores of glory. His treasure is in heaven, and his heart is there also.

5. As a pilgrim he travels onward towards the city of habitation.

He goes from stage to stage From experience to experience. From faith to faith. From dawn to day. From infancy to mature years, and on to old age. He advances in knowledge, love, obedience, and holiness, and thus increases in heavenly mindedness, and fitness for the society and services of the celestial Jerusalem. Genuine religion is progressive—deepening, expanding, and persevering to the end. Consider,

II. The Qualifications and Duties involved in it.

1. A pilgrim's heart.

And that is a renewed heart. One delivered from the love of sin and the world. A new heart. Heavenly nature. One under spiritual attractions, and moved by spiritual influences. Of all qualifications this is first and chief. A man must be born from above, before he will live for it, and seek it.

2. A pilgrim's head.

A knowledge of his way. Of the good old way. The way revealed in the holy scriptures. A way written in the luminous words of God. A way trodden by all preceding pilgrims journeying to Zion. Without a clear and full knowledge of this, all would be dubious and perplexed.

3. A pilgrim's spirit.

The spirit which has animated every child of God.

    1) Of devotion and direct intercourse with God.

    2) Of praise: singing his statutes, and rejoicing in his grace.

    3) Of self-denial: sacrificing self, and Submitting fully to the will of God

4) Of faith and hope: believing and trusting in the truth and goodness of the promises of God.

5) Of vigilance to watch against enemies and perils.

6) Of perseverance: holding on his way.

4. A pilgrim's resources.

These are generally of a very humble character. No chariot, or retinue, or luxuries. No ease, or rest, or worldly pleasures. But he must have

1) His *staff* on which to lean. And this is the pledged promise of God, that his own presence shall go with him, and never, never leave him.

2) His provision. Bread and water given him from heaven. The true manna and the streams of salvation. "If any man thirst," "Lord, evermore give us," &c.

3) His houses of entertainment. Places where he can be welcomed to the hospitable board, and chamber of repose. These are the ordinances of religion, and the various social and private means of grace. "The Lord is my shepherd," &c.

4) Suitable raiment, and especially sandals for his journey. "Thy shoes shall be iron and brass," &c. "Feet shod," &c.

Application

1. How really happy is the Christian pilgrim. His sorrows and crosses will soon be over, and that forever. His present comforts and blessings are rich and numerous.

2. How glorious the end of his journey. The heavenly Jerusalem. The city of God. World of light, and life, and glory.

3. Urge sinners to set out on this spiritual pilgrimage.

65. THE CHRISTIAN SOLDIER

"A good soldier." —2 Tim. 2:3

THE text is equally applicable to the private Christian, as to the apostle or bishop of Jesus Christ. All disciples are alike engaged in spiritual warfare. All are called to fight the good fight of faith, and to endure hardness as good soldiers of Christ Jesus. Martial language is often applied to the servants of God. And true religion involves in it a necessary and continued conflict with sin and the powers of hell. Observe,

I. The Christian Soldier becomes such by a voluntary Enlistment into the Army of Jesus.

He abandons his former course, and freely and cheerfully surrenders himself by faith to God. He ceases to be an enemy, which he was in his carnal state in the enmity of his mind. He has felt the evil of opposing the counsel and authority of God. He has been convinced of the folly and infatuated wickedness of fighting against God, and now he accepts of God's gracious offer, and voluntarily engages to war against all evil, and to devote himself fully and forever to the service of the Lord.

II. The Christian Soldier is clothed in the Armor of Salvation.

This is fully described by the apostle, Eph. 6:13.

> 1. It will be seen that the loins are to be girt with truth.

> 2. The breastplate is to be righteousness.

> 3. The shoes or sandals, the preparation of the gospel of peace. Then there is,

> 4. The shield of faith.

> 5. The helmet of hope. And the offensive weapon is,

> 6. The sword of the Spirit, which is the word of God. The whole of this armor is to be used in connection with the spirit of incessant prayer. For the apostle adds, "Praying always," &c. Now this is the authorized legitimate armor to the preclusion of all other. No other will secure us from evil, or give us victory over the enemy.

III. The Christian Soldier fights under the Standard of the Cross.

The cross is that which is the center of attraction to all the soldiers of Jesus. This is that by which the conquests of the Savior are effected, and his spiritual dominions enlarged. This is the power and wisdom of God to the pulling down of the strongholds of sin; and this is the object of glorying to all the disciples of Christ, "God forbid that I should glory," &c.

IV. The Christian Soldier is commanded by Jesus, the Captain of Salvation.

Christ is emphatically styled the "Captain of their salvation," Heb. 2:10. He has gone before his followers, and overcome in their nature all our foes, and was made perfect through suffering. He leads and commands all the spiritual army of God. He was beheld by John as seated on a white horse, having a bow and crown given unto him, and going forth conquering and to conquer, Rev. 6:2. As their captain, Jesus possesses every qualification to encourage his troops, and to head them in all their conflicts, until they have finished their course, and "fought the good fight."

He has given express orders, and specific directions, for infallibly ensuring success to all who fight under his banner He is their captain and commander to the exclusion of every other. He is infinitely wise,—undauntedly courageous,—invincibly strong,—compassionately tender,—inviolably faithful,—and ever victorious.

V. The Christian Soldier has to wage War with many Enemies.

He has to wrestle with flesh and blood; to overcome the evils of his own nature—the unsubdued corruptions of his own heart. Within are fears, and doubts, and unbelief, much ignorance, self, pride, &c. These must be subdued. All slain. Flesh mortified. Spirit have the ascendency and reign. There are also *foes without,*—the *world,* in all its evils and opposition to God. With these are leagued the *powers of hell,*—Satan and the legions of darkness With these enemies there is manifest kindredness and combination. United they are formidable and dangerous. To wage uncompromising war, and overcome them, is the duty and end contemplated by the soldier of Christ. After all, for the Christian's encouragement, they are represented as being subject to God's controlling power, finite, of limited means of evil, and have, in myriads of instances, been triumphantly vanquished by the soldiers of Christ.

VI. The Christian Soldier must Fight and be faithful unto death.

His campaigns will extend through life, and the last enemy he must conflict is death. His martial toils must be patiently and meekly borne, and his defensive and offensive fighting maintained, until he tramples on the neck of the king of terrors, and exclaims, "Thanks be to God, who giveth me the victory," &c.

VII. The Christian Soldier shall receive a Glorious and Eternal Reward.

Having suffered with Christ, they shall be "glorified together," Rom. 8:17. Having overcome they shall have dominion, Rev. 2:26; be clothed in white raiment, Rev. 3:5; sit with Christ on his throne, Rev. 3:21; eat the hidden manna, Rev. 2:17; and receive from Christ's hands the crown of eternal life, Rev. 2:10.

Application

1. Let the soldier of Christ rejoice in the sources of comfort, provision and victory, which are presented to him in the word of God. How necessary that he keep his armor bright. That he be vigilant; zealous; devoted to God; valiant in spirit. That he cleave closely to Jesus; obey his commands, and tread in his steps.

2. Urge the thoughtless sinner to cease his rebellion, sue for mercy, and obtain a place and name in the army of Christ.

3 How certain the destruction of the enemies of Christ.

66. BELIEVERS SPIRITUAL MERCHANTS

"For the merchandise of it is better than the merchandise of silver, and the gain thereof, than fine gold." —Prov. 3:14.

GOD often addresses men in his word under the character of buyers, and offers a variety of things unto them for their purchase. By the prophet Isaiah, he says, "Ho every one that thirsteth, come ye to the waters; and he that hath no money; come ye, buy, and eat," &c., Isa. 55:1. He urges that "we buy the truth, and sell it not," &c. And shows the value of his blessings by comparing them to treasure hidden in a field, which a man possesses by selling all things that he had. Solomon represents the whole course of wisdom as one of merchandise, wherein it is better than the merchandise of silver, &c. Notice,

I. The Propriety of the Comparison.

The godly man is like unto a merchant. The calling of a merchant is,

1. Honorable.

Some of the most distinguished persons in the world have been merchants. A man who may happen to possess wealth, and lives in indolent luxury, is a contemptible character, in the eyes of mankind, compared with the enterprising merchant. The Christian is a dignified character. His calling is one honorable to his judgment, and spirit, and character. It is a course vindicated by wisdom, and which enjoys the especial approbation of God.

2. It is a calling of activity.

It involves the employment of energies, and the constant use of means for improving opportunities which may present themselves, &c. Much of the success depends on the measure of activity which is devoted. &c. So with the Christian merchant, his energies and means must be diligently and actively laid out. Fervent in spirit. Glowing with zeal. Giving all diligence, &c.

3. It is a calling of risk.

The merchant is liable to losses. His property is exposed to the contingencies of sea, and thieves, and fire, &c., &c. A merchant therefore must be vigilant, and employ great prudential care. Such also is the state of the Christian. He is the subject of numerous enemies. He is liable to many contingencies, therefore he must watch, and be vigilant, knowing that his adversary, &c. The apostle speaks of some who had made shipwreck, &c. "Hold fast that which thou hast," &c. Generally,

192

4. It is a calling of great profit.

The prudent, diligent merchant often greatly increases his wealth, &c. The diligent hand makes one rich. Godliness is profitable for all things, &c. It is profitable to body and soul. For time and eternity. Then observe,

II. The Way in which the Christian Merchant should conduct his Affairs.

1. To trade in proper commodities.

He must buy those things which are lawful, necessary, and useful. Of these there are 1. Food. Heavenly manna, the milk and wine of the divine word. 2. Raiment. The white linen, which is the righteousness of the saints. 3. Medicine. Spiritual eye salve, Gilead's balm, &c. 4. Riches. Fine gold, and the holy ornaments of the graces of the Spirit. The wise merchant will not expend his money in that which is not bread, or that which does not satisfy.

2. He must be prompt and regular in his engagements.

This will be the basis of his reputation, which will be essential to his prosperity. He must draw daily on the bank of heaven by fervent prayer, and honor all God's goodness by sincere and hearty thanks giving. In all his concerns with God and mankind "He must do justly, love mercy," &c.

3. He must avoid speculations.

How many thousands have been thus ruined. The success of the few is the exception rather than he rule. Now the Christian merchant must be content to pursue the old path, the good way, and avoid a spirit of novelty and change Religion, as God's work, admits of no improvement, and allows of no alteration or addition. Religious speculators of all men are most miserable.

4. He must constantly act so as to secure the patronage of the court of heaven.

All his means, and stock, and privileges are from above. He is a trading citizen of Zion. He sails under the flag royal of heaven. And this patronage is essential to his prosperity and success. God will order all things for him. He will bring all the ways committed to him to pass. His smile will ensure happy results, &c. Then he must do all, so as to honor God and show forth his praise.

III. The Superior Advantages which this Merchandise yields.

"For the merchandise is better," &c. Now the advantages of the spiritual merchant over those who trade in earthly treasures is manifest,

1. From the intrinsic worth of the commodities in which he trades.

He trades in spiritual things, adapted to the mind; necessary to the soul; suited to the powers and capacities of spiritual intelligences. Gold and silver are worthless here. The treasures of the earth are inapplicable, and therefore in reality valueless.

2. From the certainty of success ensured.

In human affairs all is contingent. The race is not always to the swift, &c. Human policy, diligence, &c. often unavailing. The Christian merchant has success guaranteed. He has God's promises and engagements, to render the results favorable and prosperous. If he trades therefore he succeeds. God will give him success. Providence and grace are combined to ensure it.

3. From the nature of the profits derived.

The advantages are of a better kind. The gain of an abiding and immortal character. His riches will not fly away. Nor pass into other hands. Or ever fail. They are exhaustless and eternal. He secures a portion, proof against time, death, and eternity. He obtains an inheritance, incorruptible, &c. An exceeding great and eternal reward.

Application

1. Invite sinners to invest ail they have in the trade of wisdom. Everything else will finally fail. Nothing else superlatively important.

2. Urge believers to diligence in their heavenly calling.

3. Incite all wisdom's merchants to cheering hope as to the glorious results which shall crown their spiritual trading.

4. Those who trade in ignorance and sin will be ruined in body and soul forever and ever.

67. SAINTS THE RELATIVES OF JESUS

"And he stretched forth his hand toward his disciples, and said, Behold my mother and my brethren! For whosoever shall do the will of my Father which is in heaven, the same is my brother and sister, and mother." —Matt. 12:49, 50.

JESUS exhibited perfect rectitude in all the relationships he sustained. It is said of him at an early period of his life, that he went to Nazareth, and was subject to his parents, and grew in wisdom and favor with God and man. It cannot be supposed that Jesus would ever act at variance with the tenderest affection for his honored and beloved mother, especially when it is remembered, that while he was suspended in anguish on the cross he feelingly committed her to the guardian care of the disciple John. Yet it might appear from the paragraph with which the text is connected that he did not. manifest to her preeminent attention. "Then one said," &c. All other things were subordinate with Christ to his Father's glory, and the great end of his mission to our world. Whatever aspect the conduct of Christ may appear to have to his relations after the flesh, it is full of comfort and promise to his true disciples to the end of the world. Let us contemplate,

I. The spiritual Relatives of Jesus.

"The same is my mother," &c. Now this relationship is exceedingly close and intimate.

1. All true saints have one Father with Christ.

He taught his disciples to say, "Our Father," &c. "I ascend to my Father and to your Father," &c. He who testified to Christ as his Son, also says of all his saints, "I will be a Father," &c.

2. They have one nature with Christ In our original state we have the nature of the earthly first Adam. This is that which is carnal, called the flesh. In regeneration we have the heavenly nature, that of the second Adam, the Lord Jesus Christ This is the new man which born of the Spirit is spirit.

3. They have one mind with Christ.

"Let the same mind," &c. No Christianity without having the mind of Christ. Now this includes that lowly mind, that devout mind, that holy and benevolent mind, which Jesus ever displayed.

4. They have one name with Christ.

If called saints, which signifies holy, it is through Christ being made unto them righteousness, &c. Christian embodies the very name of Jesus. Disciples, signify the

195

followers, the pupils of Christ. Here then are the fourfold bonds of affinity and relationship to Christ. Observe,

II. The great Principle of this Relationship.

Now this is clearly expressed. "Who soever shall do the will," &c. Now this great principle is obedience. It accords with other passages. "Ye are my friends if ye do," &c. "If ye love me, keep my commandments." My sheep "follow me." The will of God is the great rule of all righteousness. What God wills is essentially pure, and just, and good. Now wo notice,

1. This will is revealed to us.

"God in times past, and in divers manners," &c. We have it fully, perfectly, and intelligibly in this blessed book. Nothing here superfluous. Nothing trifling. Nothing deficient. Now, it is the expressed will of God, that first of all sinners should repent of sin, and believe in Jesus Christ. And this lays the foundation for a proper superstructure of inward and practical righteousness.

2. Obedience to this will must be evangelical.

In Christ's strength. In dependence on his grace, by the aid of his Spirit.

3. Obedience to this will must be affectionate.

From love to God. "This is the love of God," &c. "The love of Christ constrains us," &c. Not of legal terror. Not of pharisaic arrogance, &c. But of humble love. This obedience,

4. Must be full, not partial.

Have respect to all his commandments.

Not dare to select. This would be presumptuous. Whatsoever he enjoins it right, and we must believe it to be so, and do it as such.

5. It must be constant and enduring.

It is service for life, for death, and for eternity This is also reasonable, and necessary, and best for us. He that endures to the end, &c. Be thou faithful unto death, &c. Consider,

III. The Advantages of this Relationship.

1. Can you think of more exalted honor.

To be recognized as the kindred of Jesus, the blood-royal of heaven. Kings and priests to God. Fellow-heirs with the Father's anointed one. O what dignity! Glory which angel and archangel have not. It exalts over the loftiest seraphim and cherubim of the skies.

2. It must include the bestowment of the greatest blessings.

Christ will not withhold from his kindred any real good, they are co-sharers of all his bliss, and joy, and treasures. "All are yours," &c. Every blessing of time and eternity.

3. Everlasting security.

He will now guard and defend. Save them from their enemies. Keep them in the day of mortality. Own them in the great judgment. Elevate them to his right hand forever and ever.

Application

1. Let Christians rejoice in the illustrious relationship they sustain.

2. Especially walk worthy of it.

3. Let degraded, wretched sinners now come and have life.

68. THE CITY OF GOD, WITH ITS RIVER AND GLADDENING STREAMS

"There is a river, the streams whereof shall make glad the city of God." —Ps. 46:4

THE text no doubt refers literally to Jerusalem, and the advantages derived from the river Kidron, with its streams. It must be manifest a river is of the very utmost importance to the health, and comfort, and prosperity of a city. None can dispute that the chief source of wealth and health to our metropolis is the river flowing through it. But the text is to be considered metaphorically in reference to the church of God Zion is one of the appellations commonly given to her. The apostle says of the New Testament church—"Ye are come unto mount Zion," &c. The church is the holy city of God. Let us then consider,

I. The city of God.

Now the city of God, or the church, must be considered,

1. As to its inhabitants.

Of whom is it composed? Of the communion of the faithful believers, separated from the world and consecrated to God. By regeneration partakers of the divine nature. And by adoption invested into all the privileges and immunities of the spiritual Zion. All spiritual persons are inhabitants of this spiritual city.

2. As to its governor and head.

This is the Lord Jesus Christ. "He is head over all things," &c. The Father hath given all things into his hands. He is Lord of all. And he has no deputy, no vicegerent. He says to all who dwell in it, "One is your master," and all ye are brethren.

3. As to its laws and regulations.

These are exhibited in the city statute book,—the living oracles of God. Now these relate to the admission of citizens; to the conduct of citizens towards the head, and towards all the brethren. They refer also to cases of offence and discipline. The New Testament is a perfect code of laws, here all our duty is fully and plainly revealed. Then,

4. As to the immunities and privileges of the city.

These are *numerous, precious,* sure, and everlasting. All the citizens are interested in the riches of the city. And these are infinite and exhaustless. They have a full supply from the *stores* of the city, and they supply all their need. They are beneath the protection and defense of the city. Angels are their guard, and God is their munition of rocks. No weapon formed against them can prosper. They are watched every moment. God keeps them as the apple of his eye, he holds them in the hollow of his hand. Then,

5. As to the dignified prospects of the citizens.

They are *eligible* to the greatest honors in this world and to unfading glories in the world to come. They have a title to immortality and eternal life Their flames are enrolled on high When they die, the) become denizens of the city of the new Jerusalem, the palace of the heavenly king. Notice then,

II. The river connected with this City.

Now this river is the love or favor of God. All the blessings of the church of God are derived from this source. See Ps. 36:7, 8; also Isa. 33:21. Now the love and favor of God to his people may well be compared to a river.

1. Like a river it has its channel of communication.

The torrent may sweep over a district, but in doing so it is often destructive and soon subsides. But a river has its specific course and channel. Christ is the channel through whom all spiritual blessings are conveyed lo the soul. He is the depositary of all the blessings both of grace and glory. God in all things treats with us by Jesus Christ. In him all fulness dwells.

2. As a river it is distinguished for its freeness.

Cisterns may be private property. Rivers are for the common good of the country through which they flow. Love and grace of God are for the common good of the church, for all the inhabitants of the city of God.

3. As a river it is characterized for its overflowing abundance.

All created sources may be exhausted. But God's infinite fulness cannot undergo diminution. The love of God cannot be bounded, it is illimitable. Its length, and height, and depth, and breadth, surpass all human understanding.

4. As a river it is noted for its constant perpetuity.

It is the same in all ages, in all dispensations. It is identical with the unchangeableness of God. His mercy is from everlasting, &c. His mercy endures forever, &c. "This is the God whom we adore." Observe,

III. Its gladdening Streams, &c.

"The streams whereof make glad," &c.

1. There are streams of ordinances, and these make glad the city of God.

What is it that makes ordinances so delightful,—so refreshing? It is because they are the wells of salvation. There they see God's beauty, and enjoy the beams of his smiling face. There they drink of the streams of salvation. Of the river of God. Hence said David, "I was glad," &c. "I had rather be a doorkeeper," &c.

2. There are streams of promise, and they make glad the city of God.

These are so many drafts on the bank of heaven, by which we often obtain a full supply from the riches of grace. How sweet and precious they are. How they support, and cheer, and sustain. All sure—and all ours by faith in Christ Jesus.

3. Streams of divine influences, and these make glad the city of God.

God pours out his Spirit, as streams of water on the parched ground. As showers upon the mown grass. Now these influences quicken, cheer, revive, comfort, and sanctify. Fill with hope and joy unspeakable, &c.

Application

1. How honored and happy are the people of God.

2. Let us act worthy of our citizenship.

3. Invite those around to partake of our privileges and blessings.

69. MINISTERS FISHERS OF MEN

"I will make you fishers of men." —Matt. 4:19.

THESE words were addressed by Jesus to Simon Peter and to Andrew his brother. When Christ met with them they were following their occupation as fishermen, and he said unto them, "Follow me, and I will make you fishers of men." Their cheerful, prompt obedience is then related,—"And they straightway left their nets and followed him." Gospel ministers are fishers of men. Let us see,

I. The Appropriateness of the Figure.

Here several things are implied.

1. The world is the sea, the scene of their labors.

Its restlessness is employed to set forth the anxious, peaceless condition of the wicked. A fit emblem of our mutable, changing world. Its storms and dangers, indicative of the moral perils, and fearful dangers, to which in this wicked state man is exposed.

2. This sea is densely peopled with human beings.

As the sea contains a vast variety and great number of fish, so the world is full of human beings. The lowest computation, eight hundred millions, peopling it at the same period.

3. The world as a sea is the natural element of unrenewed men.

As the sea is the natural element of fishes. Ungodly, rebellious, unholy men, feel at home in a world bearing the same ungodly and rebellious features. Unrenewed men are of the world, worldly. They have its spirit, and they are its children.

4. Yet the world will be a sea of destruction to those who remain in it.

In it we are necessarily distant from God; from his likeness, favor, and salvation. And it is on account of the misery and danger of this state, that God has mercifully set on foot a blessed expedient, for rescuing immortal souls from the depth of its perdition.

5. The gospel is the net for the extrication of deathless souls from the sea of sin.

It is an instrument adapted to their condition, suited to their misery, and every way calculated to bring them to God, and the knowledge of his great salvation. It reveals their state; it exposes their danger; and it brings gracious help and deliverance unto them. It is full of argument and motive, and power: it is the grace of God bringing salvation.

6. But the gospel net must be employed.

It may be fit and suitable, but it must be cast into the sea. So the gospel must be preached; the word of salvation must be declared. And for this Peter and Andrew were called: and in this work they labored, and lived, and died. This is the work of the Christian minister, to preach the gospel to every creature within his sphere and reach. This will lead us to consider,

II. The Duty to be discharged.

1. This net must be employed.

It is God's appointed remedy. To the eye of the carnal it may appear a foolish, ill adapted means; but nineteen centuries has proved it to be the "power of God to salvation."

2. It must be constantly and diligently employed.

Diligence and zeal do not *necessarily* suppose corresponding success. But generally as the rule they do so. An indolent, indifferent fisherman; cannot be expected to succeed, as the laborious, faithful, and persevering do.

3. This net only must be employed.

Other means may be useful as auxiliaries, but the gospel is God's great and blessed remedy, for the restoration of sinners to himself. The gospel is the infinitely wise and merciful instrument for the deliverance of men from sin and the power of darkness. In the discharge of this duty,

> 1) Constancy is necessary. The Christian minister must be "instant in season and out of season." In the morning and in the evening, not knowing which effort will prosper, this or that.

> 2) Skill is necessary. The fisherman, taught by experience, adopts the most probable means of success. So must the Christian minister. He requires a large supply of knowledge and wisdom. He must be wise as a serpent, &c. So was the great apostle of the gentiles. Times, and seasons, and circumstances, must all be consulted.

> 3) Perseverance is necessary. Often the fisherman may toil all night and take nothing. We cannot command success, but we can always be using God's own means, in dependence on his divine blessing. We may just add, that some Christian fishermen are more successful than others. But all and every one ought to be solicitous for it, and labor and pray for it. To urge to faithfulness in this duty, we have, the preciousness of souls,—the glory of God, and our own great and eternal reward, to influence us.

Application

1 Let the Christian fisherman rightly understand his net, and the appointed way of using it. What attention and study is requisite. Who is sufficient for it? What need of reading, contemplation, and prayer 2. Let success be the grand object of attention. Nothing can make up for lack of this. To be learned, or even highly personally pious, ought not to satisfy the faithful minister. He ought to ask, Are souls saved? Do I bring men out of the sea of sin? Where are the living saved proofs of my ministry?

3. Should not our hearts be cheerfully and devotedly in the work? Constrained by the love of Jesus and love to souls, we would freely sacrifice ease and comfort, and all things, that the glory of Christ might be promoted, and immortal being; rescued from the wrath to come.

4. Our resources are infinite and exhaustless. All the fulness and efficiency of divine grace are at our service.

70. MINISTERS SOWERS

"Bearing precious seed." —Ps. 126:6

JESUS, in one of his most instructive parables, likened the preaching of the word to a sower, who went forth to sow, whose seed fell upon various kinds of ground. Some by the wayside, some upon stony places, some among thorns, and some upon good ground. In that delightful parable he might have especial reference to himself, and to his own labors. But he parable is equally applicable to all his servants, and to the labors of every Christian minister, who goes forth proclaiming the doctrines of the kingdom of God. The text truly expresses that character. He goes forth "bearing precious seed." We ask then,

I. What Seed the Christian Minister sows?

The seed is the word of God. The holy truths of the divine mind. Those truths revealed expressly to make men wise to eternal life. Now this seed is to be sown in its original purity, without any admixture of what is human, and therefore probably erroneous. Now of this seed we notice,

1. It is living.

Word of life. Has in it the vital germ. So that if lodged in right ground, it will live and grow. It contains living principles and truths. It is the word of the living God. The living breath of the Holy Spirit from whom it emanated, and whose impress it bears. Not a dead letter, &c.

2. It is incorruptible.

Not only is it living, but as its source, it decays not, it perishes not. It produces spiritual life, which is not as the grass that withers, but abides forever. The fruit produced by this seed is incorruptible; it is the seed which is followed by the blessings of immortality.

3. It is precious.

So called in the text. Precious in its author and origin. Precious intrinsically. Precious in its effects. Precious as it has no possible substitute. It has been precious to the righteous in every age. It was given to the Jews as a solemn, invaluable deposit. It was to them worth more than thousands of gold and silver. See how it was estimated by the psalmist, Ps. xix., and cxix. God has exhibited his regard of its value, in preserving it amidst the enmity of all generations, and maintaining its purity even to the present period. It is as precious as the air, for it is the atmosphere of the renewed life. As bread, for it is the staff and support of the saints. As light, for without it we should be enveloped in mists and darkness. It is the water of life, flowing from the throne of God and the Lamb. We ask,

II. Where must it be sown?

The world is the field. Every human heart is the ground where we must labor to deposit it. "Go ye into all the world," that is the sphere. "Preach the gospel to every creature," there is the soil for its reception. Every human being needs it. To every human being it is adapted. For every living soul it is provided and sent. Then wherever the Christian minister may be, he cannot be beyond, or without, the sphere of duty and labor. Wherever he meets with one of Adam's race, he may say, according to the very letter of his commission, "To you is the word of this salvation sent." We inquire,

III. How it must be sown.

We reply,

1. Skillfully.

There is art even in sowing, and there is much art in rightly preaching the word. For this, spiritual knowledge is indispensable. Wisdom from above. Judgment by which the word may be rightly divided, truly expounded, and properly diffused abroad. Auditories differ. The condition of the same congregation varies. Varied classes must be appropriately addressed. A suitable portion must be given to each order, and to each man. And in the word of God there is that endless richness of variety, which a skilful sower will turn to good account. What a model of skill do we perceive in the great apostle of the Gentiles. See his varied discourses, epistles, &c. It must be sown,

2. Faithfully.

The whole counsel of God with fidelity made known. No part compromised, or kept back, or adulterated. Every man left without just excuse.

3. Diligently.

The whole time of the ministerial sower is the Lord's. In the morning, and in the evening, and at noonday. It must be his meat, &c. Great end of life. Chief end of all his studies, and contemplations, and solicitudes, where and how he may best scatter the seed of eternal life.

4. Plentifully.

Not with sparing hand. No need of this The sower's resources are infinite. Word of God, like the ocean, is calculated to fill the channels of the wide world. Enough for all, and for each, and for evermore.

5. Prayerfully.

For the divine blessing to succeed the labors and means employed. That he may make it to grow. That his rain and sun may produce vegetation and fruitfulness That his glory may be promoted, and converts increase, until they become as the drops of the morning dew.

Application

Learn,

1. The true nature of the ministerial office. It is to sow the word of God. To bear precious seed. Not a scientific or literary profession. Not a business of politics or commerce. But to spread divine truth. To preach the gospel of Christ.

2. The end of the ministerial office. The spiritual and eternal life of our fellow men. That they may be born again of the precious and incorruptible word of God.

3. The responsibility of those unto whom the word of God comes. They are responsible for hearing, receiving, and savingly profiting by it.

4. The assistance which all Christians may render in sowing the word of the kingdom. How very much they may assist their minister by counsel, kindness, co-operation, and prayer. Also by circulating the divine word. Teaching the rising age to read and understand it. By exemplifying its holy and benevolent fruit in their lives and conversation.

71. MINISTERS WATCHMEN

"They watch for your souls" —Heb. 13:17

THE apostle is referring to the duties which the churches owe to their pastors or rulers, and inculcates upon them obedience and submission, and this he urges from he responsible station which they officially hold. For he says, "They watch for your souls as they that must give an account." The same view of the sacred office is given in the prophecies of Ezekiel. See ch. 33:1-9. Let us then look at the office of the watchman, and see the appropriateness of the figure when applied to the ministerial office. Observe,

I. The Office of Watchman is one of Appointment.

He is chosen and designated to the work by some superior authority. He is not self-appointed, &c. The Christian minister acts under the firm conviction and persuasion, that he is called to his office by God. That he is moved to it by the Holy Spirit, through the call and voice of the church. Those who invade the office through principles of avarice, or ambition, or love of ease, are not Christ's watchmen, but deceivers, both of themselves and others.

II. The office of Watchman is an office of Trust.

He is called to watch for the security of property, life, &c. To watch against the secret or open enemies of the city where he exercises his office. The inconceivable weighty trust committed to the Christian minister, is the charge of immortal souls. To watch for their instruction, admonition, warning, &c. To secure their best interests. To prevent their ruin by the great enemy. To rescue them from the path of evil. To restore them to the favor and family of God. To bring them to the enjoyment of present salvation, and finally everlasting life. The Christian watchman has two distinct departments of duty. One relating to unconverted sinners, whose conversion is to be the leading object of his efforts, and the other, the preservation of those who have believed, that they may not apostatize from the truth, make shipwreck, &c. What a trust! How vastly beyond all the treasures of earth. How much greater than the mere security even of the present life. The life of the soul. The interests of eternity. How sublime! How momentous! Who is sufficient for these things?

III. It is an Office of Responsibility

The watchman is responsible for the right and faithful discharge of his duties. He is responsible,

> 1. For his time.

> That he truly occupies the sphere appointed. Not absent from his duty, &c. With what propriety this applies to the Christian minister He is ever to stand on the walls of Zion. To be instant in sea son and out of season.

2. For his diligence.

Not only duly, but diligently discharging it. How dreadful is apathy and indolence in the Christian minister.

3. For his vigilance.

The very term includes this. To watch, not sleep, or even doze. Lethargy totally unfits for being watchmen. Whoever sleeps, the Christian watchman must not. For the enemy sleeps not. Every hour is one of peril to souls. Then with unceasing assiduity, he must ever be on his tower, announcing the state of the city, and ready to warn against any enemy or peril.

4. For his fidelity.

Not to compromise the safety of the city. Not to deceive or neglect to warn. But with the utmost conscientiousness, with the fear of God before his eyes, and the love of souls in his heart, he is to act as with the judgment-seat of Christ immediately before him. "As one that must give account." He must be faithful to God. To sinners,—to saints,—to his own soul. And faithful to death.

Application

We learn,

1. The solemn character of the ministerial calling. A calling which demands great personal piety, as well as high spiritual gifts and qualifications.

2. The arduous duties of the ministerial office. So arduous as to claim all the faculties of the mind, and all the energies of the body. A work for which an angel's resources would not be too great or extensive.

3. The great necessity that they should receive Christian sympathy and comfort. How the Christian watchman should be esteemed, and loved. How his hands should be lifted up and his heart encouraged. How his wants should be cheerfully supplied. How unceasing prayer should be presented to God on their behalf. And in this way they may be efficiently aided Their burdens may be lightened, and their anxieties and toil greatly lessened. Consider, 4 The personal responsibility of those over whom they watch. The minister, if faithful, clears his own soul. On every man rests the responsibility of rightly improving and benefiting by the watchman's labors. "Whosoever heareth the sound of the trumpet, and taketh not warning, if the sword come and take him away, his blood shall be upon his own head," Ezek. 33:4.

5. Jesus, the great and blessed keeper of Zion, is the model every Christian minister should study and imitate. His zeal, his constancy, his fidelity, his unwearied perseverance, until he had finished all his work. He hath left Christian ministers an example, &c. &c.

72. MINISTERS BUILDERS

"A wise master builder." —1 Cor. 3:10.

THE Christian church is likened to a house, a temple, a city. Under each of these metaphors believers are considered as the materials—the stones of which it is composed. And the character the Christian ministry sustains is clearly the same. God is the great architect. Jesus is the foundation and head of the corner. Ministers are builders; as such the apostle Paul, keeping this idea in view, says of the church at Corinth, "According to the grace of God, which is given unto me, as a wise master builder, I have laid the foundation:" and of those who followed in his steps he says, and "another buildeth thereon, but let every man take heed how he buildeth thereon," &c. Observe,

I. The Christian Minister is a Builder.

1. He builds up the spiritual house or temple of God.

He is to labor to carry on this spiritual structure towards its final completion; towards its perfection. Its walls are to be elevated, until it is fit for the head stone.

2. He builds upon the one great foundation, Christ.

"Other foundation," &c. He is the chosen of God. The elect, precious, sure, and everlasting basis of this great and glorious structure. Here must rest the weight of every saved soul, and of the whole church.

3. He builds with the living stones of believers.

No other materials will be admitted by the great architect. To this the apostle obviously refers, when he speaks of some building with hay, straw, &c., material that will not stand the fiery ordeal of judgment. Improper persons may be added to the visible church, but the fire, which tries every man's work, will destroy them, and the builder will lose his expected reward. His work shall suffer loss, &c., see 5:13, 14, 15. Ministers are to preach the gospel that men may hear and believe; and when believers, that they may be built up living stones in Christ's holy and living house.

4. He builds according to the divine word.

Here are all his directions given. Here he has all the implements or means of building provided. Here his duty, his encouragement, and his resources are provided. Well acquainted with its truths, and he cannot fail in obtaining a knowledge of his work, and of all things necessary for securing success in his undertaking. This leads us to consider, that the Christian minister,

II. Ought to aim at being a wise Master Builder.

But we ask,

1. What is implied in this?

Evidently it means to be qualified with every gift requisite for its arduous duties; sufficient knowledge of the divine word; a personal and experimental acquaintance with the principles and practice of Christianity; a clear understanding; a sound judgment; a ready perception, &c. Not a novice; not an ignorant person: but well instructed in the knowledge of divine things. It includes, too, the improvement of those qualifications, and the practical exercise of all the powers, &c., in this great work. To be wise and act wisely It also includes the efficient and successful character of the ministry, in carrying upwards the walls of this spiritual structure. "He that winneth souls is wise." We ask,

2. What is requisite to this?

Reading, meditation, and prayer; the exercise of the work; make it the preeminent object of our solicitudes, &c. full consecration of all to God. We notice,

3. The motives which should urge to this.

1) Our own success. For unless we are wise master builders our labors will be entirely in vain

2) Our comfort and personal happiness. For if we feel rightly, we cannot enjoy real comfort, unless the pleasure of the Lord "prosper" in our hands.

3) Our own safety, too, is deeply concerned: for unless we build wisely and successfully we may well doubt as to our call, &c., for the work. Our motives ought to be rigidly searched, examined, &c.

4) Our final glory is identified with it. "They that turn many to righteousness," &c. The wise builder shall have joy and honor from his work in the day of the Lord. But the unwise laborer will only be saved himself, and "as by fire," 5:15.

Application

1. The subject is of great importance to the Christian ministry. Let it lead to self-investigation, &c.

2. It is of importance to all who profess to be a part of Christ's spiritual building. Are you of the saved? Living stones, &c.

3. How fearful the end of those who are merely hay, wood, stubble. The fire shall consume them.

73. GOSPEL MINISTERS SHEPHERDS

"The shepherds of Israel." —Ezek. 34:2.

THE prophet is referring to the indolent unfaithful shepherds who neglected the flocks committed to their care, and thus brought upon themselves the displeasure of God. It is, however, with the term itself that we have to do. Jesus Christ is the great and good shepherd, and ministers under him are the shepherds or pastors of their respective flocks.

It was the gracious promise of God that he would give his people "pastors according to his own heart," Jer. 3:15. And the appointment of this office is directly designed for the comfort, well-being, and safety of the people of God. Observe,

I. Christian Ministers as Shepherds have devolving upon them the care of Christ's Flock.

Believers are likened to sheep,—the sheep of the Lord's pasture. In their collective capacity, they are compared to a flock. The flock of God. They are exposed to many evils. Are surrounded by numerous enemies. Are liable to many wants and diseases. Are entirely insufficient for their own preservation, &c. To promote their comfort and safety, God sends his servants to take the oversight of them and to care for them as the shepherd cares for his flock. This is an office, then, connected with the appointment of God, and for which he gives every necessary qualification.

II. Christian Ministers as Shepherds must feed their Flocks.

They must do this by leading them into green pastures, &c.

> 1. The pastures of the divine word. Where there is an exhaustless fulness and variety of refreshing promises.

> 2. The pastures of divine ordinances. Where God showers down the manna of heaven,—bread of life,—the rich provision of his house. "I will abundantly bless her provision," &c. Now the shepherd is to render the word instructive and consolatory, and the ordinances refreshing and edifying. He is to do this by clearly explaining and opening the treasures of God's word. And by giving to each of his flock a portion of meat in due season.

III. Christian Ministers as Shepherds are to watch over their Flocks.

To warn them against danger,—"Warning every man." To admonish, to counsel, and to direct them into safe and plain paths. Their dangers are numerous. From the world, from Satan, from false professors, from their own weakness, &c. Against each and all these sources of evil, the shepherd is to watch for the safety of the flock. How necessary then is a spirit of holy energy, vigilance, &c.

IV. Christian Ministers as Shepherds are to regard especially the Weak and afflicted of the Flock.

Sheep are peculiarly liable to disease. In Christ's flock many are the infirmities and sicknesses which prevail. What spiritual weakness,—what imperfection of knowledge,—what self-trusting and complacency. "Who can understand his errors?" How often is spiritual disease evident in the mind, in the heart, in the spirit, in the conversation, in the walk and conduct. Now it is for the shepherd to labor for the healing of these maladies. To lead his afflicted people to the great physician, and to the balm of Gilead. He is to bind up their wounds; to strengthen the weak; to recover the straying; and to seek the perfection and eternal well-being of all.

V. Christian Ministers as Shepherds must give an Account of their Flocks.

They are responsible to God. God will demand an account. He is now observant of all they do. He will summon shepherds and flocks before his solemn tribunal. Faithful shepherds shall receive from the hands of the great shepherd "a crown of glory that fadeth not away," &c., 1 Peter 5:4.

Application

1. How truly solemn is the office of the Christian shepherd—the charge of souls. The responsibility of deathless souls.

2. How necessary for its right discharge are divine qualifications and help Christ is the great, model,—the Bible, the pastor's guide. The grace of God his daily and sufficient resource.

3. Faithful shepherds should have the kind sympathy and aid of all the members of the church. How the apostles were thus assisted; by pious deacons,—often by holy women, &c.

4. How glorious the meeting when all the flock of God, with each shepherd, shall appear before Christ to receive his blessing, even life for evermore.

74. MINISTERS STEWARDS

"And stewards of the mysteries of God." —1 Cor. 4:1.

A STEWARD is one who presides over the household affairs of a family, and is appointed to make provision for it. The church of Jesus is a family. A family of regenerated persons, the sons and daughters of the Lord Almighty. It is a household. "The household of faith." God is the father of this family, for they are all the children of God by faith. Jesus is the exalted and blessed elder brother, with whom is invested supreme and universal authority over it. And Christian ministers are stewards to live and labor for its welfare and comfort. The text refers,

I. To the Ministerial Office.

"Stewards."

1. This is a subordinate office.

"Stewards," not lords, not masters. All power and lordly authority belongs to Jesus. He is the head of the body,—the church. To the disciples Jesus said, "One is your master, even Christ, and all ye are brethren." Christianity has suffered irreparable loss from the lordly spirit and conduct of those who have occupied the ministerial office.

2. It is an appointed office.

Not a self-assumed one. No man puts himself into the stewardship. The apostle Paul was exceedingly susceptible on this point. He often refers to his call of God, &c. "Paul, a servant of Jesus Christ, called," &c., Rom. 1:1. "Paul, called to be an apostle of Jesus Christ," &c., 1 Cor. 1:1. "Paul an apostle, not of men, neither by man, but by Jesus Christ," Gal. 1:1. The Christian minister is not called miraculously as was Paul, or by an audible voice, as most of the apostles, but he professes to feel moved to undertake the stewardship by the voice of the Holy Spirit, the constraining power of the love of Christ, and the invitation of the church of God, which is the pillar and ground of truth.

3. It is an exalted office.

Workers together with God, 2 Cor. 6:1. Of the same vocation with Jesus, the prince of preachers—that great shepherd of the sheep. Every other calling is insignificant when compared to that which has immediately to do with the glory of God, and the eternal salvation of human beings.

4. It is a responsible office.

Every steward is responsible to his lord. So the Christian steward must give an account of himself and of his charge to God. He is responsible for the *talents* with which he is furnished. For the *time* and *opportunities* with which he is entrusted; for the right discharge of his *duties;* for *faithfulness* to the interests of his Lord; and for *affectionate fidelity* to the souls of his flock. How great the trust! How weighty the charge! How solemn the responsibility!

"'Tis not a cause of small import,
    The pastor's care demands,
But what might fill an angel's heart,
    And fill'd a Savior's hands."

Notice,

II. The great Subject of their Labors.

"Stewards of the mysteries of God." The mysteries of God are the great truths of the gospel. The gospel as a whole, is a clear revelation of the love and mercy of God to mankind, in and through the atoning sacrifice of Jesus Christ. As such it is adapted to the plainest capacity. And as such when expounded by its great teacher, it is said, "The common people heard him gladly." Yet this gospel has its great and sublime truths. It has its lofty and glorious doctrines. To these we are referred by the apostle Paul.

1. The mystery of Messiah's person and incarnation.

"Great is the mystery of godliness," &c., 1 Tim. 3:16; Luke 1:35.

2. The mystery of salvation through his cross.

Christ crucified, the great theme of the gospel ministry, is still to the Jews a stumbling block, and to the learned speculating philosophers of the world, foolishness. Yet to the believer, it is the power of God to salvation, 1 Cor. 1:18-25.

The mystery of the resurrection of the body.

Read the truly sublime representation of it as given by the apostle, 1 Cor. 15:12-54. Now the Christian steward is to publish and expound the mysteries of God. He is to make known all the divine counsel. To break to the household of Christ's family the bread of life. To study the variety of character and state of each member. To give the sincere milk of the word to babes. To give strong meat to the mature and aged disciples, and a portion of spiritual food to all in due season. In doing this effectually, and being faithful to the solemn trust, it will behoove him to be diligent, fervent, studious, prayerful. Much reading and meditation will be indispensable, and he must give himself wholly to the work.

Application

1. Let the stewards of Jesus reflect often on the solemn, arduous nature of their work.

2. Let them use all possible means for being thoroughly and ably furnished for fulfilling their calling.

3. Let Christian stewards have a deep place in the affectionate regards and prayers of the church. "Brethren, pray for us," &c. Hold up their hands; encourage their hearts, and pray down blessings upon their souls and work.

75. WORD OF GOD COMPARED TO FOOD

"Man shall not live by bread alone, but by every word that proceedeth out of the mouth of God." —Matt. 4:4.

THE text is the reply of Jesus to the tempter, who urged him to employ his power in changing stones into bread. To this Jesus replies, "It is written, (Deut. 8:3,) Man doth not live by bread alone, but by every word," &c. Christ's reply to Satan included this idea, that although bread is the staff of life, yet God can sustain and keep alive by anything, or by any means he pleases. Bread will not invariably ensure life, but the will of God is ever sufficient, under all circumstances, to do so. But the soul hath its necessities as well as the body, and it is a clear and important truth, that the food of the soul is the word of God. Thus Job said, "I have esteemed the words of his mouth more than my necessary food," Job 23:12. Consider,

I. The Propriety of the Metaphor.

The word of God may be likened to food.

> 1. As it is essential to the life of the soul.

> The body cannot live without food. The soul in like manner cannot have spiritual life, without receiving a constant supply of the divine word. The word of God is the incorruptible seed by which believers are begotten, and by which they become the children of God. And this life is sustained by the same word, which as milk nourishes, so that they grow thereby. We live, by the word of God living and abiding in us.

> 2. As it is the source of strength.

> Food when digested gives strength and vigor to the system, and by it the necessary supply of nutrition is communicated. So the word of God renews the strength of the soul. By it, holy desires and purposes receive energy and power. By it, the whole spiritual system is rendered healthy and powerful. With the vigor it imparts, the Christian is sufficient for all he duties and engagements to which he is jailed of God. Observe,

II. Its peculiar Characteristics.

This food is,

> 1. Heavenly and divine.

> It cometh down from above. The mind and will of God flowing to us from his heavenly throne on high. Not human wisdom. Not of the earth, but of God, and celestial in its nature and source

2. It is superabundant.

Not only enough, but infinitely more than the largest capacity can fully receive and digest. The word of God in its Spirit and fulness seems to resemble the infinity of its blessed author. The most studious, the most devout, the most diligent peruser of the holy scriptures, can only approach, as it were, the margin of that ocean of blessedness the word of God contains. The Bible is a never-failing, exhaustless mine of unspeakable treasure. Observe,

3. Its endless variety.

In temporal food God has given us not only plenty but variety. He has given man a right to every wholesome herb of the field,—the fruit of the earth, and of every clean beast, or fowl, or fish, Gen. 9:2-4. The word of God possesses still greater variety. In it there is everything to enrich the sanctified imagination, to enlighten the understanding, to counsel the judgment, to purify the conscience, to exalt the affections, and to meet all the spiritual desires of the soul. It contains food for every grade of character,—for every age and condition,—for all ranks, and degrees, and classes, in the kingdom of Jesus Christ. For the young and old; for the weakly and the strong; for pastors and people; for every member of the household of faith. Notice,

4. Its gratuitous bestowment.

The spiritual food of the word of God, is given by God to his people. He bestows it without any consideration or condition on our part. It descends as freely as the rain or snow from heaven. In this God acts according to the exceeding riches of his grace. This food is not to be bought by human price, or obtained by meritorious labor. Notice,

5. Its universal communication.

God giveth food to every living thing. He feeds all the beasts of the field, and the fowls of the air. All living creatures wait upon him, and he supplies the wants of all. So the food of the divine word is the common property of the whole family of man, It is suited and sent alike to all. It is the bread of life to a perishing world. Notice,

III. Our Duty with respect to it.

In reference to this heavenly food,

1. We should thankfully receive it.

God sends it. He gives it freely to us. Ungodly men despise it, reject it, and thus starve and die. We ought to receive it with sincerest gratitude, with all readiness and gladness of soul. Such a reception all give it who know their spiritual condition.

2. We should believingly feed upon it.

The word may be in our dwellings, may be the subject of our reading, and yet not profit us. By faith we make it our own. By faith it enters the heart, and thus only is indeed real food to the soul. Faith lives on what God has spoken, this faith is the life of the Christian.

3. We should grow, and improve by it.

The word of God exerts a holy transforming influence on the soul. Where God's word is cordially received, it will be exhibited in the spirit, life, and conversation. This food should make us strong in the things of God, and fit for every good word and work. We should grow in knowledge and prudence, in love, and in general holiness of heart and life.

4. We should constantly apply to it.

Every day we should gladly use God's word as the portion of our souls. Especially in the morning of the day we should avail ourselves of it, that we may profitably meditate upon it all day long. We shall need it during our whole probation; in life, sickness, and death. Then we shall exchange it for the fruit of the tree of life in the paradise of God.

Application

1. Urge the importance and value of the word of God upon all.

2. Upon the especial attention of the people of God.

76. WORD OF GOD LIKENED TO MEDICINE

"He sent his word and healed them." —Ps. 107:20

THE morally diseased condition of the human race is the subject of repeated testimony, in the holy scriptures. The description of Israel is not unsuitable to the whole family of man; "The whole head is sick, and the whole heart faint, from the sole of the foot," &c., Isa. 1:5. Of the moral malady of the soul, David was deeply conscious; hence he prayed, "Lord, be merciful unto me, heal my soul, for I have sinned against thee." Hence also he prayed on another occasion, "Have mercy upon me, for I am weak: heal me, for my bones are vexed; my soul is also sore vexed." It is probable that the text refers to bodily diseases, and the mercy of God communicated in healing them in answer to prayer. But the same gracious power and means will heal spiritual maladies, the moral diseases of the soul. Notice,

I. The diseased state of the Soul.

1. The disease itself.

It is sin. An unholy nature. Derangement of the moral powers of the mind and heart. All impurity is disease. All sin is unhealthiness. Consider,

2. Its source and origin.

This is the fallen condition of our nature through the first transgression. Adam transmitted to his posterity his own depravity. As the fountain was corrupted, the stream necessarily became impure. Diseased by his transgression, his children derived the germ of moral evil hereditarily from him.

3. Its universal influence.

It affects the whole man. Every faculty of the mind, and passion of the soul, are diseased. In the understanding there is blindness. In the judgment error. In the will perverseness. In the conscience defilement. In the affections corruption and earthliness. In the thoughts and desires evil, and that continually.

4. Its increasing virulence.

It deepens and expands, and becomes more powerful with the growth and habits of men. It yields not to education,—paternal influence,—example, &c. It never exhausts itself. It is not curable by change of place or society, or any self-exerted moral restraints.

5. Its fatal tendency.

It is a disease which ever ends in death. It is the deadly leprosy. The fatal plague No alternative but cure or death. Notice,

II. The Influence of the Word in healing it.

It is not the application of the mere letter of God's word, which removes the guilt and depravity of the soul. The blood of Jesus Christ cleanses from all sin. And it is by the Spirit's influence on the heart that the old depravity of the soul is removed, and all things become new. The Spirit changes the heart, and transforms it from a state of stone and impenitence, to a state of susceptibility and love to God. The Spirit quickens, renews, and sanctifies the soul; yet it may be truly said, that the word of God heals the soul.

1. As it reveals the divine recipe for our salvation.

It makes known the one great and in fallible remedy. It announces the one physician. The one catholicon for all moral diseases of mankind.

2. As it makes known the course necessary to our restoration.

It shows what we must forsake. What habits abandon,—what society relinquish. It shows the necessity of reflection, turning from all evil, genuine repentance, and hearty faith in the atoning death of the Lord Jesus Christ.

3. It publishes the offer of healing to every diseased soul.

Not only describes our sickness and misery, but makes known God's gracious desire to restore us to health, and happiness, and eternal life. It expostulates and says, "Why will ye die," &c. "Is there no balm in Gilead," &c. "Wilt thou be made whole," &c.

4. It affirms the ability and readiness of Jesus to heal all who come to him.

It exhibits his gracious regards, and his tender solicitudes. It refers to the prodigies of his healing power in the days of his flesh. It avers his sufficient ability to save all, and to the uttermost who come unto God by him. It re-echoes his compassionate invitation, "Come unto me," &c.

5. It is in the cordial reception of the word that restoration is enjoyed.

When the sick believed in Christ's word they were healed. When the father believed in Christ, his son was restored. So the woman of Canaan: so also when the multitude believed Peter, who preached the word, they were baptized into Christ, and added to his church, Acts 2:41. See also Rom. 10:17. Hence it is styled the "word of salvation." And the gospel is represented by the apostle as the "power of God," Rom. 1:16. A knowledge of the truth makes free. Reception of the truth is connected with regeneration. And abiding in the truth is essential to spiritual growth, and progress in divine things, John 17:17.

Application

1. How thankful we should be for God's word.

2. Its design should never be forgotten. It is sent to heal our souls. It is the message of eternal life.

3. Its possession involves great responsibility.

4. Its rejection is that unbelief which is threatened with damnation.

5. Invite the sinsick of every class, to hear and believe, and be healed.

77. THE WORD OF GOD COMPARED TO LIGHT

"The entrance of thy words giveth light." —Ps. 119:130.

"And a light unto my path." —Ps. 119:105.

LIGHT is the emblem of Deity, "For God is light, and in him is no darkness at all," 1 John 1:5. Christ is the light of the world. Saints are children of the light and of the day. The gospel is the glory of God, shining forth in the face of Jesus Christ. The holy scriptures are as a light shining in our dark and benighted world. The pious psalmist felt they were to him "as a light unto his path," and rejoiced in the experience expressed in the text, "The entrance of thy word giveth light." Notice,

I. The Resemblance of the Divine Word to Light.

1. There is the manifesting character of light.

Light makes manifest. Through it we behold the wonders of the divine works Thus the word of God is a revelation of God's mind, and of his saving work. It is the visible discovery of God's love and mercy to our world. What could we know of God,—of creation,—of ourselves,—of the divine will,—of eternity, without the light of God's blessed word?

2. There is the clear character of light.

Through its transparent medium we behold things distinctly and fully. So the word of God is a clear medium of knowledge. We have in it, the truth, distinctly and amply. It is not like the vague equivocal answers of the pagan oracles, or the ambiguous guesses of human fallible knowledge, but it makes known every great and important subject lucidly and simply.

3. There is the beautiful character of light.

It is light which invests every external object in nature with its color and hue. So all the subjects of God's word possess a celestial beauty and heavenly hue. It is unlike every other volume, and as superior as the heavens are higher than the earth, or the works of God superior to those of men. This will apply to the narratives, histories, prophecies, doctrines, and poetry of the sacred volume.

4. There is the purity of light.

Water is easily defiled or poisoned. The air is liable to the influence of contagion. But light, fair emblem of its author, ever retains its transparent purity. Such is the purity of

222

God's word. It has no admixture of error. It is as pure as the mind of its immaculate source. It is all pure, and God has preserved it through all the ages since it was written from human corruption. "Every word of God is pure." Notice,

5. The universal character of light.

God has diffused it throughout our world. It is one of God's great blessings to the earth on which we dwell. It is sent for all, free to all, and enjoyed by all, (except the blind.) Such is the character of God's word. His gift to the whole world. It is designed for the enlightening of every human being. None are excluded from its benefits but those who dwell in pagan darkness, or willfully close their eyes against it. Observe.

II. The Nature of that Reception we should give it.

1. We should behold the light.

God calls us to do so. He has given us the faculties to understand it. And he calls us to open our eyes, and, with attention and the spirit of seriousness, to know the things which God hath revealed, and which belong to our peace.

2. He calls us to rejoice in it.

It is, and ever ought to be, pleasant to see the light. But the light of God's word is still more precious, and ought to excite in our minds the liveliest emotions of grateful joy. We ought to hail the light of God's word with fervent thanksgiving to his holy name.

3. He expects our improvement from it.

The entrance of God's word must be experimental. It must enter the heart. Be received into the affections. Retained in the memory. And "dwell richly" in us. Influencing our thoughts, and purposes, and actions. "Thy word have I hid in my heart," &c.

III. The Important Benefits we derive from it.

"The entrance of thy words giveth light." By the cordial reception of God's word we obtain,

1. The light of the divine favor.

His word, says the psalmist, converts the soul, Ps. 19:7. By receiving his word, we yield to his divine authority, and own his right to exercise his authority over us, John 5:24,8:32.

2. The light of holy joy.

His word rejoices the heart, Ps. 19:8. It is as a spring of living water, spreading happiness and peace through the soul. The word impresses its own likeness and spirit on the soul. See 1 Pet. 1:8.

3. The light of cheering hope.

By the regenerating power of the incorruptible seed of the word of God, believers are begotten to a lively hope, &c., 1 Pet. 1:3. As the word converts and renovates the soul, so it opens before the mind the prospect of heavenly and eternal glory. And the entrance of God's word gives light under all the changing circumstances of life. It gives light in adversity,—in trouble,—in temptation,—in affliction,—under bereavements. And it illumines the dark valley and shadow of death. The divine word is the light of God's sanctuary,—of the Christian family,—of the believer's closet.

Application

Learn,

1. How thankful we should be for the word of God.

2. With what diligence we should peruse its sacred contents.

3. With what prayer for the Holy Spirit's assistance should we devoutly meditate upon it.

4. How anxious we should be for its diffusion. How desirable that all the world should possess it, and walk in its saving, joyous light. "O Lord, send out thy light and truth," &c.

78. THE WORD OF GOD LIKE A FIRE AND HAMMER

"Is not my word like as a fire? saith the Lord and like a hammer that breaketh the rocks in pieces?" —Jer. 23:29.

THE faithful Jeremiah is here called by God to prophesy against false prophets, and to denounce the displeasure of God against such as mixed their own dreams and imaginations with the word of God. Hence the Lord says, "I have heard what the prophets said, that prophesy lies in my name, saying, I have dreamed, I have dreamed. How long shall this be in the heart of the prophets that prophesy lies in my name?" &c. Then God says, in reference to these prophets, "The prophet that hath a dream, let him tell a dream," that is, let him only make it known as a dream, not as a revelation from God. "And he that hath my word, let him speak my word faithfully. What is the chaff to the wheat? saith the Lord." Then follow the words of the text, "Is not my word like as a fire," &c. Observe,

I. What the Text implies.

Various figures are employed to describe the word of God, and these figures have reference to the influence which the word exerts, and the effects which are produced by it. As a sword, it pierces and cuts asunder. As a medicine, it heals. As a lamp, it illumines, &c. The figure of fire evidently implies, 1. That man is the subject of dross. That he requires refining or that, 2. he has within him much that is as stubble, that must be burnt up. Perhaps the prophet had his mind directed to chaff which was cast into the oven &c. The figure of the hammer implies, the hard and rocky condition of the human heart. And this is directly taught in God's word. He is said to have a "heart of stone," Ezek 11:9. Like the rock, 1. Man's heart is barren. 2. Hard. 3. Resisting. And this is the natural state of every unregenerate soul. Notice,

II. What the Text affirms.

For the interrogatory phraseology of the text evidently sets forth the truth of God's word,—As a fire, and as a hammer, &c.; the word of God,

> 1. Is a fire.

> Celestial fire. Fire from heaven. Holy fire. Fire that searches the conscience. Fire that burns up the dross, and purifies the soul. Fire that changes into its own nature all that comes into contact with it. And it contains threatenings which will consume all sinful tares with unquenchable fire. This divine fire burns out the carnal principles of the heart. It burns up all earthliness and worldly-mindedness,—all inward sin. It sends its flame into all the interstices of the soul. And sanctifies even the imaginations of the heart. "Sanctify them through thy truth, thy word is truth," John 17:17. See John 15:3. God's word,

2. Is a hammer.

Adapted to impress and to break even the rock in pieces. As a hammer, it breaks in pieces the obduracy of the heart,—the impenitence of the heart,—the unbelief of the heart,—the apathy of the heart. It produces conviction of sin,—contrition for sin,—separation from sin. We see it exerting this power, 1. On the children of Israel at Bochim, when an angel spoke unto them the word of the Lord, "And the people lifted up their voice and wept," &c., Judg. 2:4. 2. On the Israelites in the time of Ezra. See Ez. ix. 10:3. On the people under Peter's sermon; "Who, when they heard this, they were pricked in their hearts, and said unto Peter, and to the rest of the apostles, Men and brethren, what shall we do?" Acts 2:37. So also in the case of the jailer at Philippi, &c. In every age of the world, God's word has proved itself as a hammer breaking the rocks in pieces. In our own country, how many skeptical, profligate hearts have been broken in pieces. The history of modern missions also confirms the truth of the text. This hammer has been exerted on every grade and character of human beings and everywhere it has been as a purifying fire, and as a hammer breaking the rock in pieces.

Application

Learn,

1. The importance of maintaining the purity of God's word. Science, philosophy, and literature, are utterly powerless as to the renewal of the heart of man. They may civilize, and polish, and expand the mind, &c., but they cannot convince of sin, or convert the soul. This is to be effected by the word of truth, the gospel of God, the hammer of the holy scriptures.

2. The necessity that exists for the employment of the divine word. The hammer must be used, the word of God must be preached. "For faith cometh by hearing, and hearing by the word of God." See Rom. 10:14-17. Now the employment of the divine word devolves upon the church. Jesus has left his word with his people, that they may convey it into all the world, and exert its influence on every creature. However excellent in itself, of adapted to save the soul, it is powerless, unless it be brought to bear upon the hearts of men. The hammer is adapted to break the rock, but it must be lifted up and made to fall with power upon it. The word of God is adapted to save the soul, but the hand of the servant of God must bear it, and smite with it the consciences of sinners, as Peter, and Paul, and the apostles did. We must not forget,

3. That men may resist the word; and in this man differs from the rock. Hence the word is full of moral power, the power of truth, and the power of grace, but it exerts no physical energy on the mind, but leaves every man accountable to God Then we must urge men to hear, to consider, to believe, &c.

4. The incorrigible sinner it will destroy. To such it is the savor of death unto death. "What shall the end be," &c. "How shall we escape," &c.

79. WORD OF GOD LIKENED TO THE RAIN AND SNOW

"For as the rain cometh down, and the snow from heaven, and returneth not thither, but watereth the earth, and maketh it to bring forth and bud, that it may give seed to the sower, and bread to the eater: so shall my word be that goeth forth out of my mouth," &c. —Isa. 55:10, 11.

ALL the elements of nature are under divine control. God directs and disposes of all things according to the purpose of his all-wise and righteous pleasure. He gave nature her original laws, and he is the great source of that order and harmony which prevails throughout his works. In all the diversified kingdoms of nature, he has caused one thing to depend upon another. Hence the fruitfulness of the earth greatly depends on the produce of the clouds. These empty their moistening contents upon the thirsty earth, and thus cause it to bring forth and to bud, and also to yield to the husbandman a supply of fresh seed-corn, and sufficient bread to those who labor for its cultivation. Observe then the analogy in the kingdoms of nature and grace, between the rain and snow and the divine word. We see the resemblance,

I. In the Origin of both.

The rain, although naturally produced, is yet obviously the work and gift of God. He prepares it; stores it up; bears it on the wings of the wind; and freely pours it upon the earth. So also the word of life is his own production. He inspired the minds of the writers with the ideas, thoughts, and gave them infallible directions and aid in revealing his mind to mankind. The scriptures are thus directly from heaven, and bear the sublime impression of their divine and blessed author. We see the resemblance,

II. In the Mode of communicating both.

He gives the rain,

 1. At peculiar seasons.

 Periods when its bestowment is desirable and necessary. So God gave his word, during the various seasons of our world's history, in divers manners, and at various periods, to the fathers by the prophets. Just as God exercises his infinite skill in giving rain from heaven—so also did he give the words of truth and salvation to the world. He gives the rain

 2. Abundantly.

 Hence the earth does not lack this great and essential blessing. So also he has fully, abundantly revealed his will in his holy word. We possess fulness of spiritual knowledge. Enough for all the par poses of personal piety, present usefulness, and to make us meet for eternal glory. The apostle says, "It is profitable for doctrine, for reproof, for correction for instruction in righteousness, that the man of God may be perfect, thoroughly furnished unto all good works." 2 Tim. 3:16. He communicates the rain,

3. Discriminately.

We say not according to his sovereignty, for he exercises that glorious prerogative in all his works and government. But the rain is not given to all countries in like manner, as to seasons, abundance, &c. So with respect to his word, he de posited it originally with the seed of Abraham. To them pertained his oracles. They had God's word, while the rest of the nations were in darkness. They had the copious showers of truth, while other lands were sterile and barren as to the true knowledge of God. So it has ever extensively been, and so it is even yet. As a nation we have been greatly favored. But other countries are only now receiving in their own tongues the wonderful testimonies of God's word. He communicates the rain,

4. Freely, gratuitously.

It is one of his free gifts to man. It comes bountifully from his beneficent and gracious hand. So also the word is his free gift to man. A gracious revelation of his love, and, like every other blessing, conferred without money and without price. We see the resemblance,

III. In the Design of both

The rain is sent to make the earth fruitful, to cause it to bring forth and bud. Now we observe,

1. The earth, like the heart of man, without this would be unfruitful.

The earth requires rain,—is barren without it. The heart of man requires the word of God, and is dark, hard, frigid, and barren without it. Nothing will answer as a substitute for rain, and nothing meets the exigencies of the soul but the word of God. We observe,

2. The adaptation of both for the end contemplated.

Rain softens and moistens the earth and produces fruitfulness. The word of God enlightens, impresses, alarms, convinces, and converts. It is the instrumental means of regeneration and holiness. Wherever it is received it produces these delightful effects. They resemble each other,

IV. In the Results arising from both.

The rain and snow answer the end for which they are sent. Thus God's word shall not be ineffectual. It shall accomplish God's pleasure. That is, it shall produce results pleasing to God; answer the great end he contemplated; produce fruit to the honor and glory of his name.

1. It shall make barren souls fruitful.

See Rom. 6:22. It has ever done this. Wherever it has been borne, sin and iniquity have been effaced, and holiness and goodness produced. Men have been turned from sin to God, from darkness to light, &c. What a striking example is the case of the Corinthian church. 1 Cor. 6:9, 11.

2. It shall increase the means of doing good.

"Give seed to the sower." The fruitful earth yields thirty, sixty, and a hundred-fold. Thus too all converted persons are as seed-corn, they have been produced for the reproduction of others. They shall be useful as well as fruitful. Thus as disciples are increased the power of doing is increased to the church. They are additional lights in the world, &c.

3. It shall reward the laborer.

The Christian minister is a sower, and his reward is given from the fruitful earth. He depends upon the earth yielding her increase, the earth depends upon the rain, and the rain upon God. The minister's chief reward will be the trophies of the truth. Those converted by the gospel. And if it is the joy of the Savior, how much more should it be the joy of the servant. Phil. 4:1; 1 Thes. 2:19.

4. It shall satisfy the author.

"It shall prosper whereto I send it." God will be eternally glorified in the achievements of his word. God will derive united and eternal praise from the spirits of the glorified, who have been made fruitful and righteous by his holy word. It will attain all God intended and expected from it.

Application

1. Let us not be unmindful of the source and value of temporal blessings. God sends us rain from heaven, fruitful seasons &c.

2. Let. spiritual blessings especially be gratefully received. The word, next to the Son and Spirit of God, is the greatest and most precious of these.

3. Have the ends and purposes of God been answered in giving us his sacred and precious word. Do we bear fruit to the glory of his grace.

4. Unfruitfulness under superior privileges will greatly add to our condemnation at the great day.

80. THE GOSPEL TREASURE

"But we have this treasure in earthen vessels that the excellency of the power may be of God and not of us." —2 Cor. 4:7.

THERE are two distinct similes in the text. One relates to the ministerial office. Ministers of Christ, whether apostles or evangelists, are earthen vessels. Vessels to hold and convey their contents to others. The gospel is presented to us in the text under the similitude of treasure, and this treasure is borne in the earthen vessels of the ministry, and the design of this arrangement is, that the glory may all redound to the power of God. At present we confine our thoughts to the gospel as a treasure.

I. It is so on account of its intrinsic Excellency.

In it is concentrated all that is really valuable and precious to man. It is a treasure,

1. Of divine knowledge.

The knowledge of God,—of Jesus Christ,—of immortality and eternal life.

2. Of divine grace.

The tender compassion of God to the soul. The free bounteous favor of the Lord. Favor better than life. It is described as the "unsearchable riches of grace,"—"The grace of God," &c.

3. Treasure of divine comfort.

It brings the unspeakable treasure of a peaceful conscience to every believer It includes the consolations of God's love and the comforts of the Holy Spirit.

4. Treasure of heavenly glory.

It makes believers citizens of heaven. Subjects of the heavenly kingdom. Exalts them to sit in heavenly places. Gives clear title to the heavenly inheritance; to the throne and crown which never fade away. It produces heaven upon earth and offers the enjoyment of life in heaven, for evermore.

II. It is a Treasure as it confers upon Man that which is most precious

1. It is a treasure of food.

It gives the bread of life—manna from heaven. It spreads the festive board. Invites to the marriage feast. See Isa.; Matt. 22:2.

2. It is a treasure of medicine for sinsick souls.

Here is the balm of health. The elixir of life. Medicine for every malady of the diseased soul. That which produces health, and vigor, and life.

3. It is a treasure of raiment.

It confers the costly robe of salvation. The garment of praise. See Psa. 45:13.

4. It is a treasure of ornaments and jewels.

It gives golden graces to the soul. It decorates the spirit with all the real and unperishing ornaments of love, meekness, gentleness, and truth. It confers that which is far better than gold, or silver, or pearls. It impresses the soul with the likeness of God, and transforms into his glorious image. 2 Cor. 3:18. Observe,

III. Some of the Characteristics of this Treasure.

1. It is spiritual.

Not material treasure. Not earthly and liable to decay. Not suited to the body or influenced by time. But a treasure suited to the mind. Spiritual blessings adapted to the spiritual necessities and capacities of the soul.

2. It is invaluable.

We cannot conceive of its cost to deity. We cannot conceive of the worth of the blessings it confers. It gives life—eternal life. There is no substitute for it. The whole globe is worthless compared to it.

3. It is abundant.

It is boundless as God's infinite love and power. It enriches every believer with infinite good. It has enriched countless myriads. There is a sufficiency for an infinity of worlds. It is utterly exhaustless. Then,

4. It is enduring treasure.

It is not liable to be lost, or decay as earthly treasures. The moth or thief cannot destroy or steal it. It enriches its possessor throughout life, in death, and through all the ages of ages of the worm to come.

It is a kingdom which does not pass away a crown that does not fade; an inheritance incorruptible, &c.

5. It is a treasure freely offered to all.

The gospel is designed and adapted to all men. Christ has sent it to all the world. Every creature has a gracious right to its blessings. And nothing is required but to feel our need, and cordially receive its riches 6. It is a treasure which can only be secured in the present life.

We have the mine in this world, and we must seek, and explore, and obtain it now, or be poor forever. The gospel in adapted to man as a sinner and probationer The gates of the celestial city are only open to those who, by repentance and faith, enter in during the period of that probation.

Application

1. With what joy should the treasure be received. The tidings of it should fill with gladness, with exultation, with delight.

2. With what care it should be secured. We should guard against the enemy who robbed our first parents. Against shipwreck. We should think of Demas, &c. And with holy jealousy and vigilance preserve and secure it. Think of the inspired admonition, "Hold fast that which thou hast that no man take thy crown," Rev. 3:11.

3. With what thankfulness should it be enjoyed. We ought every day to give God thanks for it. It ought to fill us with joy unspeakable and full of glory.

4. How we should urge poor sinners to come and be enriched by it. Ministers should urge it,—all Christians should speak of it. Tell the miserable and perishing of that treasure which will enrich them for both worlds. Tell them how freely it is offered, and beseech them to seek it now. "For now is the accepted time," &c.

81. THE GOSPEL TRUMPET

"The great trumpet shall be blown, and they shall come which were ready to perish." —Isa. 27:13.

DOUBTLESS this prophecy had a literal reference to the restoration of the Jews through the instrumentality of Cyrus. A prophecy which had a most exact and faithful fulfilment. But we intend the accommodation of the text to the joyful proclamation of the gospel of Christ. Blessed as were the captive people of God when they heard the proclamations of Cyrus to return to their own country; yet more blessed are they who hear the joyful tidings of salvation, as published by the heralds of the cross. Let us notice, in applying the great trumpet to the gospel,

I. The Significance of the Metaphor.

The gospel may be likened to a trumpet,

    1. As an instrument of sound.

It is intended to make specific announcements,—to arrest attention,—to give directions. Now this is the design of the gospel. It announces the grace of God to man; his love to a perishing world; and a free and full salvation to every repenting believing sinner. But it is described,

    2. As a great trumpet.

Great in its author; great in itself; great in its design; great in the universality of its application to the whole world; great compared with the use of all other trumpets. Immediately connected with the great God,—the great Redeemer,—the great concerns of souls,—and the great destinies of the eternal world. Now consider,

II. The Nature of its Proclamations.

    1. It proclaims peace between God and man.

This was the song of angels, "Glory to God," &c. Preaching peace by Jesus Christ. It is the ministry of reconciliation. Thus as trumpets proclaimed the cessation of arms, and gave the announcement of peace, so the gospel proclaims the favor and peace of God towards our fallen world.

    2. It proclaims war between man and sin.

Sin has the usurped dominion over men. It reigns as a despotic tyrant. It keeps the sinner in a state of hostility towards God. But the gospel brings the recipient of it to wage war with all moral evil. He now becomes a soldier of Jesus Christ. He puts on the gospel armor, and fights the good fight of faith. He rallies round he standard of the cross, and obeys the sound of the great trumpet in this holy and spiritual war.

3. It proclaims the assembling together of the army of Jesus.

Thus, as trumpets were employed to bring together the scattered troops, and likewise to collect the tribes in the desert for their religious assemblies, the gospel calls men to the assemblies where the soldiers of Jesus meet together, and where the congregation of the Lord worship his holy name. "Forsake not the assembling," &c.

4. It proclaims the acceptable year of the Lord.

The jubilee was introduced with the sound of trumpets. This was indeed a joyful sound,—to the poor,—to captives,—and to the people in general. Thus Jesus at the commencement of the gospel jubilee, sounded the great trumpet,—"And when he had opened the book he found the place where it was written, The Spirit of the Lord is upon me, because he hath anointed me to preach the gospel to the poor," &c., Luke 4:17-20. Consider,

III. The Blessedness of its Effects.

"They shall come," &c. Observe,

1. The characters.

"Ready to perish." A striking description of unconverted sinners. In a state of misery, wretchedness, and disease. Slaves groaning in their chains. Borne down by the yoke of the tyrant. Without strength And as to their own power, without hope. Exposed to eternal death. In the gall of bitterness, &c. In the horrible pit, &c.

2. The influence the gospel exerts.

They must of course hear it. And the text supposes that they hear it with interest—with joy: so hear it, as to be influenced by it. Now this influence is seen in the movement produced—"For they come," &c.

1) From whence? From the dreary region of death. From the land of oppression. From their exiled slavish condition.

2) To what do they come? They come to the kingdom of God's grace. To the cross. To the house of prayer. To the fellowship of his saints. No longer aliens or foreigners, but fellow-citizens, &c.

234

3) How do they come? With weeping on account of their sins. With gladness on account of their redemption. With faith in the gospel's proclamations. With heartfelt joy to receive the blessings of salvation.

Application

1. How blessed are our ears, who have been favored with the sound of the great crumpet.

"Jesus! transporting sound!
The joy of earth and heaven;
No other help is found,
No other name is given,
By which we can salvation have,
But Jesus came the world to save."

2. The dignified yet responsible office of the Christian preacher. To blow the trumpet. To convey the sound of mercy to the perishing. To blow it loudly, distinctly, incessantly.

"O for a trumpet's voice,
On all the world to call," &c.

3. The duty and interest of sinners. To hear, and come to Christ for life and salvation.

4. Neglecters and despisers are their own destroyers.

82. THE GOSPEL REPRESENTED AS THE WATER OF LIFE

"And the Spirit and the bride say, Come. And let him that heareth say, Come. And let him that is athirst come. And whosoever will, let him take the water of life freely." —Rev. 22:17.

THE word of God contains many free and delightful invitations to lost and perishing sinners: many of these are met with in the prophecies, in the gospels, and in the epistles. But as if the Holy Spirit, in concluding the holy writings, wished to give one enlarged and expansive view of the divine benignity to man, the copious, tender, universal, and urgent entreaty of the text was penned. To explain and enforce the invitation will be the end of our present address. Observe,

I. To what the Invitation refers.

"It is to the water of life." By the water of life we clearly understand the blessings of salvation, the enjoyment of the favor and love of God. This salvation is variously represented. As treasure to the poor. As a robe to the naked. As medicine to the sick As food to the starring. And as the water of life to the polishing, thirsty sinner.

The stream from the smitten rock was a striking type of it. The prophets often dwelt with delight, when using the metaphor, "Ho, every one," &c. "With joy shall they draw water &c. The psalmist said, "There is a river &c. "In that day," said Zechariah, "a fountain shall be opened," &c. Jesus very often employed the same expressive phraseology, "In that last great day of the feast," &c. "To the woman of Samaria," &c. Thus the language of the text. Now this is called the water of life, as.

> 1. It springs from the fountain of life.

> See ver. 1, of this chapter. So Christ said let him come unto me. He is the source of all life, and these streams flow from the ocean of his godhead. "Every good gift," &c. All the blessings of salvation are the gifts of his grace.

> 2. It communicates spirit and life.

> A man may have natural life and yet be dead to God, and to holy and heavenly things. And this spiritual death, if not removed, will end in eternal death. Now it is only by the reception of the gospel stream that the soul is quickened, and renewed, and lives.

> 3. It terminates or is consummated in eternal life.

> Spiritual life of God in the soul is the germ of eternal life. This is "life eternal," &c.; this is the first degree, the firstfruits, &c. Now the saving grace of God not only renews, but sustains: by it we not only begin, but continue to live; and it matures and perfects the life

of God in the soul, and then at last it gives us the full ocean of the blessedness of eternal salvation.

II. The Persons to whom the Invitation is given.

The invitation respects two kinds of characters.

1. Those who feel need, and desire it.

"Him that is athirst."

1) Now thirst arises from conscious need. So, many are conscious of their need of Christ—they admit it and feel it. By the word read or preached they have been convinced of their true state and condition.

2) Then thirst is a condition painful and distressing. Many of you have felt this. Know how it rendered everything worthless and unsatisfying.

3) Then there is no substitute for fluid to the thirsty. Nothing will do instead. So to the convicted sin-smitten sinner; the man truly sensible of his state, cannot find in all the world an equivalent, &c. Now these are invited—conscious, anxious penitents. Then the invitation refers,

2. To all who are willing to receive it.

"And whosoever will." There is one condition—"will." No respect to your character, age, sex, or condition. No respect to merit, or righteousness, or fitness, but to the will. If you will, you may, and shall have the water of life, and if you will not you must perish, and hat too because you will perish, by rejecting the merciful offer of a gracious God. Observe,

III. From whom the Invitation issued.

1. The Spirit invites.

Now every invitation contained in the holy scriptures is the invitation of the Spirit. "Holy men of God," &c. "All scripture is given," &c. In those passages we quoted all were indicted by the one blessed Spirit of God Just as a monarch or nobleman issues his mind by the ambassadors of his court, and the servants of his palace So Christ by the Spirit inspired men to speak his word and mind to the human race. Remember, the words of the scriptures are the words of God.

2. The church invites.

The church is the bride, the Lamb's wife. And she is expected to feel and make Christ's interests her own, and he has commanded her to shine and speak, and witness before men that they may be saved. Now the church, possessing the Spirit, wishes what the Spirit wishes, and enters into all the mind of the Spirit. The people of God under all dispensations felt and acted thus. Thus Moses invited his father-in-law, "Come thou," &c. Thus David prayed, Ps. 67:1, 2. But more fully did the church of Christ by her apostles and evangelists, go forth and invite. So they were commanded to visit the whole world, and invite every creature.

3. Everyone who hears invites.

"Let him that heareth." That is, all who have heard, obeyed, and found the water, may and must invite. No specific call, office, or talents are requisite. As a Christian you may do it. As a Christian you ought from love to God and love to man. But perhaps the idea is this, that all who hear must invite those beyond, then those must invite the still more distant, until all the earth shall see the salvation of God. In our

Application

We notice,

1. The duty and interest of those invited. You are to "come" to God's "gospel." To his "throne of grace." And you are to "drink." Enjoy and profess his salvation. Approach first, and then drink of the water of life freely.

2. Let this course be urged upon your practical attention. Think of the worth and preciousness of the water of life Think of its abundance and freeness. Think of your present and eternal interest. Come now. Come as you are. Come all of you, and take of the water of life freely.

3. The duty of the church and of every member. To echo the will and the words of the Spirit earnestly, prayerfully, and continually.

83. SIN THE LEPROSY OF THE SOUL

"And immediately his leprosy was cleansed." —Matt. 8:3.

ONE of the results of sin is the fearful catalogue of bodily diseases which it has introduced. Man was formed free from affliction, sorrow, and pain; neither was he liable to death. But sin has filled the world with disease and misery. Hence,

> "Fierce diseases wait around,
> To hurry mortals home."

Every part of the body is alike vulnerable, alike in danger, alike susceptible of affliction and agony. Some are tedious in their progress, and men groan beneath them for years. Others are rapid in their course, and speedily cast their victims into the gloomy grave. Some are curable, while others defy the physician's skill and power. During Christ's mission on earth, he employed his benevolent power in healing the diseases both of body and mind. Our text refers to one delightful instance, to which we invite your attention on the present occasion. Consider,

I. The Individual referred to.

"A leper." Perhaps no condition was more truly awful and distressing. Leprosy was common in Palestine, and is so still in various parts of the east. At present we shall consider it as exhibiting a striking representation of sin, the leprosy of the soul. Now the leprosy,

1. Was generally hereditary.

Thus from Adam and Eve, sin has spread into every country, and down through every generation. Men are not only born under the effects of the guilt of sin, but under its depraving and defiling power.

2. It was small in its first appearance.

A small spot on the countenance, of an inflamed red character, was the first sign. Those unacquainted with it might suspect no danger. Now sin is little in its beginning. Look at children in their tempers, &c. Look at individuals who at one period were amiable, and then became thoroughly vile.

3. It is deeply seated and inveterate in its nature.

The heart and blood are under its influence So with sin;—the heart is the seat, he soul is the spring and root of all the evil.

4. It is universal in its prevalence.

All the man affected. From the head through all the extremities. No part of a leper clean. So with sin and the sinner,—"the whole head," &c. All the faculties of the soul. All the senses of the body, &c.

5. It is very loathsome in its appearance.

The eyes and countenance assumed a horrid and disgusting appearance; painful; and it rendered the person a burden to himself, and life itself a curse; such also is sin,—it renders man abominable to God and holy angels, and fills him with anguish and misery.

6. It excluded from society and rendered them objects of terror to all around.

However close by the ties of kindredness, their breath was dreaded, it was the breath of disease, to touch them was to receive their malady. Not allowed to mix with the healthy, or to go into the congregation of the Lord. Travelers feared to meet them, &c. So sin infects and excludes from the family and presence of God.

7. It was incurable by human power, and generally produced a most awful death.

It raged until the whole person became one mass of foulness and pollution: then the vital organs being powerfully attacked death terminated the career of suffering Such, also, is the leprosy of the soul. No man can recover himself from it. No created power can restore. It never cures itself. "Sin when it is finished brings forth death." Such was the condition of the man who applied to Christ. Notice,

II. His Address to the Redeemer.

"Lord, if thou wilt," &c.

1. It was an address of humble respect.

"Lord." He acknowledged him as a dignified person. Received him as the Messiah, worshipped, &c.

2. It was associated with faith.

"Thou canst." Not ordinary faith. He would not have said so to any other person on earth. Christ had the power, and this was the power of God.

3. It contained an affecting appeal as to his misery, and Christ's goodness.

"If thou wilt thou canst make me clean." Nothing so important to him as this. This was his heart's desire. He appealed to Christ's disposition, "If thou wilt," &c.

III. The Conduct of the Savior.

1. Christ responded to his appeal.

And said, "I will." His love and mercy as great as his power. Christ's willingness is established on the most immoveable truths and facts.

2. His word was omnific, and conveyed the healing power.

He might have willed it, and effected it silently, but he spoke, &c.; so he did in creation, so in all his miracles. At the grave of Lazarus,—to the devils who possessed the demoniac,—to the raging sea, &c.

3. He put forth his hand to testify to his cleanness.

A touch would infect, and in any case ceremonially defile, but JESUS now touched him, to show that the foul disease was gone. What a cure!—how complete!—how instantaneous!—how free!—how precious!

4. He sent him to the priest that his recovery might be duly attested.

The priest was appointed of God to testify when a person was cleansed and fit for society. Now this case might have been disputed, &c. He was to go at once, for fear the priest might hear, and through prejudice refuse to attest &c.

5. He was to present a gift unto the Lord.

See Lev. 14:10, and if poor, 5:21. Now Christ enforced this to show that he came to fulfil the law, &c. And to elicit a grateful spirit from the leper. Now let one turn to the leprous sinner.

> 1) See how you are to obtain healing and purity. From Christ. By personal, humble, and believing application to him.

> 2) See the way in which Christ will receive you. He will freely and graciously deliver. He desires to do this, &c. He can do it now, &c.

> 3) See what Christ expects from those he has healed. Dedication of yourselves and all you have to the Lord.

Application

1. Bless God for health of body.

241

2. Especially be anxious for health of soul.

3. Praise God for the almighty Savior, and the means of spiritual health and felicity.

4. We now invite all to be healed.

84. SINNERS CAPTIVES

"Deliverance to the captives." —Luke 4:18.

THIS is a part of the Savior's first sermon. He began his public ministry by exhibiting the riches of his grace to sinners. His ministry was eminently one of mercy and love. In him dwelt an infinite fulness of grace and truth. He was in all things a Savior suited to the exigencies of our ruined race. He came to redeem us from all iniquity, and from its effects both in this world and in that which is to come. Hence, knowing man's enthralled condition, he proclaimed, "Deliverance to the captives." In the text observe,

I. The State of Mankind supposed.

"Captives." That is, in a state of vassalage. One who has been made prisoner in war. Man fell through the agency of Satan, and became the victim of his infernal tyranny. Now, as captives,

1. Sinners are in bonds.

Enfettered in spirit, and bound with the manacles and chains of iniquity. Of these bonds there are ignorance,—superstition,—slavish fear. Now, as captives,

2. Sinners are in exile.

Excluded from their original country and inheritance. Far from God, and from holiness and peace. In an enemy's territories, &c. They are captives,

3. In darkness.

It was an ancient practice to put out the eyes of distinguished prisoners of war, and otherwise to maim them. See the case of Zedekiah, Jer. 39:7. Now Satan, as the god of this world, blinds his victims He keeps them in a state of darkness, &c.

4. In prison.

Under the reign of Satan, sinful men are as in prison. Strangers to holy freedom and spiritual liberty. As such, his captives are,

5. Wretched and miserable.

Their professed pleasures are fictitious—imaginary—mere delusions. They are without peace; without solid enjoyment, and without hope. This captivity is connected,

6. With extreme peril of eternal ruin.

It is the design of Satan to involve his victims in everlasting misery. He intends their unending ruin. Hence, those who are not liberated from his power, and translated out of his kingdom, will go down into the dark abyss of wo, to be tormented with the devil and his angels forever and ever. Observe,

II. The Deliverance announced.

This deliverance has been rendered,

1. Possible through the redeeming power of Christ.

Jesus is the deliverer. He came to rescue us from the power of the devil. He has bruised the head of the serpent. He has overcome all his enemies by his triumphs on the cross, and his resurrection from the dead. He hath opened a glorious highway for the return of Satan's captives to the liberty and favor of God,—from the regions of death to the kingdom of life This deliverance,

2. Is proclaimed in the gospel.

It is the design, the great end of the gospel, to offer liberty to the bound, and deliverance to the captives. The gospel is the gracious annunciation of hope and life to wretched perishing sinners.

3. This deliverance is offered to all.

God addresses men as sinners, and all such are invited to enjoy the redemption of the gospel. There is no restriction, no limitation. Whosoever will, may freely come, and not one of such shall be cast out

4. This deliverance is obtained by faith.

The hearty belief of the gospel proclamation gives instant deliverance to the captive. The truth known, at once makes free. The gospel to every believer is the power of God to salvation. God says, it is not by works of righteousness, but by grace, and through faith. But this faith is the exercise of the heart, and embraces the whole gospel, and yields implicit homage to the authority of Christ.

5. This deliverance is connected with blessings of indescribable value.

It is connected with remission of sins; renewal of the heart; adoption into God's family; enjoyment of internal peace; and the hope of eternal life.

Application

1. To enslaved sinners. How deplorable your state. How infatuated to reject the deliverance. O be wise and turn unto the Lord.

244

2. To emancipated freemen. Rejoice. Bless your deliverer, Jesus. Show forth his praise. Tell others of it.

"Point dying sinners to his blood,
And say Behold the way to God."

85. THE GOSPEL THE CHARTER OF LIBERTY

"And ye shall know the truth, and the truth shall make you free." —John 13:32.

WE perceive from the preceding verses that many of the Jews had believed on the Savior. This was an event highly joyous to Christ, and of the utmost benefit to themselves. But the Redeemer, knowing the difficulties and dangers of their path, now endeavors to strengthen and comfort them, by urging the importance of steadfastness and constancy upon them, ver. 31. How very necessary is this truth to be remembered, that we must not only receive but continue in Christ's word; and thus only can we be his disciples in deed, ver. 31. And it is only thus we can realize all the advantageous ends of our high and heavenly calling. In this way we shall "know the truth, and the truth," &c. We have to consider in the text,—*The Truth,—The Knowledge of it,*—and *Its Influence.* Let us consider,

I. The Truth.

It is a term variously employed in the holy scriptures. It means often, *veracity* in opposition to falsehood; *substance,* in op position to types and shadows. "The law was given," &c. It often means the whole word of God. It is one of the titles of the *Messiah,* "I am the way, the life, the truth." "He is faithful and true." In the text it clearly refers to Christ's holy and blessed gospel. Now the gospel includes every other definition of truth. It is *veracity,* nothing fallacious in it. It is *substance,* no mere shadows. It is full of Christ's person and glory. Gospel of Christ. Its histories are truth; its revelations are truth; its doctrines are truth; its promises are truth; it is divine truth; heavenly truth; gracious truth; infinitely precious truth; eternal truth. Consider then,

II. The Knowledge of the Truth

Now this may, 1 Be merely mental.

By hearing or reading the gospel we may know all its facts and statements the same as we may know anything in science or history. Now thus we may go through the whole length and breadth of scripture statements, without any effect being produced on the heart or life. There may be a state of non-belief, or it may, 2 Be experimental.

That is, when I have tried and tested and felt what is represented as truth; when I *visit* the places described by the *traveler,* —when I *try* the experiments stated by the philosopher,—when I *prove* the medicine prescribed by the physician. Now this is experimental knowledge, to which the soul can bear witness. And all who cordially hear and believe the truth know it thus. The woman of Samaria knew it thus. The man born blind knew it thus. Saul knew it thus. All who are converted know it thus. Now this experimental knowledge is *alone saving.* No extent of speculative knowledge can give true comfort, or lay the foundation for eternal glory. Observe

III. The Influence of the Truth.

"It shall make you free." Now the bondage or slavery of man is here premised. And such is the declaration of the holy scriptures. All men are naturally the slaves of sin and the devil. In the prison house of depravity, guilt, and condemnation, Now an experimental knowledge of the truth makes free,

1. From the condemnation of guilt.

We are all guilty, and against all, the sentence of condemnation has gone forth. He that believeth not," &c. Now the truth points to the only way of pardon and life. It exhibits the surety, the sacrifice. It shows where God has punished sin, and where he will forgive the guilty. "Be it known unto you," &c. It makes free,

2. From the enslaving fetters of depravity.

Forgiveness is not holiness. We must be changed,—converted,—born again,—sanctified. The truth points to the source of regeneration. The blood of sprinkling. The fountain opened. And by knowing the truth we are sanctified by it. "Sanctify them," &c.

3. From harassing fears of wrath.

Guilt and sin are ever associated with fear and dread. The sinner, whether he looks within, behind, onwards, or above, he is alarmed. God is against him, &c. Under the curse. But the truth reveals the Holy Spirit, the pacifier, comforter, the pledge of divine love, the earnest, &c. of glory. And in receiving the truth, he receives the Spirit of truth, who fills the mind with peace and joy through believing. He bears witness, &c.

4. From the anxious cares of life, and the dread of dissolution.

Nothing more is necessary to our misery than for the worm of care to be gnawing upon the soul. To have anxiety as our constant guest. Fearing a thousand imaginary ills. Never content. Never really happy. Especially cherishing dark forebodings of death, and gloomy, horrifying views of the grave. Now the truth makes free from all these. It points to Christ's universal reign. It shows that all things are managed by infinite wisdom and love. That all things shall work together, &c. That the presence of Christ shall be ours in life and death, and that to live will be Christ, and to die everlasting gain.

Application

1. Let believers rejoice in their spiritual freedom.

2. Avoid the trammels of human authority in matters of religion.

3. Invite sinners to receive the truth.

86. THE GOSPEL DISPENSATION AN IMMOVABLE KINGDOM

"Wherefore we receiving a kingdom which cannot be moved, let us have grace, whereby we may serve God acceptably with reverence and godly fear." —Heb. 12:28.

THE apostle had just been presenting in contrast the two dispensations:—that of the law and the gospel; of Moses, and Christ; Sinai and Zion. Having shown the vast superiority of the Christian economy, he then urges reverential obedience to the authority of Christ, "See that ye refuse not," &c., ver. 25. Then he refers to the power which accompanied his voice when he gave the law, as contrasted with that which he now possesses as heir of the worlds and Lord of all. Then follows the practical and experimental deduction of the text, "Wherefore we receiving," &c.

I. The Kingdom specified.

Now this kingdom is clearly the spiritual rule or reign of Jesus in the soul. The Christian dispensation is a kingdom. As such John the Baptist cried, "The kingdom of heaven is at hand." Into this by faith and through regeneration we are introduced: born into it of water and the Spirit. This is the opposite of Satan's kingdom and of this world, which are in hostility to God. But the text relates not only to that, but to the spiritual reign or kingdom which is erected in the soul; of which Christ said, "The kingdom of God is within you." Now this kingdom is a kingdom,

> 1. Of spirit and power.

> Not a lifeless form; not a mere name or profession. It is a vital and blessed reality. Life of God in the soul,—power of salvation diffused through all its energies and powers.

> 2. It is a kingdom of experience and practice.

> It has its seat in the affections, and is connected with our warmest emotions. It is love constraining the soul, and this is followed by righteousness of life. Holiness to the Lord is the essential characteristic of this kingdom. Not a system of ceremonial institutions,— "Not meat and drink, but righteousness," &c. Not saying, "Lord, Lord, but doing the things," &c.

> 3. It is an abiding and changeless kingdom.

> "Cannot be moved." Now in this the kingdom of Christ differs,

>> 1) From all earthly kingdoms. Where are the renowned empires of ancient times? Where the proud Assyrian,—the rich Persian,—the learned Grecian,—the mighty Roman? Where their ancient capitals, and their splendid palaces? Where indeed is the ancient kingdom of which Jehovah at one time was the only king. Palestine is in the hands of the false prophet,—the temple is razed,—the city itself in ruins.

2) In contrast with preceding dispensations. The patriarchal first appears in rural simplicity, the head of the family being both its lord and priest. Then followed the Mosaic,—at first with its movable tabernacle, and afterwards with its magnificent temple, numerous rites, bleeding victims, and costly services. But that waxed old and has gone forever. Now no daily sacrifices, no ministering priesthood of Aaron's order. Its worshippers have been dispersed through every region of the globe. But this kingdom is fixed on a better basis, established by promises, and is destined to overthrow every other, until it shall comprehend within itself every nation, and people, and tongue.

Now there are connected with this kingdom several features which indicate its immovability.

1) Its moral glory. It cannot in this respect be exceeded except by the purity of heaven. We cannot have more holy precepts, example, or influences, &c.

2) Its triumphs in past ages. It never will have more learning, talent, and power, arrayed against it; yet it stood and conquered. If so in the time of its infancy, what shall impair it during the period of its maturity and strength.

3) Its universal adaptation to every country in the world. No other religion, or form of religion, is adapted to the whole earth. Judaism was not,—Mohammedism is not;—nor any one form of Paganism. Christianity is alike at home everywhere. It suits the Arab in the desert,—the Hottentot in his kraal,—the philosopher in his study,—and the monarch on his throne. Like the light it is adapted to the world; like the air it is the breath of life to all human beings.

II. We refer to the Reception of this Kingdom.

Now this supposes the promulgation and offer of it. This is what is done when the gospel is preached. It announces, it offers to men the dominion and the blessings of his reign. It is in this way that it is to be extended to the end of time, and throughout the habitable earth. Now in receiving this kingdom,

1. We must relinquish the kingdom of Satan.

Cannot be identified with both. One light, the other darkness, &c. We abandon the one when we receive the other. We must come out and be separate. This is called a translation, passing from death unto life.

2. We must with faith cordially and humbly receive Christ and his administration.

The faith must be that of the heart, "If thou shalt believe with thine heart," &c. And the humility must be that of the child, "For except ye be converted and become as little children," &c. Look at the simplicity of spirit, the docility of mind, and humble tractableness of a little child. In that way we must receive the kingdom of God. Observe,

III. The Duties arising therefrom.

1. We must exhibit loyal obedience.

"Serve God,"—not ourselves, not the world, nor sin. These are to be forsaken. We must yield loyal obedience to Jesus, keep both his, and his Father's words. Act as becometh the subjects of his reign. Notice,

2. This obedience must be that which God prescribes and demands.

"Acceptable."

> 1) According to his revealed word. Not will-worship, not acts of human fancy.

> 2) In the way and spirit he requires.

> 3) To the end he has appointed,—his own glory, and the honor of his grace.

> 3) This obedience must be connected with due homage and fear.

> Not in a light and trifling spirit, not carelessly, but with holy feelings of profound respect and veneration; a proper fear of offending him; with just views of our littleness and sinfulness. To enable us to do this,

> 4) We must seek the aid of heavenly grace.

> "Let us have grace." guiding, supporting, sanctifying grace. "Thy grace is sufficient," &c.

> 5) It is to be had at the throne of grace.

> It must be sought, cherished, and exercised; we must hold it fast; grow in grace.

Application

1. To the happy and dignified subjects of this kingdom, we say, cultivate a public generous spirit; seek its prosperity, peace, and glory.

2. Urge wretched sinners to receive it. It is come to you. Believe, and be saved.

3. Let us anticipate its final triumphs and universal diffusion.

> "Jesus shall reign where'er the sun
> Does his successive journeys run,
> His kingdom stretch from shore to shore,

Till suns shall rise and set no more."

87. CHRIST'S SPIRITUAL BODY

"For as we have many members in one body, and all members have not the same office," &c. — Rom. 12:4, 5.

SCRIPTURAL views of the church of Christ would go far towards promoting a right state of mind in believers towards one another. Most persons acknowledge but one true church, but then all are eager to show that their own party forms that church, to the exclusion of all who do not walk with them, bear their name, and pronounce their peculiar sectarian shibboleth.

One of the great causes of this mistake arises from confounding uniformity with unity. The one we believe is not possible, the other is specifically enforced in the divine word. Our text may greatly aid us in comprehending the mind of God on this important and interesting subject.

I. The Church of Christ is composed of many Members.

Now this is not contradictory of those passages which represent the flock of Christ as small, or the number of the righteous as few;—compared with the great mass they are so. But truly in the abstract they are many; were so in the apostles' time; are so now; many more than we know of; Elijah calculated wrongly. See 1 Kings 19:8, 10. Bigotry often does so. The great completed family will be innumerable. No man shall number them. The seed of the Shiloh is to exceed the sands of the sea shore and the countless stars of heaven.

II. The Members of Christ's Church are diversified in Character and Office.

In the human body the variety and use of the various members is beautiful and wonderful. Some of these are less distinguished and less important, but all essential to the completion of the body. All have their distinctive functions, &c. One sees for the body, one speaks, one hears, one bears burdens, &c. Now in this way the church of Christ is constituted. Some minister, others teach, exhort, rule, &c. ver. 6-8. But let it be observed here that all the members have an office, all a part which is assigned by the great head and Savior, Jesus Christ.

III. The numerous and diversified Members of Christ form "one" Body.

One member does not make a body, nor yet several, but all. The unity of the church is especially taught by the apostle, Eph. 4:4, &c. Now this body of many members is one in the following parts.

1. One common Father.

Just as all human beings are the creatures of God, so all believers are the spiritual sons and daughters of God; "Our Father" is the common universal language of all the family of faith.

2. One common nature.

Just as the human species have only one human nature, however form or features may differ, so there is only one spiritual divine nature which all possess who have been born of God

3. One pervading animating spirit.

If so ye be, ye are the sons of God, the Spirit of God dwelleth in you. "If any man have not," &c. One spirit, but diversity of operations.

4. One in vital union to Christ,—"In Christ."

He is the great center where all the lines of truth meet. The one foundation on which all rest. The one mediator in whom all trust. The one great head to whom all the members are united influenced, directed and whom they love and obey.

5. One in entire dependence upon divine grace.

Without the Savior we can do nothing. However intellectual, experienced, and talented, all and each are helpless without him.

IV. All the Members of Christ's Body are Members one of another.

However dissimilar in age, office, &c. All spiritual persons belong to one spiritual community, one building, one body. As such,

1. They have mutual blessings.

All heirs of the same covenant and promises. The same bread and water of life Same benefits and privileges.

2. They have mutual perils.

The adversaries, snares, and dangers, are the same. The evils of the world, of the carnal mind, of the raging lion, &c.

3. They have a mutual and common destination.

All journeying to the same place which the Lord hath prepared, &c., shall walk the same streets, worship before the throne, join in the same songs, and enjoy the same bliss forever and ever.

4. They are mutually dependent on each other in their way to this blissful destination.

There can be no independence in the church of Christ. All depend on God, all dependent on each other; just as in the body, the eye sees for it, &c. The least is necessary and important, so the greatest; so the learned and the illiterate; the rich and the poor; the man of ten talents and the man of one.

Application

1. Learn what constitutes a true Christian. Being a member of the body of Christ; believing we are united to Jesus and his people.

2. What necessity there is in the body for the individual members to exercise the spirit and graces of Christianity.

1. Ought there not to be great forbearance? We ought not to expect from any, but that, which an imperfect Christian can present.

2. Ought there not to be sympathy? It is so in the natural body,—if one part suffers, the whole nervous system feels.

3. Ought there not to be love, and love unbodied in active mutual aid? What man will not aid any weak or maimed member.

4. Prayer. "Pray for one another, &c.

88. EARTHLY AND HEAVENLY DWELLINGS OF BELIEVERS

"For we know that if our earthly house of this tabernacle were dissolved, we have a building of God, an house not made with hands, eternal in the heavens." —2 Cor. 5:1.

CONSIDERABLE doubt has been expressed by critics as to the meaning of the apostle in this passage. Some have contended he evidently intended to teach, that at death, believers had prepared for them a kind of vehicle, or vestment, in which the so, should dwell, until the resurrection of their bodies at the last day. We feel better satisfied with the general exposition of the text, as referring to the heavenly dwelling, into which at death the saints have a glorious happy reception. Observe then,

I. The Christian's present Residence.

This is the body, figuratively styled the "earthly house of this tabernacle."

1. It is a house.

The residence of the soul. The dwelling for the immortal spirit. It is a most wondrous and beautiful structure. Fearfully and wonderfully made. Of which God was the all-skillful artificer. It is wisely adapted for the lofty tenant which occupies it.

2. It is an earthly house.

Originally made of red earth. Of the earth, earthy, &c. Formed of that which is material, in contradistinction to the spiritual character of the soul. The body is earthly, as its supplies are from the earth. Its foundations are in the dust. And it is destined to return to the earth from whence it originally proceeded. "Dust thou art," &c.

3. It is a movable house or tabernacle.

Not a stable, fixed, abiding building. But calculated and adapted for removal from place to place. Like a shepherd's tent, now pitched here and then elsewhere And as such it is destined to be taken down. At death it is unpinned. Then it is that it ceases to be the abode of its spiritual inhabitant. Now this taking down or dissolving of the tabernacle, is an event,

> 1) Most certain. The living know that they must die. All, whether sinners or saints, &c. "I know that thou wilt bring me to death," &c. All the great and distinguished servants of God, who once dwelt on earth, and served God in their respective generations, have had their tabernacles dissolved. "The fathers, where are they," &c.

2) It is an event most necessary. We must be dislodged from this earthly house, before we can inherit immortality and eternal life. "Flesh and blood cannot inherit," &c.

3) It is an event demanding solemn thought and holy preparation. It is desirable that the tabernacle should be taken down in hope of a part in the first and blessed resurrection. But especially before the ejectment of the spirit, that we should have a clear and satisfactory prospect of a better residence in the heavenly state. This leads us to consider,

II. The Christian's future Residence.

Now this residence is clearly that of God's glorious kingdom and presence above. The saint's future residence,

1. Is a building.

As such it, is likened to a glorious city. The new Jerusalem. The heavenly temple. This is the place spoken of by Jesus, "My Father's house." Palace of God. Imperial residence of Deity. As such it will be worthy of his greatness, and majesty, and glory. As such it will be capacious,—resplendently beautiful, sublimely magnificent.

2. Building of God.

His own residence. Full of his glory. Building which God has designed to be the residence of holy beings.

3. Not made with hands.

Not formed as God made the human body.

4 A celestial building.

In the heavens. Not having its foundations on this mutable decaying earth. But in the highest and most glorious part of God's universe. The highest heavens. Heaven of heavens.

5. An eternal building.

The body is fragile, dying; will be consigned to the earth. But the heavenly building, like its founder and maker, is "eternal." Unaffected by change. Eternity is engraven upon the walls of that building. Its foundations are immoveable Death is unknown. Immortality is the atmosphere of heaven. The tree of paradise is the tree of life, endless life. The river which flows from before the throne, is the river of life. Heaven in its enjoyments is "eternal life." Let us notice,

III. The Influence which a Knowledge of this should produce.

The apostle expresses one knowledge which believers have of this "We know," &c. From God's own infallible record from the inviolable promises of his word, they know with blessed and certain assurance, the certainly of that glorious state of felicity, which he has in reversion for all his saints.

1. This knowledge should wean the mind from love of the world.

They should consider themselves but strangers and pilgrims here, &c. Knowing that time is short, we should buy and sell, and weep and rejoice, &c. as remembering that the fashion of this world passeth away.

2. We should habitually live in a state of preparedness for death.

Our bodies are journeying to the grave. These tabernacles must be dissolved. Then let us wisely consider this, and live as those who know that they must die. "Be ye therefore ready," &c. The event is certain—the time unknown.

3. We should cherish joyful hope as to the future.

The Christian has a good hope. His best state is future. He is an heir of glory. He has a house on high,—a building in glory. His body too shall be raised again; raised in beauty,—in health,—in vigor,—in immortality. O blessed hope O rapturous prospect! Meditate and cherish those feelings this subject is calculated to inspire.

We would remind the ungodly of that fearful state to which their sins and impurity of nature are evidently exposing them When their earthly tabernacle is dissolved, there will be no habitation to receive them but the dark, hopeless regions of death, the prison of hell, and everlasting weeping and gnashing of teeth. O fear, tremble, repent and seek mercy.

89. HEAVEN LIKENED TO A FAMILY

"The whole family in heaven." —Eph. 3:15

THE Christian is a traveler on his way to Zion. This is not his rest. The traveler oftentimes directs his attention to the end of his journey, to the city of his habitation. The mariner often casts a look of hope over the waters which separate him from the desired haven. The prince who is the crown heir, often anticipates the riches and magnificence he will possess when he arrives at age. Now the Christian is a traveler passing through this desert world to the city of the new Jerusalem: and he often sings,

> "Jerusalem my happy home,
> Name ever dear to me,
> When shall my journey have its end,
> When shall I come to thee?"

The Christian is a tempest-tossed mariner, sailing to the celestial haven, and often does he long to behold the quiet shores of the heavenly world. The Christian is a child of God, and an heir of glory, and he looks forward when he shall receive from the hands of the chief shepherd the crown of life, &c. Our subject leads us to the contemplation of the heavenly family. Now let us notice,

I. The Members of the Heavenly Family.

1. There is the supreme head of the family.

Jehovah, the universal Father of the spirits of all flesh. The Father and origin of all beings. So called in reference to Jesus. Angels too are his sons—believers his adopted children—the human family his intelligent offspring—all animated beings his creatures.

2. There is the elder brother, the mediator between God and man.

Jesus stands midway between essential Deity and creature man, closely and inseparably allied to each. He has the essential nature and perfections of the Father. "He and the Father are one." He had absolute glory with him before the world was. Then he has, in connection with the divine nature, the nature of man. He was "made of a woman," &c. "God manifest in the flesh." Now he is the light and glory of heaven. The sun of the Heavenly temple. The tree of life, &c.

3. There is an innumerable company of angels.

Now these are called "morning stars," "sons of God," "Jehovah's host," "his ministering servants." It is said of them that their number is "ten thousand times ten thousand, yea, thousands of thousands." Now all these are clad in habiliments of unspotted purity, and from their zeal and benevolence, are likened to flames of fire.

4. There will be a countless number of glorified children.

The old monstrous doctrine of the reprobation and eternal perdition of infants is now nearly exploded from the world. Of the felicity of all who die in childhood there can be no doubt. The Father of mercies cannot rejoice in their destruction. Besides, Jesus said with great complacency and delight, "Suffer," &c.

5. There will be the whole collected body of believers.

Now this will of course include the truly pious, 1. Of all ages. From Abel downwards to Noah. Noah to Moses,—Moses to David,—David to Christ,—from the Baptist to Stephen,—Stephen to Constantine:—from thence to the reformation and to our own day. 2. Of all countries "They shall come from the east," &c. Of every clime and tongue, color and people. Of all these only one grand essential:—a living, purifying, and obedient faith; for every believer shall be saved, &c.

II. The Unity of the Heavenly Family.

The "whole family." Observe,

1. There is one family house.

On earth this cannot be. Diversity of sentiment and worship render it desirable, that in separate companies we should go up to the heavenly Zion. Besides, no house on earth could hold the congregation of the faithful. But there is a house not made with hands, &c. Jesus said, "In my Father's house," &c. This unity is ever kept prominent. Kingdom,—inheritance,—city,—temple.

2. All of this family have the same employments.

Worship God and the Lamb. His servants shall serve him, &c.

3. All have the same enjoyments.

They see God. Enjoy God. The Lamb leads them to living fountains of water, &c. Same rest. Same sources of joy. "In thy presence," &c.

III. The glorious Characteristics of the Heavenly Family.

1. Absolute purity Not one spot, or one infirmity. Not one selfish or envious or angry member.

2. Perfect blessedness.

Nothing that disturbs or grieves. No enemies without. No fears within. No darkness of mind. No sin, or pain, or disease. The eye weeps not, the heart aches not. There is,

3. Glorious permanency.

Immutability is engraved upon the walls and pavement of the celestial city. The church of God on earth is like a vessel on the waters tossed hither and thither. There are removals to other churches; apostasies from the truth; the scythe of death: the king of terrors visits the sanctuary, and one and another he marks as his victims. None of these in the family above.

Application

1. Have we not all some friends and kindred who form part of the family in heaven?

2. Are we living and acting so as to get there ourselves?

3. Invite sinners.

90. CHRIST THE SUBSTANCE OF TYPES AND METAPHORS

"But the body is of Christ" —Col. 2:17

THE apostle had been treating of Jewish ceremonies and festivals, and these he describes as being "a shadow of things to come." Only designed to prefigure some approaching event or blessing. Not possessing any real intrinsic value, but instituted to lead the pious, believing mind to look forward for that which was thus symbolized. The apostle then exhibits the whole of these shadows as terminating in the Savior. "But the body is of Christ," or, as some versions read, "The body is Christ." It does not however follow that we are to look for the substance of all the ceremonies in the person of Christ, or even in his work, or benefits. Many of the ceremonial institutions pointed to the economy of the gospel; to the ordinances of Christianity; and to the mystical body of his church. Yet Jesus being the foundation, the sum and substance, the Alpha and Omega, of the Christian religion, it is not difficult to perceive with what propriety the apostle says, "The body (or substance) is of Christ." Observe then by way of concise recapitulation,

I. That Christ is the Body or Substance of the Personal Types.

Adam, the Father of the human race, was a figure or type of him that was to come,—even the father of the world to come. Noah, in his name, lift ministry as the deliverer of his family, and the founder of a new world, exhibited Jesus the preacher of righteousness, and the deliverer from the wrath to come. Thus, too Melchizedek was a distinguished type of the kingly and priestly offices which Jesus should sustain. Isaac evidently typified the beloved Son of God, who was really and truly offered for the sin of the world. In many things we behold a beautiful similarity in the interesting events of Joseph's life, and those of the world's Redeemer. Moses was confessedly a personal type of the world's great teacher and deliverer. Joshua, who led Israel as the captain of Gods host, to the goodly land, was a type of that still more distinguished person, who was given to be a leader and commander to the people. The exploits of Samson evidently referred to some of the greatest of Christ's achievements. David in many things acted a typical part, and shadowed forth the truly beloved of God and his people. In Solomon we have several striking traits which were only exhibited, in all their fulness and lustre, in Solomon's Lord and Savior. Jonah, the wayward prophet, with all his weakness, was a sign of the death and resurrection of Jesus. The substance of all these typical excellencies is Christ.

II. Christ is the Body or Substance of many Scriptural typical Things and Events.

He is the true ladder, or way of communication between heaven and earth. He is the real paschal lamb, our Passover sacrificed for us. He was typified by the rock smitten for the supply of Israel's congregation with water in the desert. He is the manna from heaven, the true bread of life. He is the substance, both of the goat that was dismissed into the wilderness, as well as the goat that was slain, "for he bare our iniquities," and "died for our sins." As the brazen serpent was the medium of healing to the wounded Israelites, so Jesus is the great evidence of God's love to the world, and the medium of life to all believers. He is the ark of God's covenant, embodying his law, and the mercy-seat, or propitiatory, by whom we have access to God, and obtain forgiveness of sin. He is the great high priest, having our nature, ever living to make intercession for us. He is our sure and accessible refuge, by whom we are saved from the wrath to come.

III. Christ in his Church and Gospel was typified by many of the Institutions and Services of the Levitical Dispensation.

His church was symbolically set forth in the bush enveloped in flame, yet unconsumed; in the priesthood under the law, seeing his spiritual people are a "royal priesthood;" in the tabernacle, which was preparatory to the erection of the temple of Solomon; in Jerusalem, which typified the Jerusalem from above, the mother of all believers; in the Jewish nation, which shadowed forth the separated character and glorious privileges of the church of Jesus. The gospel of Christ was evidently typified in many of the festivals of the Jewish religion, especially in the year of jubilee, to which the Redeemer alluded, as the "acceptable year of the Lord." But we observe,

IV. All Types and Metaphors but feebly shadowed forth the Glories and Excellencies of Jesus.

"All are too mean to set him forth,
Too mean to show the Savior's worth"

It will be needful that we select all that was holy and eminent from all the personal types, and concentrate them, as in one, to judge rightly of Jesus. Then his excellencies and perfections, his work and benefits, are only feebly presented before us. He is the infinitely holy and absolutely perfect Son of God. In him dwelt all the fulness of the godhead, bodily. He is the glory of heaven, the object of angelic worship and praise, the joy of redeemed spirits, and the light of eternity. He is the sun of the universe, the life of the world, and supreme Lord of all. Then how we should study his character, meditate on his glories, be solicitous of his favor, and joyfully anticipate the vision of his glorious face, in the heavenly temple. In the divine oracles every tiling is full of Christ. We find him as the golden thread in its eventful histories. We find him as the perfection, the substance, and end, of its holy biography. We behold him as the beauty and significance of its rites and institutions. He is the theme of holy song. The subject of constant prophecy. The riches of all the precious promises. The peerless pearl of the field of revelation. Finding him, we are rich for both worlds. Possessing him, "all things are ours." Joint heirs with Christ, and we are thus "heirs of God," and of all the glories of the world to come

91. CHRIST CRUCIFIED

*"For I determined not to know anything among you save Jesus Christ, and him crucified." —*1 Cor 2:2.

THIS is Paul's noble avowal to the church of Christ at Corinth. The occasion of it is to be found in the declining of that church from the purity and simplicity of the gospel. After Christianity had been established there for some time, they became ambitious of gifts and miraculous powers. In addition to this, they divided themselves into respective parties, and some said they were of Paul, others of Apollos, &c. In this way they became unsettled, and exhibited a most unhappy and unsightly appearance to the other churches of Christ. Paul endeavors in this epistle to show them the evil of such a course, and that Paul, Apollos, or Cephas, were only servants of the one Lord, Jesus Christ. And it was on this account that he thanked God he had baptized so few of them. See 1:14, &c. He also shows them that he never attempted to gain any improper influence over them; his sole design being to preach Christ, and him crucified, &c. So also in the text, "For I determined," &c.

I. The Subject of Paul's Declaration.

"Christ and him crucified." Now this accords with what he affirmed to the Galatians, "God forbid," &c. Christ crucified is the great theme of the Christian ministry. Now this will be evident if you observe that,

1. This is the great end of all revelation.

The types and sacrifices of the ancient economy all referred to this. So did the prophecies; they testified beforehand of the sufferings of Christ, &c. Jesus declared the certainty and character of his death. "The Son of Man must be delivered," &c. "Thus it was written, and thus it behooved," &c. This is the sum of the gospel testimony, &c., that "Christ died for our sins," &c.

2. Here alone is exhibited the infinite love and mercy of God.

Here we see how much God hated sin, and yet loved the sinner, &c. "Greater love hath no man than this," &c. How great the gift!—how vast the price! Who can compute it? Contrast heaven and earth,—glory and infamy,—the throne of the eternal, and the cross of Calvary.

3. Here only has the sinner life and salvation.

Where can the sinner go but to the cross? There is the sentence against sin. Sin punished. The surety dying. The blood of redemption flowing. There is the fountain opened for sin, &c. "See there my Lord upon the tree," &c. Before the cross we are humbled, made contrite, and drawn to love the Redeemer. "We love him," &c. Here then is the ground, the immoveable ground of our hope, &c. "As Moses lifted up," &c.

II. The Nature of his Declaration.

1. It intimated that nothing pertaining to himself should have the place of the cross.

The human mind is capable of being influenced by a variety of principles and feelings. But all the ordinary things so highly esteemed by men in general, the apostle sacrificed in preaching Christ crucified. *Mental dignity* had to be sacrificed. The Jews who had the oracles, stumbled at the cross. To the Greeks it was foolishness, and the preachers of the gospel were deemed fools by all. One said, "Much learning hath," &c. Well, says the apostle, be it so, call me idiot or madman, "For whether we be beside ourselves, it is to God, or whether we be sober, it is for your cause," &c. Nothing was so offensive to the learned as salvation by the crucifixion of a reputed malefactor. Yet, says Paul, "I am determined," &c. The approbation of friends, the associates of his youth, had to be sacrificed. His chosen friends. His own countrymen. Yes, to elevate the cross was to excite all their scorn their hatred, malevolence. His name would be ranked with apostates, and his character associated with the base, the refuse of the world. What a sacrifice! Yet in spite of all this, he resolved to know nothing, &c.

The ease and affluence of life had to be sacrificed. The cross exposed him to the loss of all earthly good. In preaching Christ, he had to endure hunger, and weariness, and pain; perils by land and by sea; the loss of all earthly riches, and the possession of all poverty; the loss of liberty; yea, and life itself was in jeopardy every hour. Nevertheless, he said, "he was determined," &c. He preferred Christ to all things, and was resolved to preach him, whatever might be the cost. His determination included,

2. To preach nothing that was contrary to Christ crucified.

Hence he had to denounce human merit, the ancient sacrifices, the works of the law, and all systems of religion then in existence. The cross knew of no compromising. No mixture. It was to overthrow all creeds and forms; and these, however ancient, popular, and powerfully patronized and supported. Paul knew this, yet he "was determined," &c.

3. To make Christ crucified the grand center of all other truths which he might proclaim.

Such as the goodness of God,—the truth of God,—the holiness, and the mercy of God,—the recovery of man from sin and ruin,—the hope of man. All doctrines in reference to this,—all duties,—all blessings, and privileges in reference to this. All that Christ did, and taught, and wrought out. Incarnation,—humiliation,—preaching,—miracles, &c.

4. To proclaim Christ crucified in all places, at all times, and to all persons.

This was his theme everywhere—at Corinth, Athens, Rome; the theme by which he began his ministry, with which he carried it on, and which he manifested to its termination. To the rich and the poor; to the wise and the illiterate; to the young and the old; to every man he made known Christ and him crucified. Consider,

III. The Reasons by which this Declaration may be Justified.

1. This was the design of his office.

As Christ's ambassador; Christ's witness. It was his business. His great work. He was called, &c. to this. Not to acquire languages; to examine the productions of nature; or the effects of science. Not to visit ancient monuments,—inquire after antiquities, &c. Not to collect manuscripts and visit the seats of learning. No, but to lift up the cross,—to say everywhere,

> "'Tis all my business here below,
> To cry, Behold the Lamb."

2. This alone would prove saving to souls.

This to all believers is the power of God, and this the wisdom of God. Here is pardon, peace, and holiness for every sinner, and nowhere else.

3. This alone would glorify Christ.

"If I be lifted up," &c. He endured the pain and the curse &c. that he might see his seed, and witness the travail of his soul, and be satisfied. In this way Christ's kingdom is to be extended, and the world to be subdued to his authority and will.

Application

1. This subject is the basis of hope to the sinner.

2. The ground of triumph to believers.

3. And the joy of heaven forever.

Printed in Great Britain
by Amazon